W9-CGQ-238

# MOVING UP THE ECONOMIC LADDER: LATINO WORKERS AND THE NATION'S FUTURE PROSPERITY

## State of Hispanic America 1999

EDITED BY
SONIA M. PÉREZ

National Council of La Raza
Washington, DC

# National Council of La Raza

The National Council of La Raza (NCLR), the largest constituency-based Hispanic organization in the nation, exists to improve opportunities for the more than 30 million Americans of Hispanic descent. A nonprofit, tax-exempt organization incorporated in Arizona in 1968, NCLR serves as an advocate for Hispanic Americans and as a national umbrella organization for more than 230 formal "affiliates," community-based organizations serving Hispanics in 37 states, Puerto Rico, and the District of Columbia. NCLR seeks to create opportunities and address problems of discrimination and poverty through four major types of initiatives:

- Capacity-building assistance to support and strengthen Hispanic community-based organizations.

- Applied research, public policy analysis, and advocacy on behalf of the entire Hispanic community, designed to influence public policies and programs so that they equitably address Hispanic interests.

- Public information efforts to provide accurate information and positive images of Hispanics in the mainstream and Hispanic media.

- Special catalytic efforts which use the NCLR structure and reputation to create other entities or projects important to the Hispanic community, including international projects consistent with NCLR's mission.

NCLR is headquartered in Washington, D.C. and has program offices in Chicago, Illinois; Los Angeles, California; Phoenix, Arizona; San Antonio, Texas; and San Juan, Puerto Rico.

Copyright© 2000 by National Council of La Raza
1111 19th Street, N.W., Suite 1000, Washington, D.C. 20036

ISBN: 0-615-11386-9

Printed in the United States of America
All rights reserved. No part of this book may be reproduced in any form without written permission from NCLR.

# Contents

# Acknowledgments

A book – even an edited book with many "official" contributors – is always the product of many more people than those included in the formal credits. I am especially pleased to acknowledge below the colleagues and supporters who deserve special mention.

This book was the brainchild of Raul Yzaguirre, President of the National Council of La Raza (NCLR). He shared his vision of ways in which researchers, advocates, and academics could collaborate to produce policy-relevant and educational documents with a Latino focus. I appreciate the opportunity and challenge he put before us, as well as his insight, historical perspective, and commitment to the Latino community.

I would like to thank members of the NCLR Hispanic Employment Policy Project Academic Advisory Committee for their collaboration and support (see list included at the end of this volume). Over a two-year period, Advisory Committee members met to share their knowledge and ideas about how best to contribute to the field of employment policy research. In addition to their time and brainpower, both NCLR and I appreciate their interest in building bridges between research and policy. Similarly, I want to thank the authors of the chapters included here for their patience, dedication, and contributions. It has been a long process, but I have gained much from the experience of working with each of them and am grateful for their willingness to collaborate on such an effort. As a group, they have all demonstrated their interest and genuine concern for areas in which policy can help Latino workers succeed. The guidance they provided not only produced NCLR's first book, but also shows that research has an important role to play in shaping policy and creating opportunities for Latinos. I especially thank Cordelia Reimers for her interest, disposition, and good will, and for sharing her knowledge with us on related projects.

I would also like to acknowledge the significant support received from many colleagues at NCLR. Jonathan Njus, former NCLR Employment Policy Analyst, was extensively involved in the book's conception, development, and coordination. He served as able coordinator and co-editor before leaving NCLR to attend the University of Chicago Graduate School of Public Policy. The authors have let me know how much they appreciate his work on and contributions to early versions of the book. I especially thank him for his enthusiasm, continued interest in, and commitment to the completion of the book – and to this field.

Other colleagues at NCLR also provided important assistance. Eric Rodríguez, Senior Policy Analyst, reviewed two of the book's chapters and provided valuable comments that strengthened their clarity. Joel Najar, Immigration Policy Analyst, provided useful suggestions for the chapter on immigrant workers and pointed me to helpful references for background information. Lisa Navarrete, Deputy Vice President for Public Information, provided a fresh perspective to help me think about the book's message. Cecilia Muñoz, Vice President, helped in reviewing and clarifying sections related to immigration. Lorena Méndez, Administrative Assistant, provided a range of support to coordinate the numerous phases of the book's publication – I thank her for her help and computer assistance. Computer thanks also go to Allen Kadis, Management Information Systems Director, who helped us convert and format tables and charts, and rescue missing information. I thank Cristina Bryan, Editor, for providing expert editorial and proofreading oversight, preparing the book's index, and offering encouragement and comprehension along the way. Yael Flusberg, NCLR Consultant, also provided editorial assistance during the early versions of the book. I am grateful for the teamwork of Rosemary Aguilar Francis, Director of the Graphics & Design Unit, Ofelia Ardón-Jones, Design Specialist, and Carlos Acosta, Design Consultant, who were responsible for the book's design and layout, and who were helpful and patient throughout the publishing process.

Others outside of NCLR also made the completion of this book possible. I thank my parents, Luz and Pedro, who worked harder than I will ever have to and who serve as a constant reminder of why I care about these issues. My husband and *compañero*, Luis Duany, knows as much about this book as I do. He untiringly listened to all the developments along the way, believed in its value, and with humor and love provided encouragement and the final push to help me get to the finish line. Two friends also lent support. Cynthia Ferguson, my seventh sister and *mejor amiga*, often asked me how the book was going and patiently listened to details when I responded, even though this is not her field. And I thank Félix Matos Rodríguez for sending encouragement from a distance and for understanding the value of policy-oriented research.

The production of this book was made possible by funding from the Rockefeller Foundation, through its support of NCLR's Hispanic Employment Policy Project; from the Ford Foundation, through its support of NCLR's Economic Mobility Project and its general support to the organization; and from the John D. and Catherine T. MacArthur Foundation for its support of NCLR's Policy Analysis Center. The content of this book is the sole responsibility of NCLR, the editor, and the book's contributors, and does not necessarily reflect the opinions of its funding sources.

Sonia M. Pérez
San Juan, Puerto Rico
May 2000

# Foreword

From Amazon.com CEO Jeff Bezos, pioneer of e-commerce, to the Latina health care worker in Chicago, to the street vendor selling oranges by a Los Angeles freeway, to the latest "hot" Hispanic entertainment act, Latinos have never been more visible in the workforce. And this is just the beginning; according to *The Economist* magazine, 40% of net new job entrants in the U.S. labor force in the late 1990s were Latino. Moreover, few issues dominated policy-making in recent years as the drive to put people to work. Components of that effort ranged from the severe – dramatically thinning welfare rolls – to the more benign, such as a major revision of the nation's job training system. In addition to massive demographic changes over the past two decades, the data confirm that Americans – especially Hispanics – are working harder than ever before. Furthermore, the remarkable performance of the U.S. economy in the 1990s has resulted in the longest period of sustained economic growth in history.

Normally, one might think that the combination of unprecedented visibility, rapid growth, substantial policy attention, a powerful attachment to the labor force, and a "rising economic tide" would translate into significant improvements in the economic status of all workers, including Latinos. Unfortunately, while the vast majority of Hispanics are successfully moving up the economic ladder, a disturbingly large number are struggling.

Clearly, many of the "conventional" explanations for economic success – or the lack thereof – do not apply to Hispanic workers. For instance, the simplistic notion that anyone can get ahead through hard work alone is very much alive and well. It has also become fashionable in some quarters to assert that the nation's immigration policies are responsible for the lack of economic progress in the Latino community. These proponents suggest that the number of low-skilled immigrants entering the U.S., many of them Latino, distort the U.S. Hispanic economic profile. If immigration were reduced, they contend, the problem would be alleviated over time. When questions are raised about the impact of discrimination on economic mobility, many believe the issue is exaggerated and/or that little can be done. If one asks about the effect of education and job training programs, many suggest that these programs "don't work," or that they are principally local responsibilities. Many of these observers espouse the notion that for the poor, in general, and for ethnic minorities in particular, all we need is a healthy growing economy that "lifts all boats."

Although many of the theories and arguments noted above have some salience for the Hispanic community, overall, they do not explain the stagnant labor force position of many Latinos. For example, as the chapters in this book document, Hispanics display a strong work ethic, arguably more powerful than that of any other identifiable ethnic group. In addition, the book's findings suggest that one of the principal problems among Hispanics is not unemployment but underemployment; the addition of, or better access to, more low-wage jobs alone will not alleviate poverty or create wealth in our community. While it is true that all workers with high levels of education, including Hispanics, have experienced increases in wages over the past decade, it is also true that Latino wages are lower than those of White or Black non-Hispanics. Moreover, the wage gap between Hispanics and Whites has increased over this period. Additional disparities are seen when examining important benefits, like health care and pension coverage – Latino workers are less likely than other American workers to obtain these in their places of work. As for the notion that unemployment and poverty are linked to immigration, this report substantiates the mainstream view among economists that the effects of immigration have tended to be exaggerated in media and policy debates.

For much of my professional life, I have been placed in the position of trying to change misperceptions of my community. In this sense, this book follows in a long line of National Council of La Raza (NCLR) analyses that seek to inform policy-makers and the public that issues that affect Latinos too frequently are a "square peg" that cannot be made to fit the "round hole" of traditional policy paradigms.

But in another sense, this book constitutes a new, exciting venture for NCLR. It represents an intensive collaboration between NCLR and a group of distinguished academicians in an attempt to bridge the gap that too frequently divides research and policy formation. In this connection, it provides a major contribution to the field, if for no other reason than to demonstrate that many of the labor force problems experienced by Hispanics are amenable to changes in public policy. It shows that all Americans, and not just Latinos, have a vital self-interest in improving the labor force status of what will soon be the nation's largest ethnic minority. At the opening of a new century, and at a time of unprecedented economic prosperity and potential record federal and state budget surpluses, I believe that the research presented here underscores the importance of making a series of strategic investments in the nation's growing Hispanic workforce. If not now, when?

Raul Yzaguirre
Washington, D.C.
May 2000

# Introduction

As the U.S. Latino population has increased in size and extended its presence across the country, interest in how it is faring economically has grown. In recent years, there has been greater acknowledgment of the economic contributions made by Hispanic Americans. For instance, Latino-owned businesses represent the biggest source of small business growth in the nation. Latinos are also likely to be found among first-time home-buyers and are increasing their share of the middle class. This has gone hand in hand with significant purchasing power, measured at more than $350 billion annually, that has made economists and others stand up and take notice.

Among workers, Latino men are the most likely to be in a job or looking for one. Their consistently high labor force participation rate has been one of the dominant factors behind Latino economic gains. Yet despite their strong attachment to the labor force and the recent boom economy, there is a segment of Latino workers who continue to face challenges to economic prosperity. These workers typically have low education levels and limited workplace skills, and some are immigrants, but not enough has been written to document ways in which their employability can be enhanced. In particular, there is a gap in policy-relevant literature, specifically related to employment. Beyond understanding the challenges that Latino workers face as they seek jobs, what else is known about the changes in the economy that these employees will encounter? How can the nation better prepare Hispanics to move into sectors of the economy in which they are underrepresented? And how much does Latino economic status have to do with the increasing segment of the population that is immigrant?

To address some of these questions, as well as to augment the work that has been done on Latino employment issues, the National Council of La Raza (NCLR) convened an Academic Advisory Committee. These experts know the research, could help identify gaps, and have a common interest in raising the employment issues affecting Latinos to a national level in order to have policy-makers respond. This book reflects the collaborative effort undertaken by NCLR, its Advisory Committee, and other academicians over an almost-three-year period. After many discussions and several revisions, it seeks to describe the current employment status of Latino workers, and address the different factors that influence their outcomes. Moreover, it analyzes the current thinking to offer some direction for future research and for policy, with an aim toward improving not only the employment prospects of Latino workers, but also the socioeconomic status of the Latino community. This is especially timely given the demographic changes that the U.S.

is experiencing, which show that Latinos are younger than their non-Hispanic counter-parts and, as such, will make up a significant portion of the nation's workforce in the years to come.

The book begins with an assessment of human capital, and addresses the extent to which Latino labor market experiences and outcomes are shaped by characteristics like educa-tion, work experience, and skill level. In Chapter 1, Siles and Pérez present relevant data and research on Latino workers. This profile shows that low educational attainment lev-els are a significant – if not the most important – predictor of occupational distribution and earnings potential. Other factors are also reviewed, including English language skills and proficiency, work experience and training, computer literacy, and pre-employment or "soft" skills. The authors summarize these characteristics, which are then shown to influence employment levels and rates, as well as types of occupations held, and earn-ings. In addition, the authors deepen the profile by providing some discussion of diver-sity within the Latino community and its importance to labor market experiences, includ-ing gender, immigrant and foreign-born, and Latino subgroup differences. Their discus-sion suggests that policies focused on increasing educational attainment and building skills within specific segments of the Latino workforce can enhance employment prospects.

Chapter 2 explores the issues besides human capital that affect Latino labor force out-comes. Specially, Morales discusses the extent to which a host of structural changes, as well as discrimination, affects the placement and outcomes of Latinos in the workforce. As this chapter demonstrates, in the past two decades, the structure of jobs has under-gone significant transformation. Specifically, the loss of basic manufacturing jobs to high technology employment and services has coincided with demographic changes, includ-ing a major increase and shift in the composition and distribution of the Latino labor force. Industrial restructuring has helped to redefine the jobs now available to Latinos; as a result, how and where Latino workers enter the labor market and the opportunities available to them have changed. Morales notes that those workers – like Latinos – who have been most dependent upon traditional routes for upward mobility in manufacturing and through unionized, blue-collar jobs, have been adversely affected by industrial restructuring. In addition, Morales discusses other, larger, dynamics, such as political and policy decisions, that affect the status of the labor market and opportunities for low-wage workers. The chapter is strengthened by an assessment of the impact of employ-ment discrimination on Latino workers. Together, this discussion illustrates the chal-lenges of the current labor market for Latino workers.

One of the problems facing Latino workers, especially over this past decade, is high levels of unemployment. Chapa and Wacker examine this issue in Chapter 3. The authors set the larger context for the discussion by exploring the mixed economic experience of Latinos in the U.S., including their low educational attainment rates. With this as a backdrop, Chapa and Wacker turn their attention to different segments of the Latino worker population that have experienced high rates of unemployment and displacement, including Latina women and young Latinos. They also review trends in Latino unemployment throughout the 1990s to discuss what characterizes, and what explains, high Hispanic unemployment levels. In particular, the authors suggest that California's Proposition 187 and the devaluation of the Mexican *peso* are short-term factors that have influenced the Latino unemployment rate. The chapter also includes a discussion of underemployment, an important issue related to Latino unemployment. In addition, they discuss the impact of industrial restructuring and employment discrimination experienced by Latinos compared to non-Hispanic Whites, and reflect on both the future prospects for Hispanic workers and the areas in which public policy can strengthen this outlook.

Grenier and Cattan, in Chapter 4, address one of the most controversial issues in Latino employment: the effect of Latino immigrants on the labor market experiences of Latino and other low-wage workers. Their discussion examines the education, employment, and poverty profiles of Latino immigrants at the national level, and then explores patterns in these areas in key states where Latinos are concentrated, including California and New York. Their chapter also presents a summary of the research related to the socioeconomic status of recent immigrants to the U.S. and immigration's effects on jobs and wages. The authors find little evidence to support the belief that immigrants are a major factor in job loss and wage stagnation among native-born workers, and suggest that any effects are better studied at the local level, rather than uniformly assumed across labor markets.

Regardless of immigrant status, one of the most pressing issues for Latino workers is related to wages. In Chapter 5, Reimers presents new research that examines, across a number of variables, including age, education, and nativity, what has happened to the wages of Latino workers since 1990. Reimers' findings suggest that differences in wages between Latinos and other groups, and among Latino subgroups, are associated with several factors. These include the lower educational attainment levels of Latinos, as a whole, which is exacerbated by the influx of immigrants with few years of schooling. Reimers also notes that factors that encourage or discourage schooling, like school quality and financial aid policies, are also important contributors. In the case of Latinos who tend to be concentrated in large cities, these elements are important, since Latinos may not have access to high-quality schools or training opportunities. Other important factors that affect the wages of Latino workers are industrial restructuring and the decline of unionized jobs. Reimers suggests that the labor market alone cannot be relied upon to address the problem of deteriorating wages for Latinos, and offers some thoughts for public-policy-makers to consider.

Another increasingly important aspect of employee compensation addressed in this volume regards benefits. Santos and Seitz provide a thorough discussion in Chapter 6 of how employment-related benefits, a meaningful component of overall compensation in public and private-sector jobs, affect the economic well-being of Hispanic workers and their families. As this chapter illustrates, despite having the highest labor force participation rate of any group in the economy, Hispanic men are significantly less likely than other workers to receive "fringe" benefits through their employers. Overall, Latinos are not likely to have employee-provided benefits such as health care, pension coverage, dental insurance, maternity and paternity leave, and child care. The authors note that access to these benefits is predominantly determined by employment status, and, more specifically, by employment in well-paying primary-sector jobs – in which Latinos are typically underrepresented. The discussion includes an examination of benefits by race, ethnicity, and gender, as well as by native-born and foreign-born status. Latino and other workers who share certain characteristics, including participation in unions, high levels of educational attainment, and employment in large establishments, are especially likely to have access to important benefits. In light of the ongoing Social Security and health care debates, this chapter is particularly relevant to current discussions of Latino employment status.

In Chapter 7, Meléndez and Falcón bring a new perspective to the consideration of Latino employment status by examining how Latino workers search for jobs. Specifically, the authors examine the role that local "networks," organizations, and businesses play in the labor market experiences of Hispanic workers. As they note, while almost all job-seekers utilize the web of contacts available to them, not all networks are equal. The authors analyze data from the Multi-City Study on Urban Inequality for Los Angeles and Boston to show that Latinos have job search patterns different from those of other workers in those cities, and that the methods that they rely on to seek employment tend to be associated with poorer labor market outcomes. In response to this concern, the authors present two examples of effective community-based intermediary programs that serve Latinos to suggest that such organizations can play an important role in enhancing employment outcomes for Latinos.

The volume's final chapter summarizes the major issues raised by the previous discussions. In Chapter 8, Pérez and Kamasaki underscore the positive characteristics that Latino workers bring to the labor force, and suggest that tapping the strength and vibrancy of Latino workers has enormous economic potential for the nation's future prosperity. In particular, the authors argue that an "investments in workers" approach is needed to enhance the employability of Latino workers. Moreover, they suggest that many of the challenges facing Latino workers cannot be addressed solely by the dynamics of the labor market, but rather that public policy must play a role in shaping and improving Latino labor force outcomes. The authors highlight the need for investments in education and in workforce development and lifelong learning opportunities, as well as in proven strategies for making work more rewarding, like the Earned Income Tax Credit.

This book does not pretend to include all the issues that affect Latino employment status, or the related issues that are linked to jobs and the labor market, but it does provide a solid understanding of the most pressing employment issues that face Latinos – particularly those that have relevance for public policy. The interdisciplinary nature of the collection suggests that what comes next stems from many arenas. To improve Latino labor market outcomes, more research is needed in areas from gender-specific analyses to more knowledge of the experience of Latinos in unions. NCLR hopes, too, that policy-makers will pay close attention to the strategies outlined in this volume which could improve the employability of Hispanic workers. In terms of follow-up work, the response of employers to the issues raised here, especially of those who employ low-wage workers, is vital. It is NCLR's belief that those who generate the nation's jobs must also understand the importance of investing in the nation's labor force as a means to enhancing productivity. In the context of both the enormous demographic shifts that the U.S. is experiencing and the significant force that Latino workers represent, this volume is timely and relevant.

# What Latino Workers Bring to the Labor Market: How Human Capital Affects Employment Outcomes

**Marcelo Siles, Ph.D.**
*Michigan State University*
*Institute for Public Policy and Social Research, and Julian Samora Research Institute*

**Sonia M. Pérez, M.P.A**
*National Council of La Raza*

## Abstract

*This chapter examines the human capital characteristics that Latino workers possess. Specifically, it presents data related to occupational skills, such as education levels, English language ability and proficiency, work experience and training, computer literacy, and "pre-employment" or "soft" skills, such as attitude and punctuality, that influence the labor market outcomes of Latinos. The chapter demonstrates that the low education and skill levels of Hispanic workers, as a group, determine both the types of occupations Latinos hold and their earnings levels. The discussion includes a brief analysis of these data, which underscores that, despite low skills, Latino workers actively participate in the labor force. Additionally, the analysis points to the differences in labor force status between Hispanic men and women, specifically showing that Latino men appear to be trapped in low-wage industries expected to decline, while Hispanic women are making important strides in higher-wage occupations. Human capital and labor market distinctions between Latino subgroups are also reviewed and described. The chapter concludes by discussing education and workforce development issues that are critical to improving the current human capital profile of Latino workers, and their occupational and earnings status.*

The authors acknowledge the valuable comments of Dr. José E. Cruz, Dr. Sheldon Danziger, Jonathan Njus, and Eric Rodríguez on earlier drafts of this chapter. Only the authors, however, are responsible for any errors of fact or logic that remain.

# Introduction

Contrary to public perception, Latinos actively participate in the U.S. economy on both the supply and demand sides. First, Latino workers contribute their skills and services in the labor market as workers; Hispanic men have the highest labor force participation rate of all male worker groups. In addition, in the past decade, the proportion of Hispanic females who are working or looking for work has steadily increased. Second, Latinos act as consumers, with a purchasing power of more than $350 billion per year in 1996; this figure is growing at an average rate of 8% per year. However, Latino economic activity – and in particular their employment status and prospects – is constrained by their human capital characteristics.

Latinos are a predominantly young ethnic group, with a median age of 26.5 years. Almost half are under 25 years old, indicating that they are entering their prime working years. In addition, the Latino population has experienced significant population growth, fueled by both immigration and relatively high fertility rates. Because U.S. Census Bureau projections estimate that the Latino population will become the largest "minority" group in the nation by 2004, it is of critical importance to assess the potential impact of this group on the nation's labor force and overall economy.

This chapter will examine the range of employment qualifications of Latino workers that influences their placement and outcomes in the U.S. labor market. Occupational skills, including education, training, language skills, and computer literacy, as well as "pre-employment skills" and job experience levels will be discussed. The chapter also considers Latino occupational distribution and earnings levels, within the human capital context, and concludes with research and policy areas that merit further attention.

# Skill Levels

Skill levels greatly influence the types of jobs Latino and other workers obtain. For any worker, the most important skill determinant of labor market success is educational attainment. As this section discusses, significant and troubling discrepancies exist between Latinos and their peers from pre-primary through higher education levels. In addition, other relevant types of skills for the labor market, such as language skills and proficiency, work experience and training, computer literacy, and "pre-employment skills" like punctuality, attendance, and attitude are elaborated on below.

## Educational Attainment

Compared to that of other racial/ethnic groups, Latino educational status can be characterized by low school enrollment rates, starting at the pre-school stage and apparent also at the secondary school and higher education levels. In addition, while trend data for the last 30 years show that high school completion rates for the entire U.S. population have steadily increased, Latinos are still the least likely of all Americans to have high school diplomas. College completion data reflect a similar situation. The resulting – and persistently large – education gap between potential Hispanic job seekers and their peers has been a critical element in the employment status of Latinos. Specifically, as we will review later in this chapter, such low levels of education help to explain the large concentration of Hispanic workers in low-wage jobs.

A cross-sectional analysis shows differences in the percentage of persons three to 34 years old enrolled in the school system by sex and race/ethnicity at different age brackets in 1995. As shown in Table 1, we can observe vast differences between Latinos and

### Table 1

### Percentage of Persons 3 to 34 Years Old Enrolled in School by Age, Race, and Hispanic Origin, 1995

| AGE | ALL | WHITES | BLACKS | HISPANICS |
|---|---|---|---|---|
| Total Enrolled | 53.7 | 53.2 | 56.1 | 49.7 |
| 3 and 4 Years | 48.7 | 49.6 | 47.5 | 36.9 |
| 5 and 6 Years | 96.0 | 96.2 | 95.5 | 93.9 |
| 7 to 9 Years | 98.7 | 98.9 | 97.7 | 98.5 |
| 10 to 13 Years | 99.1 | 99.0 | 99.2 | 99.2 |
| 14 and 15 Years | 98.9 | 98.8 | 99.0 | 98.9 |
| 16 and 17 Years | 93.6 | 94.7 | 92.9 | 88.2 |
| 18 and 19 Years | 59.4 | 59.3 | 57.4 | 46.1 |
| 20 and 21 Years | 44.9 | 46.2 | 37.4 | 27.1 |
| 22 to 24 Years | 23.2 | 23.1 | 19.9 | 15.6 |
| 25 to 29 Years | 11.6 | 11.5 | 10.0 | 7.1 |
| 30 to 34 Years | 6.0 | 5.5 | 7.8 | 4.7 |

Source: U.S. Bureau of the Census, Current Population Survey.

the other two major racial groups at the preschool level (ages three and four). Only 36.9% of Latino children were registered in pre-primary education programs, compared to almost half of Blacks and Whites. And research indicates that the gap in preschool attendance has widened over time.[1] Moreover, Latinos have the lowest school enrollment rates at all age groupings, except ages seven to 15 years.

At the critical high school years, declines in enrollment rates reappear for Latinos. For instance, among 16-17-year-old youth, 94.7% of Whites and 92.9% of African Americans are enrolled in school; yet the comparative rate for Latinos is 88.2%. Under-enrollment is a likely element in the low educational attainment status of Latinos.

According to the U.S. Bureau of the Census, 54.0% of Whites 25 years and older had completed high school in 1970; by 1997, this figure had jumped to 83.0%. Among Blacks, about one-third (32.0%) had a high school diploma in 1970, compared to almost two and a half times as many (74.9%) in 1997. By comparison, the education gap between Latinos and their non-Hispanic counterparts is quite wide, and has not narrowed significantly. In 1973 (the first year for which such data for Hispanics are available), about two in five (38.0%) Latinos had completed high school – a rate not unlike that of Blacks at that time. By 1997, that proportion had increased to only slightly more than one-half (54.7%).

Among Hispanic subgroups, the data reveal a similar situation. Given that Mexican Americans constitute the largest proportion of U.S. Latinos, education data for Latinos as a whole give a sense of the educational status of Mexican Americans. Fewer than half of Mexican Americans (46.7%) 25 years old and over were high school graduates in 1996. This makes Mexican Americans the least likely of all Hispanic subgroups to have obtained a high school diploma. By contrast, Cuban Americans are the most likely to be high school graduates, given that almost two-thirds (64.1%) of their population had diplomas that same year. Yet, even this educational attainment rate – the highest among Latinos – differs significantly from that of both Blacks and Whites. Other Latino subgroup data show that, of those 25 years old and over, a slightly smaller proportion of Central and South Americans (62.4%), followed by Puerto Ricans (59.4%), had graduated from high school.[2]

For Latinos aged 25 to 34, data from the March 1997 Current Population Survey are more encouraging. "Other Hispanics" are the most likely to have a high school diploma (77.5%), followed closely by Cubans (76.3%). Similarly, almost three in four (74.3%) Puerto Ricans aged 25-34 are high school graduates. This compares to about two-thirds (65.5%) of Central and South Americans and more than half (55.6%) of Mexican Americans. While the rates for some of the subgroups within this age bracket are higher than the rates presented above for Hispanics 25 years and older, they are still not at the level of attainment of Whites and Blacks.

High school dropout rates are especially disturbing. In the last 25 years, Latinos have had the highest dropout rates among all racial groups. The most recent data show that 30% of young adult Latinos are not in school and have not graduated, compared to 8% of Whites and 13% of African Americans.[3]

This education gap persists through the college-age years and beyond; in 1995, among 25-to-29-year-olds, one in nine Whites (11.5%) and one in ten Blacks (10.0%) were attending some type of educational institution, compared to only one in 14 Latinos (7.1%). Thus, in addition to low completion rates and high dropout rates at the secondary school level, Latinos' insufficient educational attainment is exacerbated by poor college enrollment and completion rates.

An analysis of U.S. Census data shows that, at the college level, the percentage of persons 25 years and older who have completed college has been growing in the last two decades for all racial groups, but at different rates. For example, in 1970, more than 11.0% of Whites were college graduates, a figure that grew to 24% by 1995. African Americans, on the other hand, had a lower growth rate in the proportion of persons who had completed college. In 1970, fewer than 5% of Blacks had college degrees; by 1995, Blacks had a college graduation rate of 13.0%. For Hispanics, a positive note is that the proportion of college graduates increased from 5% in 1973 to 9.5% in 1995. However, the rate of increase was quite small over this period, relative to that of other groups, so that currently only about one in ten Hispanics 25 years old and over is a college graduate.

For the Latino population aged 25-34, data regarding completion of higher education show upward movement for almost all subgroups. In 1997, although only 7.1% of Mexican Americans were college graduates, 11.5% of Puerto Ricans, 13.7% of Cubans, and 13.2% of Central and South Americans in this age bracket had received a bachelor's degree.[4]

A review of the educational status of Latinos would not be complete without examining the status of immigrants – an increasing segment of the overall Hispanic population who often have low education levels. In 1996, more than one-third of Hispanics were foreign-born. Education data show that U.S.-born Latinos are more likely than their foreign-born counterparts to complete high school and college. Specifically, about 70% of Latinos born in the U.S. had completed high school in 1996, compared to about 42% of those born abroad.[5] With respect to college attainment, the gap is much smaller; about 12% of U.S.-born Hispanics had bachelor's degrees, compared to 8% of foreign-born Latinos that same year.[6] While the education data of immigrant Latinos do influence overall Hispanic education rates, there is still a significant gap in educational outcomes between U.S.-born Latinos and their Black and White peers.

These insufficient levels of educational attainment, at a time when other Americans are increasing the rates at which they complete secondary and higher education, have a decisive effect on Latinos entering the labor force, both in the type of jobs for which they are eligible and in their potential earnings. Moreover, the U.S. Department of Labor projects that the growth of new jobs that require at least an associate's degree will be greater than occupations requiring less education and training in the next decade.[7] Within this context, Latino educational attainment levels will need to improve significantly in order for Hispanic workers to compete and excel in the labor force of the coming century.

## English Language Skills and Proficiency

The ability to communicate in English constitutes one of the basic skills required of new employees, particularly in high-paying industries. Workers with no or very poor oral and/or written English language skills can only perform basic tasks at entry-level positions offering low wages. Among Hispanics, there is a segment of both the overall and the worker populations whose first language is not English and who may not be English-proficient. According to the U.S. Bureau of the Census, the most recent national-level data from 1990, presented in Table 2, show that just over one-half (52.1%) of Latinos who speak Spanish at home report speaking English "very well" and one-fifth (21.9%) speak English "well." By contrast, about one-quarter (25.9%) say they speak English "not well" or "not at all." These data give some indication that a notable proportion of Latinos who speak Spanish do not have a level of English language ability that permits them to enter high-paying jobs in the current labor force.

**Table 2**

**English Language Proficiency for Spanish-Speaking Persons
Living in the United States, by Region, 1996**

| Speak English | United States | Northeast | Midwest | South | West |
|---|---|---|---|---|---|
| "Very Well" | 52.1 | 51.7 | 57.0 | 54.0 | 49.7 |
| "Well" | 21.9 | 23.1 | 21.1 | 22.6 | 21.0 |
| "Not Well" | 17.5 | 18.0 | 17.2 | 15.9 | 18.8 |
| "Not at All" | 8.4 | 7.3 | 4.7 | 7.5 | 10.5 |

Source: U.S. Bureau of the Census, Population Estimates, January 1998.

Table 2 also shows that, for persons who speak Spanish at home in the U.S., the level of proficiency in English also tends to differ by region. This is an important distinction, given that the labor market experience of Latinos varies according to geographical location, and by Latino subgroup. Although there is not enough research to determine whether a greater level of English language ability has correlated with the improved economic status of Latino workers in these specific geographic regions, the preliminary information suggests that this is an area for further study. According to the data, the Midwest presents the highest level of English proficiency among Spanish speakers, with 57.0% of persons reporting the ability to speak English "very well" and only 4.7% reporting speaking English "not at all." On the other hand, the West, followed by the Northeast, present the lowest levels of English proficiency among Spanish-speakers; about half (49.7% and 51.7%, respectively) speak English "very well." These lower proportions are explained by the high share of recent immigrants in these two regions.

English language skills are necessary for almost all jobs in the U.S., particularly for those that are in growth industries and offer economic mobility. Holzer reports that for occupations in the service sector, ability to communicate in English is very important to employers; to illustrate, 87.1% of employers reported that they give high marks for the verbal skills of their employees. Indeed, several factors underscore the importance of English language proficiency to labor market outcomes for Latinos. First, given the youthfulness of the Hispanic population and that most Latino adults are at the beginning or middle of their working years, lack of English language skills can affect employment paths or job opportunities early in a worker's career. Second, since Hispanic workers are currently concentrated in slow-growth or declining occupations,[8] their chances to move into high-wage jobs and industries projected to experience growth are small if their English language skills are not at the level expected by the marketplace. Third, a recent study conducted by researchers at the University of Miami vividly demonstrates the extent to which language ability among Latino families significantly affects family income. While families who spoke only Spanish had an average income of $18,000, those with only English-language ability had an average income of $32,000. However, those with both Spanish and English language skills had the highest family income: $50,376.[9]

Latino workers' English language skills and proficiency levels are especially important in the case of recent immigrants. Carliner found that for immigrants who arrived in the U.S. in the 1950s and 1960s, English language skills contributed 6% to 18% of the narrowing of the earnings gap between immigrant and native-born workers. However, the acquisition of English language fluency and literacy is complex, especially for young adult and older immigrants, and is often hampered by the limited availability of English as a Second Language (ESL) classes or training. According to the National Clearinghouse for ESL Literacy Education, there is a high demand for adult English language classes, and many adult students are on waiting lists, particularly in urban areas. For example, in 1996 more than 4,000 adults were reported on waiting lists in San Jose, California; and a Massachusetts Department of Education survey verified that 15,000 adults were wait-listed statewide.[10] Of the ESL students currently enrolled in adult education programs, the majority is Hispanic (69%). Apart from outside classes, one way that language skills are likely to improve is with on-the-job training, but this is not a benefit that is usually available to low-wage workers, many of whom are Latino.

## Work Experience and Training

Work experience can be obtained through formal educational institutions, organized training programs, and/or years of work. Typically, "experience" encompasses general abilities transferable to different working environments, such as basic numeric skills, writing, and other communication skills. Such experience can also refer to specific education levels, abilities, or skills related to unique characteristics of a determined job (e.g., advanced computer graphic design).

Latinos tend not to have formal educational preparation, because they start school later and leave school earlier than other Americans in the workforce. However, this pattern of premature entry into the workforce, coupled with high and consistent labor force participation, and late retirement, arguably translates into long work histories, especially for Latino men, and the accumulation of work experience over time. Yet, this type of experience is difficult to quantify and has not been documented in the literature. It is particularly problematic to get a clear understanding of the type and scope of work experience of those in low-wage jobs. It might be suggested that although Latinos tend to be concentrated in low-skilled labor and may not have advanced education or high-skilled training, their work history often gives them different types of employment experience. However, the marketplace may not always value such human capital.

One body of research on work experience by both Holzer and Trejo shows that, as a group, Hispanic males and females do not reflect comparable levels of "general" or "specific" experience as their White and African American counterparts when applying for non-college jobs. In research by Holzer, only 7.8% of Hispanic males reported having "general experience," compared with 26.6% of Whites and 8.3% of Blacks in 1994. Similarly, there was a large gap between the proportion of Hispanic females (6.6%) who reported having "general experience" and White females (36.8%) with such experience. About one in ten (9.6%) Black women indicated having this experience.

With respect to "specific experience" for certain jobs, this research also shows troubling disparities. While only 7.9% of Hispanic males reported having specific experience, 26.8% of White males indicated that they had this type of experience. A comparable proportion (7.1%) of Hispanic females reported having specific job experience; by contrast, 35.6% of White females said they had this type of experience.

One way to gain general and specific experience is through job training programs, sponsored by both the public and private sectors. There is a body of literature that has examined the representation and participation of Latinos in federal training programs. These studies have found that while Hispanics tend to be underrepresented in most federal government training programs, their experience in these programs has been mixed.[11] In some cases, the issue is one of proportional representation; the percentage of Latinos eligible for participation has not been reached. In other cases, the programs have not served Hispanics well. Some Latino participants are channeled into components that are not effective at moving workers into the job market, or are not offered sufficient "basic skills" or English language training to prepare them for more rigorous training opportunities that can result in high-paying, stable jobs. Additionally, research has documented that Hispanics have not adequately been able to participate in other types of programs or arrangements that have helped to move young adults successfully from school to work, including apprenticeships.[12]

However, at least two national-level programs (as discussed in Chapter 7) and a host of small community-based efforts have successfully helped to move Latinos into stable or better-paying employment. While it is beyond the scope of this chapter to present a discussion on training programs and Latino workers, it is essential to underscore that the skills that any worker brings to the labor force can be greatly enhanced by effective training. We believe that one component in the human capital equation for Hispanics is training gained outside of formal schooling. To the extent that Latinos have not proportionately benefited from government training programs or private sector on-the-job training, the experience that they bring to the labor market and the skill level at which they can compete with other workers are greatly diminished.

## Computer Literacy

In the last two decades, the increasing use of computer-based technology at work has meant that employers are looking for workers with at least a basic knowledge of computers. According to Holzer, of employers who offer jobs that require the use of computers, 51% of these jobs require daily computer use, 5.2% weekly computer use, and 2.3% monthly use. Two in five (41.5%) jobs evaluated by Holzer do not require the use of computers. These tend to be in the managerial and administrative support, and manufacturing sectors.

There are few data on the levels of computer literacy of Latino workers, but recent research by Fisher, et al. provides an indication of how Hispanic youth – tomorrow's workers – are faring in this regard. Between 1984 and 1993, more than half (57%) of Hispanic and African American (55%) students in grades seven through 12 used a computer at school, compared to almost two-thirds (64%) of White students. During this same period, home use of a computer was significantly lower for all groups, especially Latinos. More than one-third (37%) of Whites and about one in ten Hispanics and Blacks (10% and 11%, respectively) reported using a computer at home. These data suggest that minority students do not have the same exposure to this important new workforce tool that White students do. While further data are needed for a more complete assessment of Latino computer literacy, these preliminary findings suggest that Hispanics are not gaining sufficient experience with and preparation in the use of technological equipment, which is critical for success in the workplace of the 21st century.

## Pre-Employment Skills

There is a subcategory of issues that helps to round out the picture painted above regarding the employment attributes of Latino workers. "Pre-employment skills" are a set of human capital characteristics that, while difficult to measure, have recently engaged the interest of researchers and policy makers because of their relevance to long-term unemployed workers or those considered "hard-to-serve" by training programs. These skills include characteristics such as attendance habits, punctuality, work effort, and attitude. To date, few studies exist which measure these characteristics or the role they play in labor market success, specifically for Latino workers. However, there has been growing public policy attention to the relevance of such "soft skills" to occupational placement and retention, especially within the context of workers with long absences from the labor force, such as welfare recipients.

For example, in Denver, Colorado's Adult Career Educational Services (ACES) Program, a training program under the former Job Training Partnership Act and Aid to Families with Dependent Children programs, emphasis was placed on such general employment skills. As the program literature explains, clients "may participate in a simulated work environment where they have the opportunity to role play as if they were at an actual place of employment . . . Supervisors evaluate their punctuality and attendance, appearance, communication skills, work quality, attitude, and other aspects of their performance. Assessment of clients during these sessions is used to determine their readiness for training and, eventually, placement."[13] A 1998 study on the job prospects of welfare recipients from the perspective of employers noted that "willingness to work, motivation, reliability, and ability to be trained" are attributes that employers seek in entry-level candidates.[14] When asked to rank such skills, the employers who participated in this survey rated the following four qualities as "most important" for entry-level positions: "have a positive attitude," "are reliable," "have a strong work ethic," and "are punctual." While no data could be found that discuss these skills and Latino workers specifically, this small but growing body of research suggests that these general characteristics, required by all employers, are especially important for workers entering the labor force and for those without industry-specific skills.

This brief exploration of pre-employment qualifications suggests that this set of human capital characteristics merits further study, both from the perspective of the role that such skills play in labor market experiences and from that of employer perceptions of Latino workers.

## Impact of Skill Levels on Labor Force Status

The discussion above illustrates that an employee's education, training, and abilities are important determinants of overall employment status, including likelihood of labor force participation, types of occupations held, and earnings. The human capital characteristics of Latino workers help to explain their labor force status, examined in greater detail below.

### Employment Levels and Rates

The U.S. labor force has grown significantly in the last 30 years. In 1976, more than 96 million people were working or actively looking for a job; by 1996, the civilian labor force was close to 134 million. The U.S. Bureau of Labor Statistics (BLS) projects an increase of 15 million people over the 1996-2006 period, reaching 149 million in 2006. As shown in Table 3, there are noticeable differences in the annual growth rates of the civilian labor force among the different racial/ethnic groups. Asian and Pacific Islanders, followed very closely by Hispanics, are expected to be the groups with the highest annual civilian labor force growth rates between 1996 and 2006. Specifically, BLS anticipates that the Hispanic civilian labor force will experience an annual growth rate of 3.1% up to the year 2006. While currently one in ten U.S. workers is Latino, that share is expected to increase significantly in the next century. To illustrate, data show that, in 1996, 40% of net new labor force entrants were Latino.[15] If current demographic trends continue, Latinos will become the largest minority group in the nation by the year 2004. By that time, there will be more than 17.4 million Latinos working or looking for work.

In addition to the numerical force that Latinos represent in the labor market, their influence in the workforce is reflected in their high levels of work activity. The labor force participation rates for Latinos 16 years and over have remained practically constant since the mid-1970s, when the federal government started to collect data for persons of Hispanic origin. The proportion of Hispanics working or looking for work in the labor

**Table 3**

**Civilian Labor Force by Sex, Age, Race, and Hispanic Origin,
1976, 1986, 1996 and Projected 2006 (Numbers in thousands)**

| Group | Level | | | | Annual Growth Rates (%) | | |
| --- | --- | --- | --- | --- | --- | --- | --- |
| | 1976 | 1986 | 1996 | 2006 | 76-86 | 86-96 | 96-06 |
| Total* | 96,158 | 117,834 | 133,943 | 148,847 | 2.1 | 1.3 | 1.1 |
| Men* | 57,174 | 65,422 | 72,087 | 78,226 | 1.4 | 1.0 | 0.8 |
| Women* | 38,983 | 52,413 | 61,857 | 70,620 | 3.0 | 1.7 | 1.3 |
| 16 to 24 | 23,340 | 23,367 | 21,183 | 24,418 | 0.0 | -1.0 | 1.4 |
| 25-54 | 58,502 | 79,563 | 96,786 | 101,454 | 3.1 | 2.0 | 0.5 |
| 55 & over | 14,317 | 14,904 | 15,974 | 22,974 | 0.4 | 0.7 | 3.7 |
| White* | 84,767 | 101,801 | 113,108 | 123,581 | 1.8 | 1.1 | 0.9 |
| Black* | 9,561 | 12,654 | 15,134 | 17,225 | 2.8 | 1.8 | 1.3 |
| Asian & other* | 1,822 | 3,371 | 5,703 | 8,041 | 6.3 | 5.4 | 3.5 |
| Hispanic Origin* | ----- | 8,076 | 12,774 | 17,401 | ---- | 4.7 | 3.1 |

*16 years and over

Source: U.S. Department of Labor, "Charting the Course to 2006," November 1997.

market increased by only one percentage point between 1986 (when it equaled 65.4%) and 1996 (when it equaled 66.5%). This labor force participation rate is expected to reach approximately 67% by the year 2006.

Data disaggregated by gender show that Latino men have always had the highest participation rates in the labor market among all the racial/ethnic groups. In 1986, 81.0% of Latino men were participating in the labor force; this rate declined to 79.6% in 1996, but edged up again to 80.1% in 1998. Although this rate is expected to decrease over the next decade to reach 77.1% in 2006, even at this level, Latino men will continue to

## Table 4

## Civilian Labor Force Participation Rates by Sex, Age, Race, and Hispanic Origin, 1976, 1986, 1996 and Projected 2006

| Group | Participation Rate (%) | | | | Percentage Point Change | | |
|---|---|---|---|---|---|---|---|
| | 1976 | 1986 | 1996 | 2006 | 76-86 | 86-96 | 96-06 |
| *Total, 16 Yrs. & over* | **61.6** | **65.3** | **66.8** | **67.6** | **3.7** | **1.5** | **0.8** |
| 16 to 24 | 65.3 | 68.6 | 65.5 | 62.4 | 3.3 | -3.1 | -3.1 |
| 25 to 54 | 74.9 | 82.0 | 83.8 | 85.5 | 7.2 | 1.8 | 1.7 |
| 55 to 64 | 56.6 | 54.0 | 57.9 | 62.6 | -2.5 | 3.8 | 4.7 |
| 65 and over | 13.1 | 10.9 | 12.1 | 12.6 | -2.2 | 1.1 | 0.5 |
| *Men, 16 Yrs. & over* | **77.5** | **46.3** | **74.9** | **73.6** | **-1.3** | **-1.3** | **-1.3** |
| 16 to 24 | 72.9 | 73.0 | 68.8 | 65.8 | 0.1 | -4.3 | -2.9 |
| 25 to 54 | 94.2 | 93.8 | 91.8 | 90.8 | -0.4 | -2.0 | -1.0 |
| 55 to 64 | 74.3 | 67.3 | 67.0 | 70.2 | -7.1 | -0.3 | 3.2 |
| 65 and over | 20.2 | 16.0 | 16.9 | 17.8 | -4.2 | 0.9 | 0.9 |
| *Women, 16 Yrs. & over* | **50.9** | **55.3** | **59.3** | **61.4** | **4.4** | **4.0** | **2.2** |
| 16 to 24 | 62.5 | 64.3 | 62.2 | 62.2 | 1.8 | -2.1 | 0.0 |
| 25 to 54 | 62.3 | 70.8 | 76.1 | 79.3 | 8.5 | 5.3 | 3.2 |
| 55 to 64 | 41.7 | 42.3 | 49.6 | 55.8 | 0.6 | 7.3 | 6.2 |
| 65 and over | 8.3 | 7.4 | 8.6 | 8.7 | -0.9 | 1.2 | 0.1 |
| *White, 16 Yrs. & over* | **61.8** | **65.5** | **67.2** | **68.1** | **3.7** | **1.7** | **0.9** |
| Men | 78.4 | 76.9 | 75.8 | 74.3 | -1.4 | -1.1 | -1.6 |
| Women | 46.9 | 55.0 | 59.1 | 62.0 | 8.1 | 4.1 | 2.9 |
| *Black, 16 Yrs. & over* | **59.0** | **63.3** | **64.1** | **64.9** | **4.3** | **0.8** | **0.8** |
| Men | 70.2 | 71.2 | 68.7 | 69.6 | 0.9 | -2.5 | 0.9 |
| Women | 49.9 | 56.9 | 60.4 | 61.3 | 7.0 | 3.5 | 0.9 |
| *Asian & Pacific Islanders* | **64.6** | **65.5** | **65.8** | **65.7** | **0.9** | **0.3** | **-0.1** |
| Men | 79.2 | 75.0 | 73.4 | 71.6 | -4.2 | -1.6 | -1.7 |
| Women | 51.9 | 57.0 | 58.8 | 60.1 | 5.1 | 1.8 | 1.3 |
| *Hispanic, 16 Yrs. & over* | ---- | **65.4** | **66.5** | **65.7** | ---- | **1.1** | **1.0** |
| Men | ---- | 81.0 | 79.6 | 77.1 | ---- | -1.4 | -2.5 |
| Women | ---- | 50.1 | 53.4 | 57.2 | ---- | 3.2 | 3.8 |
| *Other than Hispanic Orig.* | ---- | **65.2** | **66.8** | **67.5** | ---- | **1.6** | **0.7** |
| Men | ---- | 75.9 | 74.4 | 73.1 | ---- | -1.5 | -1.3 |
| Women | ---- | 55.7 | 59.9 | 62.4 | ---- | 4.2 | 2.5 |
| *White, non-Hispanic* | ---- | **65.5** | **67.3** | **68.7** | ---- | **1.8** | **1.5** |
| Men | ---- | 76.5 | 75.3 | 74.1 | ---- | -1.2 | -1.2 |
| Women | ---- | 55.4 | 59.8 | 63.7 | ---- | 4.4 | 3.9 |

Source: U.S. Department of Labor, "Charting the Course to 2006," November 1997.

have the highest labor force participation rate among all male workers, as shown in Table 4.

Latinas have pushed their labor force participation rate steadily upward from 50.1% in 1986 to 53.4% in 1996 to 55.4% in 1998; it is projected to reach 57.2% in 2006. Greater numbers of Hispanic women are entering the labor force, in some cases to augment the family income provided by the low wages earned, on average, by their male counterparts. In other cases, this increase can be attributed to the need to support families on their own, since there has been a rise in the proportion of female-headed families within the Hispanic community. In fact, women workers are gaining strength and bolstering the overall Latino socioeconomic profile. While they are less likely than other women to be in the paid labor force, Latinas have increased their participation among workers, and have outpaced Hispanic men in certain high-paying occupations, as the next section will discuss.

In terms of Hispanic subgroups, data from the March 1997 Current Population Survey show that Central and South American women, followed by Other Hispanic women, have the highest labor force participation rates (59.7% and 56.9%, respectively). Mexican American and Cuban American women are equally likely to be working or looking for work (54.0% and 53.0%, respectively). Fewer than half of Puerto Rican women are participating in the labor force (49.0%). Similar data regarding males show that Central and South American men, as well as Mexican American men, are the most likely to be working or looking for work among all Latinos (81.7% and 81.1%, respectively). Other Hispanic and Cuban men have similar proportions of workers in the labor force (72.9% and 70.0%, respectively). Like their female counterparts, Puerto Rican men are the least likely among the subgroups to be working or looking for work (67.8%).

## Types of Occupations Held

A trend in employment at the national level in the last 20 years depicts a shift of the entire population from jobs in the primary sector of the economy (agriculture, mining, and manufacturing) toward jobs in the tertiary sector (wholesale and retail trade, finance, insurance, and services). During these years, the highest percentages of employed persons were concentrated in three industries: manufacturing, retail trade, and services, while the mining, agriculture, and wholesale trade industries had the smallest proportion of workers.

Consistent with their educational preparation, Hispanic men tend to be employed in industries that do not require high levels of literacy and numeracy. By contrast, Hispanic women have slowly moved into professional and managerial positions. In fact, a larger proportion of Hispanic women than men are in these types of jobs.

**Table 5**

**Industries in the United States in Which Latinos and
Other Racial Groups Are Employed: 1980, 1990, and 1996 (Percent)**

| Industry | Total | | | White | | | Black | | | Latinos | | |
|---|---|---|---|---|---|---|---|---|---|---|---|---|
| | 1980 | 1990 | 1996 | 1980 | 1990 | 1996 | 1980 | 1990 | 1996 | 1980 | 1990 | 1996 |
| Agriculture | 3.0 | 2.7 | 2.7 | 1.3 | 2.8 | 3.0 | 0.6 | 1.3 | 0.7 | 4.8 | 5.1 | 5.2 |
| Mining | 1.1 | 0.6 | 0.5 | 0.3 | 0.7 | 0.5 | 0.2 | 0.3 | 0.2 | 1.1 | 0.5 | 0.3 |
| Construction | 5.9 | 6.2 | 6.3 | 1.2 | 6.5 | 6.7 | 0.6 | 4.2 | 3.9 | 6.4 | 7.4 | 7.0 |
| Manufacturing | 22.4 | 17.7 | 16.2 | 16.4 | 17.6 | 16.1 | 17.4 | 17.2 | 15.8 | 27.1 | 20.0 | 17.7 |
| Transportation* | 7.3 | 7.1 | 7.0 | 4.1 | 6.9 | 6.7 | 5.2 | 9.3 | 9.5 | 6.4 | 6.2 | 6.2 |
| Wholesale Trade | 4.3 | 4.4 | 3.9 | 2.9 | 4.4 | 4.1 | 1.5 | 2.9 | 2.5 | 4.3 | 4.6 | 4.1 |
| Retail Trade | 16.1 | 16.8 | 17.0 | 20.4 | 17.0 | 17.1 | 11.2 | 14.1 | 14.8 | 15.5 | 18.1 | 18.7 |
| Finance, Insurance** | 6.0 | 6.9 | 6.4 | 8.5 | 7.1 | 6.5 | 6.2 | 5.9 | 5.4 | 4.8 | 5.1 | 5.5 |
| Services | 28.7 | 32.7 | 35.5 | 40.1 | 32.3 | 35.0 | 49.3 | 37.4 | 40.1 | 25.0 | 29.1 | 31.9 |
| Public Admin. | 5.3 | 4.8 | 4.6 | 4.6 | 4.5 | 4.3 | 7.5 | 7.4 | 7.1 | 4.7 | 3.8 | 3.3 |

*Transportation and Public Utilities
**Finance, Insurance, and Real Estate

Sources: U.S. Bureau of the Census, *Social and Economic Characteristics of the Population*, 1990; U.S. Department of Labor, "Charting the Course to 2006," November 1997.

Latinos experienced a clearly-defined, positive employment trend in the tertiary sector of the economy between 1980 and 1996, since the percentages of employed Latinos in the services and retail trade industries continually increased during this period. Table 5 shows that, in 1980, one-quarter (25.0%) of Latinos were working in the services industry; by 1990 the percentage had risen to 29.1%. Further, in 1996 that proportion approached the one-third mark (31.9%). In a similar fashion, the percentage of Latinos working in the retail trade industry increased from 15.5% in 1980 to 18.7% in 1996, yielding a net increase of 6.9% of workers in the 16-year period. In the other service-related industries (e.g., finance, insurance, and real estate), the percentage of employed Latinos also increased during this period, but at a modest rate. Other industrial sectors with high concentrations of Latinos include: construction, finance, insurance and real estate, agriculture, and wholesale trade. Mining is the only industry where the percentage of employed Latinos is very low and has been declining over the last 20 years; only 0.3% of Latino workers were employed in this sector in 1996.

There has been a pronounced reduction of employed Latinos in the manufacturing industry in the last 20 years. According to BLS, between 1980 and 1996 there was a 10-point drop in the level of Latino employment in this segment of the labor market. In 1980, 27.1% of Latinos were employed in this industry, and by 1996 only 17.7% remained. The transportation industry also experienced a loss in Latino employment during this period, but it was minimal. In 1980, 6.4% of Latinos worked in transportation jobs, compared to 6.2% in 1996.

Table 6A shows that in the last 20 years, male Latinos have increasingly been employed in technical sales and administrative support occupations. The percentage of Latinos employed in this sector in 1980 was 14.9%, but by 1990, close to 17% of Latinos were working in this category of occupations that includes clinical laboratory technologists and technicians, electrical and electronic technicians, chemical technicians, and legal assistants. More than 20% of male Latinos are currently working in these types of occupations, which require some degree of post-high-school education and practical training. The latest technological developments in the electronic and chemical industries will require Latinos to increase their knowledge of these operations in order to maintain their occupation levels. There is also a sizeable proportion of Latinos working as retail or wholesale sales workers, cashiers, street and door-to-door sales workers, and news vendors; and in administrative support occupations, working in supervision, distribution, and scheduling, and as adjusting clerks.

The service industry is another area of the economy with an increasing concentration of male Latinos, who work as cleaners and servants in private households or in the rapidly-growing industry of personal protection. In 1980, only 13.3% of Latinos were working in service occupations; this percentage jumped to 16.1% in 1990 and was close to 20.0% in 1996. The service occupations do not require the same education and training levels as the technical sales and administrative support occupations described above.

## Table 6A

## Occupation of Employed Males, 16 Years and Over, by Race and Hispanic Origin: 1980-1990-1996 (Percentage)

| RACE/ HISPANIC ORIGIN | Managerial Professional Occupations | Service Occupations | Technical Sales & Admin Support | Operators, Fabricators & Laborers | Precision Production Craft & Repair | Farming, Forestry & Fishing |
|---|---|---|---|---|---|---|
| *Total Population* | | | | | | |
| 1980 | 23.6 | 9.2 | 19.0 | 23.2 | 20.7 | 4.3 |
| 1990 | 25.2 | 10.2 | 21.7 | 20.3 | 18.9 | 3.8 |
| 1996 | 27.3 | 10.1 | 19.8 | 20.3 | 18.3 | 4.3 |
| *White* | | | | | | |
| 1980 | 25.0 | 8.3 | 19.5 | 21.6 | 21.4 | 4.3 |
| 1990 | 26.8 | 8.8 | 22.1 | 18.9 | 19.5 | 3.8 |
| 1996 | 28.4 | 9.3 | 19.8 | 19.2 | 18.8 | 4.6 |
| *Black* | | | | | | |
| 1980 | 11.7 | 17.0 | 15.2 | 37.2 | 15.5 | 3.4 |
| 1990 | 14.5 | 18.8 | 19.0 | 30.4 | 14.6 | 2.7 |
| 1996 | 16.9 | 18.0 | 17.9 | 31.1 | 14.2 | 2.0 |
| *Total Hispanic* | | | | | | |
| 1980 | 12.0 | 13.3 | 14.9 | 32.5 | 20.7 | 6.5 |
| 1990 | 12.0 | 16.1 | 16.7 | 28.1 | 19.7 | 7.3 |
| 1996 | 14.1* | 20.2* | 24.6* | 22.4* | 12.8* | 5.9* |
| *Mexican* | | | | | | |
| 1980 | 9.0 | 12.2 | 12.2 | 35.4 | 21.9 | 9.2 |
| 1990 | 9.4 | 15.4 | 14.2 | 30.2 | 20.7 | 10.1 |
| *Puerto Rican* | | | | | | |
| 1980 | 11.4 | 17.4 | 18.6 | 34.3 | 16.1 | 2.2 |
| 1990 | 14.0 | 19.2 | 21.6 | 27.2 | 15.9 | 2.1 |
| *Cuban* | | | | | | |
| 1980 | 22.3 | 12.4 | 23.1 | 22.1 | 18.7 | 1.4 |
| 1990 | 22.5 | 12.8 | 25.2 | 19.4 | 18.1 | 2.0 |
| *Other Hispanic* | | | | | | |
| 1980 | 17.6 | 14.5 | 18.1 | 26.8 | 20.1 | 2.9 |
| 1990 | 15.7 | 17.7 | 19.3 | 25.0 | 19.2 | 3.1 |

\* Represents data for the whole Hispanic population; there are not data available by gender.

Sources: U.S. Bureau of the Census, *Census of Population, General Social and Economic Characteristics, U.S. Summary,* 1980 and 1990; U.S. Department of Labor, Bureau of Labor Statistics, *Employment and Earnings,* January 1997.

On the other hand, the occupational categories of "operators, fabricators, and laborers," and "precision production, craft, and repair" have experienced a decrease in the percentage of employed Latinos in the last 20 years. In 1980, one in three Latinos was working as a machine operator, welder and cutter, or textile, apparel, or furnishing machine operator. By 1990, the percentage of Latinos working in these occupations declined to 28.1%, and continues to drop, due to the economic trend that has shifted jobs from this industry to the service sector. In 1980, one in five Latinos was working in mechanics and repair jobs, in various occupations in the construction sector, and in precision production occupations. The percentage of Latinos working in these occupations remained practically constant in the 1990s and continues to be about 20.0% today.

Two more occupational sectors with minimal variations in the percentage of employed Latinos in the last 20 years are managerial and professional specialties and farming, forestry, and fishing. Approximately 12.0% of Latinos were employed during this period in management-related occupations and in marketing, advertising, and public relations. Close to 7.0% of Latinos were working in agricultural occupations, mainly as farm workers or as groundskeepers and gardeners, during the same period.

Further analysis points to Latino subgroup differences in occupational distribution. Between 1980 and 1990, Mexicans and Puerto Ricans were primarily working as operators, fabricators and laborers, and in precision production, craft, and repair, all of which require some measure of manual ability and technical skills. Cubans, on the other hand, tended to work in service occupations; 25% were employed in the technical sales and administrative support areas. Other Latinos, especially from Central and South America, were evenly distributed between production and service occupations. While Cubans and U.S.-born Hispanics are more likely than other Latino men to work in white-collar jobs, the proportion of these men who hold such jobs is much smaller than that of White men.[16]

The occupational distribution of Whites during this period reflected an inverse trend relative to that observed for the total population. Specifically, the percentage of Whites working in the manufacturing sector increased from 16.4% in 1980 to 17.6% in 1990, but declined between 1990 and 1996 to 16.1%. At the same time the representation of White workers in the services sector decreased. For example, in 1980, more than 40% of Whites were working in services, but by 1990 the percentage had declined to 32.3%. Similarly, the percentage of White workers in the retail trade sector declined from 20.4% in 1980 to 17.1% in 1996.

In 1980, almost half of Blacks (49.3%) worked in service jobs, making them the most likely of all racial/ethnic groups to be employed in this industry. As with Whites, the percentage of African Americans working in service jobs declined, to 37.4% in 1990. Since 1990, however, this segment of the labor market has experienced a return of Black workers. On the other hand, in the primary or productive sectors of the economy, Table 6B shows a negative trend in the employment of African Americans. For example, the manufacturing industry showed a decrease of Black employees, from 17.4% in 1980 to 15.8% in 1996. The most recent data indicate that Blacks have, among all racial/ethnic groups, the highest proportion of employed persons in the category of jobs "public administration." In 1980, 7.5% of African Americans were employed in public administration, and this has remained constant during the past 16 years.

In general, for the total population during the period between 1980 and 1996, males were working in occupations related to the managerial and professional specialties; one in four males worked as executives or administrators, or in professional occupations. These occupations require high levels of education and training. During the same period, one in five males was working in an occupation that required a high level of practical training. The service and agriculture-related occupations also employ many men; nearly one in 10 males was working in service occupations, and only one in 20 was working in an occupation related to agriculture.

Between 1980 and 1996, females in the U.S. were notably concentrated in two occupational areas: managerial and professional jobs and in technical sales and administrative support. The percentage of females working in the managerial and professional areas increased from 21.5% in 1980 to 30.3% in 1996, with a net increase of 8.8%. This positive trend shows the progress that women have made in obtaining positions previously reserved mainly for their male counterparts. Today, more and more women work in managerial positions that require advanced levels of technical and professional training. Another occupational area with a significant concentration of females is technical sales and administrative support. These areas, unlike the previous one cited, do not require high levels of education, but instead require considerable practical training. In 1996, more than two-fifths of U.S. females were working in this area.

Latina workers have primarily been concentrated in two areas: technical sales and administrative support, in which two-fifths (40.0%) were employed in 1990, and in the service industry. Together, these two occupational areas employed almost two-thirds (62.6%) of

**Table 6B**

**Occupation of Employed Females, 16 Years and Over, by Race and Hispanic Origin: 1980-1990-1996 (Percentage)**

| RACE/ HISPANIC ORIGIN | Managerial Professional Occupation | Service Occupations | Technical Sales & Admin Support | Operators, Fabricators & Laborers | Precision Production Craft & Repair | Farming, Forestry & Fishing |
|---|---|---|---|---|---|---|
| *Total Population* | | | | | | |
| 1980 | 21.5 | 17.9 | 45.6 | 11.7 | 2.3 | 1.0 |
| 1990 | 27.8 | 16.9 | 43.6 | 8.5 | 2.3 | 0.8 |
| 1996 | 30.3 | 17.5 | 41.4 | 7.6 | 2.1 | 1.2 |
| *White* | | | | | | |
| 1980 | 22.4 | 16.3 | 47.3 | 10.8 | 2.3 | 1.0 |
| 1990 | 29.3 | 15.4 | 44.7 | 7.5 | 2.2 | 0.9 |
| 1996 | 31.5 | 16.3 | 41.9 | 6.9 | 2.0 | 1.3 |
| *Black* | | | | | | |
| 1980 | 16.5 | 29.3 | 35.2 | 16.1 | 2.3 | 0.5 |
| 1990 | 21.3 | 25.3 | 38.7 | 12.1 | 2.4 | 0.3 |
| 1996 | 22.8 | 25.4 | 38.4 | 11.0 | 2.2 | 0.2 |
| *Total Hispanic** | | | | | | |
| 1980 | 12.5 | 20.8 | 38.9 | 22.0 | 3.9 | 1.8 |
| 1990 | 17.0 | 23.5 | 39.1 | 15.2 | 3.5 | 1.6 |
| *Mexican* | | | | | | |
| 1980 | 10.8 | 22.8 | 37.5 | 22.0 | 4.0 | 2.9 |
| 1990 | 15.2 | 23.6 | 38.7 | 16.2 | 3.7 | 2.5 |
| *Puerto Rican* | | | | | | |
| 1980 | 13.4 | 15.2 | 42.0 | 25.5 | 3.5 | 0.4 |
| 1990 | 21.1 | 17.6 | 44.9 | 13.1 | 3.0 | 0.4 |
| *Cuban* | | | | | | |
| 1980 | 15.7 | 12.4 | 42.8 | 24.4 | 4.4 | 0.3 |
| 1990 | 24.1 | 13.7 | 45.5 | 12.8 | 3.6 | 0.3 |
| *Other Hispanic* | | | | | | |
| 1980 | 14.8 | 21.5 | 39.4 | 19.9 | 3.7 | 0.6 |
| 1990 | 17.4 | 28.1 | 36.0 | 14.6 | 3.3 | 0.6 |

* Represents data for the whole Hispanic population; there are not data available by gender.

Sources: U.S. Bureau of the Census, *Census of Population, General Social and Economic Characteristics, U.S. Summary,* 1980 and 1990; U.S. Department of Labor, Bureau of Labor Statistics, *Employment and Earnings,* January 1997.

Latinas. On the other hand, while only 17.0% of Latinas were employed in managerial and professional occupations, this represents a significant increase over the past decade. In fact, a higher proportion of Hispanic women than men are employed in these types of jobs. The data also show that, among all female workers, Latinas have the highest percentage of employment in another well-paying area of the economy, the precision production and craft occupations (although only around 4.0%).

With respect to differences in the occupational distribution of Hispanic women by subgroup, data indicate that Puerto Rican and Cuban women are more likely than Mexican American or Central American women to be employed in professional or managerial jobs. In 1997, 25.5% of Puerto Rican and 24.0% of Cuban women held such jobs, compared to 16.3% of Mexican American and 19.3% of Central and South American women. By contrast, these latter two groups of women tend to be concentrated in low-wage and unskilled labor, in the category "operators, fabricators, and laborers" (16.6% and 17.0%, respectively), compared to 9.8% and 7.0% of Puerto Rican and Cuban women, respectively.[17]

Table 6B also shows that almost three-quarters of White females worked in managerial, professional, technical, and administrative support activities in 1996. The participation level of White females in other occupations was relatively low; one in six White females worked in service occupations and only one in 14 White females worked as operators or laborers. In occupations that require high levels of physical activity, such as precision production, repair, and others related to the agriculture sector, the percentage of White female workers is very low, at 2.0%. Since 1980, Black women also had a high percentage of workers in the technical, sales, administrative support, managerial, and professional areas, with 61.2% of African American females working in this type of occupation. The percentage of African American females working in service occupations is higher than the corresponding percentage of White females, at 25.4%. The other three occupation categories have low levels of Black female employment.

Finally, data related to immigration status indicate that 60% of foreign-born women were employed in service and unskilled occupations. Comparatively, about 82% of Latino men born outside the U.S. worked in low-skilled jobs in factories, agriculture, or construction, which is not surprising, given their (on average) low education levels and limited English proficiency.[18]

## Earnings Levels

The prevailing differences in educational attainment levels among persons participating in the job market, the level of their practical skills, and the types of occupation in which they are employed, are some of the key factors that determine – and help to distinguish – earnings levels.  A review of earnings data show that the level of Latino full-time workers' weekly earnings was far below the level of median earnings of both White and total workers in the United States in 1996.  The median weekly earnings of all workers in 1996 were $490; Whites had the highest weekly earnings at $506, followed by Blacks with $387, and Latinos with $339.  The gap of $167 in weekly earnings between Latino and White workers represents 49.2% less earnings (see Table 7), but this is not altogether surprising, given the human capital characteristics that Latinos, as a group, possess, and their propensity to work in low-skilled, low-wage industries, as discussed above.

### Table 7

### Median Weekly Earnings of Full-time and Part-time Wage and Salary Workers, 16 Years and Over, by Race and Hispanic Origin, 1996

| Race & Hispanic Origin | FULL-TIME WORKERS | | PART-TIME WORKERS | |
|---|---|---|---|---|
| | Number of Workers (000) | Median Weekly Earnings ($) | Number of workers (000) | Median Weekly Earnings ($) |
| *Total* | *90,918* | *490* | *20,810* | *144* |
| Men | 51,895 | 557 | 6,432 | 134 |
| Women | 45,919 | 418 | 3,029 | 148 |
| *White* | *76,151* | *506* | *17,960* | *146* |
| Men | 44,428 | 580 | 5,310 | 134 |
| Women | 31,724 | 428 | 12,550 | 150 |
| *Black* | *10,871* | *387* | *2,006* | *132* |
| Men | 5,316 | 412 | 695 | 129 |
| Women | 5,555 | 362 | 1,311 | 134 |
| *Hispanic* | *9,082* | *339* | *1,711* | *139* |
| Men | 5,831 | 356 | 622 | 144 |
| Women | 3,251 | 316 | 1,089 | 137 |

Source:  U.S. Bureau of the Census, Bureau of Labor Statistics, *Employment and Earnings* January 1997.

Occupations in farming, forestry, and fishing had the lowest weekly earnings in 1996, at $294, followed by service occupations, with $305, and then by operators, fabricators, and laborers, at $391 per week (see Table 8). As discussed above, since 1980, a sizeable segment of Latino workers ages 16 and over were employed as operators, fabricators, and laborers and worked in the farming, forestry, and fishing occupations. Conversely, jobs in which smaller proportions of Latinos tend to work, such as precision production, craft, and repair, had the highest levels of earnings, at $540, followed by occupations in managerial and professional specialty, with earnings at $490, and technical sales and administrative support, with $441 in weekly earnings. There also appears to be an upward trend, since 1980, in the proportion of Hispanic workers in agriculture, retail trade, and services industries. The reported earnings in these industries were among the lowest of all occupations reviewed, but the increase of Latino workers in such jobs can be explained in part by the low educational and skill levels required by these industries.

### Table 8

### Median Weekly Earnings of Full-time Wage and Salary Workers, 16 Years and Over, by Detailed Occupation and Sex, 1996

| Occupation | Total ($) | Men ($) | Women ($) |
|---|---|---|---|
| Managerial and Professional Specialty | 490 | 557 | 418 |
| Service Occupations | 305 | 357 | 273 |
| Technical Sales and Administrative Support | 441 | 567 | 394 |
| Operators, Fabricators, and Laborers | 391 | 422 | 307 |
| Precision Production, Craft, and Repair | 540 | 560 | 373 |
| Farming, Forestry, and Fishing | 294 | 300 | 255 |

Source: U.S. Department of Labor, Bureau of Labor Statistics, *Employment and Earnings,* January 1997.

Although Latinas are likely to work in technical sales and administrative support occupations, which include the third-highest paying category of jobs, in all cases men had higher levels of weekly earnings than women. On the whole, women tend to earn less than men; for example, the largest gap in weekly earnings by gender – of $187 per week – was in precision production, craft, and repair. Similarly, male workers earned $173 more than female workers in technical sales and administrative support jobs. More-over, since 1980 there has been an increasing trend for Latino females to work in the service industry, which has among the lowest-paying jobs.

In terms of high-wage industries, the mining sector had the highest weekly salaries and wages in 1996 ($693 per week). Transportation and public utilities ($596), the government sector ($592), and finance, insurance, and real estate ($521) – areas in which Latino men and women are underrepresented – also offered high weekly salaries and wages in 1996.

In addition to human capital and occupational concentration, another important distinction that affects differences in earning levels by industry is the impact of unions and union representation. In general, unionized workers earn higher salaries and wages than their non-union counterparts. On average, there was a 10% gap in earning levels between unionized and non-unionized workers in all the industries considered (see Table 9). Latinos are less likely than other workers to be members of unions. In 1994, union membership was proportionally higher among men (18%) than women

### Table 9

### Median Weekly Earnings of Full-time Wage and Salary Workers, 16 Years and Over, by Industry and Union Affiliation, 1996

| Industry | Total ($) | Members of Union ($) | Represented by Union ($) | Non-Union ($) |
|---|---|---|---|---|
| Agriculture | 306 | — | — | 305 |
| Mining | 693 | 698 | 699 | 690 |
| Construction | 504 | 748 | 742 | 464 |
| Manufacturing | 507 | 560 | 558 | 494 |
| Transportation and P.U.* | 596 | 680 | 676 | 555 |
| Wholesale Trade | 503 | 566 | 551 | 500 |
| Retail Trade | 343 | 408 | 408 | 338 |
| Finance, Insurance, and R.E.** | 521 | 534 | 533 | 520 |
| Services | 456 | 501 | 498 | 451 |
| Government | 592 | 657 | 651 | 519 |

*Public Utilities    **Real Estate

Source: U.S. Department of Labor, Bureau of Labor Statistics, *Employment and Earnings,* January 1997.

(13%), and among Blacks (21%) than either Whites (15%) or Hispanics (14%). According to the Department of Labor, within these major groups, Black men had the highest proportion of union membership (23%), while White women and Hispanic women both had the lowest (12%).

Finally, Table 10 shows the impact of educational attainment on mean earnings. Mean earnings by gender for the total population and by race and Hispanic origin are compared with different levels of educational attainment for 1980 and 1990. To make relevant comparisons, the 1980 nominal figures were converted into 1990 constant dollars using CPI indices, and then differences were obtained in constant dollars for all the categories. For the total population, Table 10 shows that Hispanics in general, and Hispanic males in particular, experienced losses in their mean income during this period, at $56 and $1,200, respectively. Females from each of the racial/ethnic groups made substantial progress during the period, with Hispanic women experiencing a gain of almost $1,800. While this helped to offset the loss of male earnings over this time, it was the lowest increase among all women workers.

Among persons who do not have a high school degree, men and women in all racial/ethnic categories experienced substantial losses in their earnings during the 1980s. For example, Hispanic women experienced a loss of more than $2,900. The results were mixed for people who had obtained a high school certificate; all males in this category experienced earnings losses, while females saw some gains. Hispanic males lost more than $2,700, followed by Black males with a loss of $1,340. At the same time, White females who completed high school recorded the highest earnings gains at $1,250.

In general, people with some years of college, associate degrees, or college degrees experienced considerable gains in their mean earnings, because advanced levels of educational attainment qualify these workers for a range of employment options with high wages and other benefits. For example, persons with some college background improved their mean earnings by $964 during this period, while those with a bachelor's degree experienced jumps of more than $2,300. In these two categories only Hispanic males and Black females experienced losses in their mean earnings, by $420 and $1,496, respectively.

Finally, mean earnings for people with advanced degrees increased substantially for both males and females during the decade. Hispanics in this category had substantial

## Table 10

## Mean Earnings of Workers, Ages 18 Years and Over, By Educational Attainment, Race, and Hispanic Origin, 1980-1990

| Description | 1980 Total | White | Black | Hispanic | 1990 Total | White | Black | Hispanic | DIFFERENCE Total | White | Black | Hispanic |
|---|---|---|---|---|---|---|---|---|---|---|---|---|
| **Total** | | | | | | | | | | | | |
| All Sexes | 20,137 | 20,734 | 17,625 | 15,999 | 21,793 | 22,401 | 16,677 | 15,943 | 1,656 | 1,667 | -948 | -56 |
| Male: | 26,047 | 26,943 | 17,625 | 19,573 | 27,164 | 28,105 | 18,859 | 18,320 | 1,117 | 1,162 | 1,234 | -1,253 |
| Female: | 12,575 | 12,609 | 12,218 | 10,764 | 15,493 | 15,559 | 14,449 | 12,516 | 2,918 | 2,950 | 2,231 | 1,752 |
| **Not a High School Grad** | | | | | | | | | | | | |
| All Sexes | 14,064 | 15,491 | 13,389 | 12,909 | 12,582 | 12,773 | 11,184 | 10,368 | -1,482 | -2,718 | -2,205 | -2,541 |
| Male | 17,557 | 18,347 | 13,339 | 15,622 | 14,991 | 15,319 | 13,031 | 13,182 | -2,566 | -3,028 | -308 | -2,440 |
| Female | 8,368 | 11,111 | 7,449 | 7,995 | 8,808 | 8,727 | 8,946 | 5,093 | 440 | -2,384 | 1,497 | -2,902 |
| **High School Grad** | | | | | | | | | | | | |
| All Sexes | 17,989 | 18,323 | 18,385 | 16,189 | 17,820 | 18,257 | 14,794 | 15,417 | -169 | -66 | -3,591 | -772 |
| Male | 23,853 | 24,457 | 17,385 | 20,842 | 22,378 | 23,135 | 17,046 | 18,100 | -1,475 | -1,322 | -339 | -2742 |
| Female | 11,803 | 11,790 | 11,938 | 11,006 | 12,986 | 13,031 | 12,560 | 12,109 | 1,183 | 1,241 | 622 | 1,103 |
| **Some College/Associate's Degree** | | | | | | | | | | | | |
| All Sexes | 19,730 | 20,156 | 19,705 | 18,907 | 20,694 | 21,095 | 18,209 | 19,206 | 964 | 939 | -1,496 | 299 |
| Male | 25,235 | 25,938 | 19,705 | 22,786 | 26,120 | 26,841 | 21,152 | 22,376 | 885 | 903 | 1,447 | -410 |
| Female | 13,127 | 13,071 | 13,585 | 14,005 | 15,002 | 14,922 | 15,734 | 15,245 | 1,875 | 1,851 | 2,149 | 1,240 |
| **Bachelor's Degree** | | | | | | | | | | | | |
| All Sexes | 28,739 | 37,311 | 24,829 | 24,925 | 31,112 | 41,906 | 26,448 | 25,703 | 2,373 | 4,595 | 1,619 | 778 |
| Male | 37,111 | 37,847 | 24,829 | 30,566 | 38,901 | 39,781 | 29,451 | 31,485 | 1,790 | 1,934 | 4,622 | 919 |
| Female | 16,899 | 16,611 | 19,699 | 16,803 | 21,933 | 21,725 | 23,837 | 19,378 | 5,034 | 5,114 | 4,138 | 2,575 |
| **Advanced Degree** | | | | | | | | | | | | |
| All Sexes | 37,060 | 37,311 | 31,736 | 34,837 | 41,458 | 41,908 | 32,962 | 38,075 | 4,398 | 4,597 | 1,226 | 3,238 |
| Male | 44,275 | 37,847 | 37,120 | 39,181 | 49,768 | 50,385 | 39,104 | 47,479 | 5,493 | 12,538 | 1,984 | 8,298 |
| Female | 22,295 | 21,956 | 27,472 | 23,322 | 32,929 | 28,494 | 28,074 | 27,184 | 10,634 | 6,738 | 602 | 3,862 |

*In 1990 Dollars*

Source: U.S. Bureau of the Census.

gains in their mean earnings; among men, the difference was nearly $8,300, while for women the increase was over $3,200. These data clearly show that high levels of educational attainment translate into meaningful benefits in terms of earnings.

## Analysis and Implications

The primary determinants of a worker's labor force outcomes are his/her human capital characteristics. The discussion above shows that Hispanics are at a disadvantage when it comes to formal educational preparation, given that they have significantly lower levels of high school attainment, and a smaller proportion of them are college graduates, compared to other Americans. By the year 2006, Latinos will become the largest minority group in the labor market, but their educational status leaves them with very few labor market options. Currently, too many Latinos are able to seek only entry-level positions that do not require extensive human capital. For example, the high-growth service industry employs many Latinos, often in maintenance jobs or food preparation, but these tend to be low-wage occupations. Furthermore, it is difficult to acquire highly-evolved skills or general knowledge transferable to well-paying industries from these jobs, so such work limits Latino economic progress. Without advanced education or practical training, many new or promising sectors of the economy will be closed to Latino participation.

In terms of training, the experience of Latinos in federal workforce development programs has been uneven. While many programs have effective components, Latinos have not always participated in those most likely to translate into steady or meaningful employment. Furthermore, one serious and consistent problem has been the lack of proportional representation of Hispanic workers within these programs. Therefore, much needs to be done to ensure that such programs be available to Latino workers who need to enhance their job qualifications and abilities. Apart from participating in formal training programs, workers in certain industries are able to gain additional skills through on-the-job training. Yet, too many Latino workers do not receive this valuable benefit because of the occupations in which they are concentrated. Another phenomenon related to training and work experience that has not received sufficient attention is the accumulation of experience over time, even in "low" or "unskilled" jobs. Given that they tend to enter the labor force at a young age, Latino workers, overall, probably have better-than-average work experience. However, because they have less access to formal experience-gaining programs, this usually means that there is less opportunity for Hispanics to get the range of experience required by economically-mobile occupations.

To complicate matters, more than one-third of Hispanics are foreign-born, suggesting that a sizeable share of the Latino population has to overcome another barrier to labor force success: limited English proficiency. Further, Latino immigrants have low levels of educational attainment, on average, which limits their ability to compete for high-skilled jobs with promising wages and benefits.

While it is true that immigrant educational data do depress overall Hispanic educational attainment levels, data disaggregated by Hispanics born within and outside of the U.S. show that educational gaps are still quite wide between U.S.-born Latinos and their Black and White peers. Additionally, both data and research show that U.S.-born status or U.S. citizenship are not the most important determinants of educational success. For instance, Puerto Ricans – U.S. citizens by birth – do not have educational attainment rates close to those of Blacks or Whites. Moreover, the children of immigrants (or second-generation Americans) "appear to have better scholastic records, despite their parents' lower educational attainment and their limited English" than those with U.S.-born parents.[19] Immigration status notwithstanding, Hispanic education levels are substantially inadequate for the current and future labor markets. Moreover, U.S. Census Bureau data show that four-fifths of all Latinos under 18 years old were born in the U.S., and that a significant segment of Latinos are entering the labor force or are in their prime working years. This means that the U.S. economy – and the nation as a whole – will rely on these workers for its growth. Educational achievement among all Hispanics must be increased.

With respect to two additional sets of human capital characteristics, computer literacy and pre-employment skills, the information is not conclusive. Preliminary student data seem to indicate that there exists a disparity between access to and use of computers at school and at home for Hispanics, compared to their peers. Given that the global economy is increasingly computer-based, and that high-wage, high-growth industries require at least basic computer knowledge, this is an area that merits further exploration. The ability of young Latinos to compete – and excel – in the labor market is not an issue of relevance simply to their own families; as they are a growing proportion of tomorrow's workers, their success is critical to the nation's future economy. The area of pre-employment skills is still premature ground from a social science research perspective. There is a set of intangible and universal skills that employers seek and which are expected in any workplace. However, the importance of these "soft skills" to employment status and prospects has not been quantified. Further research is needed, not only to better understand employer expectations, but also, more importantly, to ensure that Hispanic and other inexperienced workers learn what the labor market requires – and how they can best meet these standards.

Their less-developed human capital characteristics relative to those of other American workers have not prevented Latinos from actively participating in the labor market. In fact, Hispanics have maintained impressively high employment levels in spite of their lack of formal education, training, or preparation for the labor market of the late 20th century. Labor force participation rates are not an area of concern. Latino men represent those most likely to work or look for work in the U.S., and a positive upward trend has been the increase, since 1990, of the Latina labor force participation rate. It is likely that the increases in labor force activity among Latino workers overall will be due mainly to the growth in the participation of Hispanic women in the paid labor force.

Still, several issues stand out. First, Hispanic men appear to be trapped in low-wage industries expected to decline. For the past 20 years, the highest proportions of Latino male workers have been in occupations in the manufacturing or other low-skilled sectors, which are expected to decrease in number of jobs. Thus, while Hispanic men are more likely to work than others, they are especially likely to experience stagnation, few opportunities for job advancement, and minimal earnings increases. Second, Hispanic women, who are the least likely of all women to work in the paid labor force, are making important strides. Over time they have increased their share of workers in high-paying professions and have already outpaced their Hispanic male counterparts in the category of professional and managerial jobs. These trends will need further study for their implications for Latino workers and their employment status to be clear. These developments also merit further examination for what they might mean for Latino families. For instance, women's employment outside of the home may challenge traditionally-defined gender roles within the Latino community, especially among recent immigrants, and may have implications for family formation and relationships.

Another notable issue relates to Latino subgroups. Data reviewed and presented above indicate that important human capital and labor market distinctions continue to exist between the various Hispanic subgroups. Cubans have among the highest levels of educational attainment and tend to work in better-paying industries than other Latinos. Their higher median age relative to other Latinos may contribute to this. While Puerto Ricans tend to have higher levels of educational attainment than Mexicans, they have the lowest labor force participation rates of all groups – despite their citizenship status and the strong economy. More research is needed to understand the reasons for this. One factor that offsets these low rates is that Puerto Ricans who do work are often employed in high-paying industries.

By contrast, those groups, like Mexicans, who tend to have a sizeable share of immigrants among their total population, are concentrated in low-paying jobs. Their overall human capital characteristics are evidently not valued by the labor market. Nevertheless, immigration status has not affected their likelihood to work, as evidenced by their very strong labor force participation rate – which is higher even than that of Whites or Blacks. What is key is not immigration status per se, but education levels, skills, and English-language ability. More attention should be paid to augmenting and increasing the human capital of workers with such a strong attachment to the labor force.

One subgroup that has not received sufficient attention in the literature is composed of Central and South Americans. Their educational attainment levels are between those of Mexicans and Puerto Ricans, but there is a fairly noteworthy proportion of Central and South Americans with college degrees. They also represent the group with the highest labor force participation rates for both genders, but their occupational distribution is mixed. More research is needed to gain a better understanding of their labor force experiences, and their contributions to the U.S. economy.

Improving the human capital characteristics and employment outcomes of U.S. Hispanics will require multifaceted responses in a range of arenas, including research, policy, and practice. Three areas are key:

(1) **Early Childhood Education.** The poor educational attainment of roughly two-fifths of Latinos is unequivocally linked to their limited labor market prospects. While the proportion of Latinos enrolled in school must increase across the spectrum, improvements in early childhood development are especially needed. Data show that the participation level of Hispanic children in pre-primary programs is not where it should be, despite much national focus on the significance of the early years for intellectual and social development. Policy can have a role here, especially with regard to Head Start – an early childhood development model that has been demonstrated to improve the school readiness and educational outcomes of poor children. Current data show that approximately 15% of Latino children participate in Head Start programs, even though about twice that number are eligible. A strong education and learning base in the early years could

translate into an upward trend in educational outcomes and workplace success for Latino students in the future.

(2) **Middle and High School Development.** As the data show, the middle teenage years, from 15 to 17 years old, is a critical period for Latino students. At this point, the difference between school enrollment levels for Latinos and their counterparts begins to widen. Schools and Latino families must work together to emphasize the importance of education and help prevent the early desertion of Latino students from the school system. In this area, community-based after-school initiatives that provide additional learning and skills building, as well as decision-making guidance and opportunities for positive social development, can be key. To strengthen young Latinos' ability to make a smooth transition to higher education or employment, school-based instruction and facilities must be relevant to the changing workforce, and Latino students should develop familiarity with computers and other technological skills that are required by employers. They should also have access to a wide range of higher education and employment options to help them plan for the future, including to those federal programs that currently underserve Latinos, like college-preparatory "TRIO" (Turning Risk Into Opportunity) and Upward Bound programs.

(3) **Workforce Development.** Given the strong labor force participation rates of Latinos, attention should be paid to strategies that will augment human capital characteristics, as well as increase the proportion of Latino workers in high-paying industries in which they are currently underrepresented. Efforts should be focused on three populations:

• **Youth.** To ensure that Latino and other American youth are well-skilled and prepared to enter the labor market, there should be a spectrum of workforce development options available to them. In addition to traditional four-year college instruction, other programs should be developed through institutions such as community colleges and community-based organizations to train Latinos for specific high-growth jobs. Apprenticeships, internships with specific industries, and other training opportunities for youth are also needed. Another source of both employment and labor market training is the Department of Defense – the nation's largest employer – and strategies should be developed to ensure that interested and eligible Latinos be encouraged to pursue all levels of military service and opportunities for civilian jobs.[20]

- **Adult workers.** Efforts must be made to increase the levels of Hispanic worker participation in existing, effective federal government training programs, at least to their proportionate levels. But the private sector should also play a role in the preparation of the workforce. Alternatives are especially needed for adult Latino workers already in the labor force. For example, this might include private-sector efforts to train and recruit Hispanic workers, thereby helping Latinos to move into higher-paying jobs in the primary sector of the economy and to reduce their concentration in poor-paying areas of the service industry. Other options might also include on-the-job training and specific career ladders within the service industry, to allow Latino workers to "move up" to management and other well-paying positions.

- **Immigrants.** Immigrants are an important segment of the workforce that helps to fuel the nation's economy, and many immigrants would benefit from basic education and GED programs to help them complete their high school degrees. In particular, programs providing English language instruction to adult immigrants should be funded and expanded to meet the demand, reduce waiting lists, and strengthen their employment qualifications. In general, businesses with large concentrations of low-wage workers should provide these and other on-the-job training opportunities to strengthen the productivity and enhance the upward mobility of their employees.

Demographically, the Latino community is close to becoming the largest minority group in the nation, and is a necessary and vital source of workers. Concerted effort is now needed from the Hispanic community, as well as from public policy makers and the private sector, to increase Latino high school and college completion rates, and effective workforce development programs that will allow Latinos to compete for high-paying jobs should be expanded. Opportunities for training for already-employed low-wage workers would also help Latinos move up the economic ladder. While Hispanic workers, on average, bring low skill and education levels with them to the labor market, their high and consistent labor force participation has contributed to the nation's strong economic growth. In addition, Latino workers often possess other non-traditional characteristics, like bilingual ability, that are valuable to the evolving global economy and can translate into good incomes. More can and should be done to enhance their employment and economic opportunities.

# NOTES

1. del Pinal, Jorge and Audrey Singer, *Generations of Diversity: Latinos in the United States*, Washington, DC: Population Reference Bureau, October 1997, Vol. 52, No. 3.

2. Fisher, María with Sonia M. Pérez, Bryant Gonzalez, Jonathan Njus, and Charles K. Kamasaki, *Latino Education, Status and Prospects,* Final Edition, Washington, DC: National Council of La Raza, October 1998.

3. *Ibid.*

4. March 1997 Current Population Survey, U.S. Bureau of the Census.

5. del Pinal and Singer, *op.cit.*

6. *Ibid.*

7. U.S. Department of Labor, Bureau of Labor Statistics. *Employment and Earnings*, Vol. 44, Number 1, January 1997.

8. Martínez, Deirdre, *Hispanics in the Labor Force: A Chartbook*, Washington, DC: National Council of La Raza, December 1993.

9. Figures taken from 1990 Census data, as cited in *Chicago Tribune*, "SPANISH FOR ALL?" Domenico Maceri, April 15, 1999.

10. Information obtained from http://www.ncbe.gwu.edu/askncbe/faqs/13adult.htm.

11. "Hispanic Participation in Selected Federal Anti-Poverty Programs," Issue Brief, Washington, DC: National Council of La Raza, July 1997. Also see Romero, Carol J., *JTPA Programs and Adult Women on Welfare: Using Training to Raise AFDC Recipients Above Poverty*, Washington, DC: National Commission for Employment Policy, June 1994. For an understanding of Latina women's experiences in training programs aimed at welfare recipients, see Cruz, José E., *Puerto Rican Participation in Job Opportunities and Basic Skills (JOBS) Programs: A Preliminary Assessment*, Washington, DC: National Puerto Rican Coalition, May 1991; Rodríguez, Eric and Deirdre Martínez, *Latinos and JOBS: A Review of Ten States and Puerto Rico*, Washington, DC: National Council of La Raza, January 1995; and Uriarte, Miren, *Latinas and the Massachusetts Employment and Training (ET) Choices Program: Factors Associated with Participation and Outcomes for Boston Latinas in ET*, Boston, MA: Mauricio Gastón Institute for Latino Community Development and Public Policy, University of Massachusetts at Boston, January 1992.

12. Gantz McKay, Emily, *The Forgotten Two-Thirds: An Hispanic Perspective on Apprenticeship, European Style*, Washington, DC: National Council of La Raza, 1993.

13. *Case Studies of Successful or Promising Welfare-to-Work Programs that Have Involved the JTPA or Employment Services Systems*, Westat, November 1997; viewed online. For WordPerfect version, see http://wtw.doleta.gov, Westat Casebook on Promising WtW Practices.

14. Regenstein, Marsha, Jack A. Meyer, and Jennifer Dickemper Hicks, *Job Prospects for Welfare Recipients: Employers Speak Out*, Washington, DC: The Urban Institute, July 1998.

15. "Immigrant assistance," *The Economist*, March 29, 1997.

16. del Pinal and Singer, *op.cit.*

17. Table 9.3, March 1997 Current Population Survey: Occupation By Race-Ethnicity, Employed Persons Age 16 and Over: Females – Values/Percents, Source: U.S. Bureau of the Census, Internet site: http://www.census.gov/population/socdemo/hispanic/cps97/tab09-3.txt.

18. del Pinal and Singer, *op.cit.*

19. Ruben G. Rumbaut, "Passages to Adulthood: The Adaptation of Children of Immigrants in Southern California," Michigan State University, 1997; and Elaine Woo, "School Success of Immigrants' Children Tracked," *Los Angeles Times*, 16 June 1997: A1,19, as cited in *Generations of Diversity: Latinos in the United States, op.cit.* For a further discussion of this anomaly for Mexican Americans, in particular, see Chapter 3.

20. For a discussion of these issues, see Heitzman, Norman R., Jr., *A Force Overlooked: Achieving Full Representation of Hispanics in the Department of Defense Workforce*, Washington, DC: National Council of La Raza, January 1999.

# 2

# What a Latino Worker Finds in the U.S. Labor Market

**Rebecca Morales, Ph.D.**
San Diego State University

## Abstract

*The nation's growth economy has not had a favorable impact on Latinos. Latinos are the poorest racial/ethnic group in the country and are continuing to fall behind economically. There are several reasons for this disparity. One is the industrial restructuring of the last two and one-half decades that has resulted in the loss of manufacturing jobs and a rise of retail trade, services, and high technology. The new employment landscape is highly bifurcated, with few occupational ladders. Jobs at the lower end are characteristically unstable and lacking social benefits. Latinos who have been unable to make the transition into the higher-skilled, higher-wage jobs have been caught in an unyielding situation. Their plight has been exacerbated by unfavorable institutional trends affecting critical assurances for Latinos, such as the minimum wage and unionization. Yet a third dimension is persistent employment discrimination. These issues are explored in detail in an effort to understand why the problem is so intransigent, and how it can be changed through concerted policies.*

## I. Overview

Since the 1970s, Latinos in the United States have fallen further and further behind as workers, in sharp contrast to both the nation as a whole and other minorities, despite their strong attachment to the labor force. This downward slide has occurred within the context of an extremely robust economy which has produced job growth and declining unemployment since the mid-1990s. The reasons for this disturbing phenomenon are complex, and the subject of continuing debate. At the core is the nature of work and the structure of jobs that have undergone a profound transformation over the last 20 years. The loss of basic manufacturing to high-technology employment and services has coincided with a major shift in the composition and allocation of the Latino labor force. Together, these factors have redefined the way Latinos have entered into and progressed through the labor market. In addition to these massive changes in the demand for and supply of workers, the political environment, affecting such institutional factors as the minimum wage and unionization, has also been permanently altered, leading to a new set of rules governing the workplace. These conditions – demand, supply, and institutional parameters – have combined with lingering employment discrimination to shape the contemporary labor market for Latinos.

This chapter examines the structural, institutional, and discriminatory dimensions that shape the demand for Latino labor, and discusses their policy implications.

## II. The Changing U.S. Labor Market

The incorporation of Latinos in the U.S. labor market over the last several decades has varied significantly in response to transformations in the national economy. As the economy has changed from one that was largely agrarian to one dominated by manufacturing, and then again to one driven by services, the nature of jobs has also changed. In particular, the manufacturing and service changes impact the current period most directly. The era of manufacturing reached its peak roughly between the 1940s through the 1960s, while the shift toward services began during the 1970s and accelerated during the 1980s. With these transformations, the way workers entered into employment, how they progressed on the job, and the benefits and wage structure they could expect – what is referred to as "the internal labor market" – were redefined, as were the way they moved from job to job and the nature of benefits between employment, or what is referred to as "the external labor market."

Seen broadly, the manufacturing era was one in which employment was relatively secure for a large segment of the population, especially for the industrial work force, which compensated workers on the basis of productivity as well as on their cost of living. The nation experienced a growth in the proportion of workers with middle-class incomes.* This combined with a decline in the difference between the highest and lowest income segments of society, i.e., a growing parity of incomes. During this period, Latinos also realized an improvement in their economic position.

With the rise of services, however, employment has become less secure, both in services and in manufacturing, and the economy has become more global in reach, which in turn has put competitive pressures on jobs in the U.S. Furthermore, the income structure has become skewed, as highly-skilled people and those with accumulated wealth have realized high returns in the labor market, while less-skilled workers have endured a decline in their real income, i.e., a growing income disparity or divergence of incomes. Throughout this period, the middle class has decreased precipitously. Similarly, from the early 1970s forward, Latinos as a whole have suffered from dramatic declines in income.[1]

## A. Industrial Restructuring

The disaggregated picture reveals the significance of the shift in greater detail. The nature of the industrial change from manufacturing to services is readily apparent when examining employment by industry (Table 1). Whereas in the 1980s employment in manufacturing was surpassed only by employment in services, by the 1990s it was also eclipsed by employment in retail trade and government, and is projected to decline to an even more distant fourth place in the 2000s.

---

* There are several ways to define "middle class." One way is simply to take the middle third of individuals in terms of equivalent income (family income adjusted for family size), which in dollar terms would consist of all individuals in families with incomes of $15,000 to $30,000 in 1993. However, "middle class" often refers to cultural perceptions, in addition to measures of income. Self-definitions are usually not helpful, since many individuals who actually live below the poverty rate or at quite high income levels consider themselves to be "middle class." Another approach is to base the upper and lower bounds of middle-class income on a chosen fixed percentage interval around median family income for a given year – for example, everyone who falls within 40% of the median. For further discussion, please see the U.S. Department of Labor's *Report on the American Workforce,* 1995.

## Table 1

## Employment Projections by Industry, 1983 to 2005

| Industry | Employment (1,000) | | | Annual Growth Rate | |
|---|---|---|---|---|---|
| | 1983 | 1994 | 2005 | 1983-1994 | 1994-2005 |
| Total | 102,404 | 127,014 | 144,708 | 2.0 | 1.2 |
| Agriculture | 3,508 | 3,623 | 3,399 | 0.3 | -0.6 |
| Mining | 952 | 601 | 439 | -4.1 | -2.8 |
| Construction | 3,946 | 5,010 | 5,500 | 2.2 | 0.9 |
| Manufacturing | 18,430 | 18,304 | 16,991 | -0.1 | -0.7 |
| Transportation/ Communications/ Utilities | 4,958 | 6,006 | 6,431 | 1.8 | 0.6 |
| Wholesale Trade | 5,283 | 6,140 | 6,559 | 1.4 | 0.6 |
| Retail Trade | 15,587 | 20,438 | 23,094 | 2.5 | 1.1 |
| Finance/ Insurance/ Real Estate | 5,466 | 6,933 | 7,373 | 2.2 | 0.6 |
| Services | 19,242 | 30,792 | 42,810 | 4.4 | 3.0 |
| Government | 15,870 | 19,117 | 20,990 | 1.7 | 0.9 |

* Projections based on assumptions of moderate growth.

Source: U.S. Bureau of Labor Statistics, *Monthly Labor Review*, November 1995.

Among Latinos, this sectoral change has resulted in a drop in the proportion of both men and women employed in manufacturing, and a rise in the percentage of both men and women working in business and professional services (Table 2).

## Table 2

## Industrial Distribution by Sex, Race, and Ethnicity

| | Latino | | | White | | |
|---|---|---|---|---|---|---|
| | *1984* | *1988* | *1992* | *1984* | *1988* | *1992* |
| *Male* | | | | | | |
| Agriculture | 6.8% | 7.1% | 7.1% | 4.3% | 3.7% | 3.5% |
| Construction | 10.7 | 11.0 | 10.0 | 10.3 | 11.0 | 10.3 |
| Manufacturing | 26.3 | 24.5 | 21.0 | 23.8 | 24.3 | 22.1 |
| Transportation | 8.2 | 7.3 | 7.9 | 9.1 | 9.4 | 9.4 |
| Wholesale Trade | 4.2 | 4.9 | 4.4 | 5.4 | 5.8 | 5.8 |
| Retail Trade | 16.9 | 15.4 | 19.4 | 14.5 | 12.8 | 13.3 |
| Finance/Ins./Real Estate | 3.9 | 4.0 | 3.8 | 5.2 | 5.1 | 5.4 |
| Bus./Prof. Services | 13.9 | 17.2 | 16.2 | 18.5 | 19.1 | 20.5 |
| Personal Services | 4.5 | 4.3 | 5.7 | 2.9 | 2.6 | 3.3 |
| Public Admin. | 3.7 | 3.5 | 3.8 | 4.5 | 4.9 | 5.3 |
| *Female* | | | | | | |
| Agriculture | 1.6 | 1.8 | 1.7 | 1.4 | 1.2 | 1.1 |
| Construction | 0.1 | 0.1 | 0.2 | 0.4 | 0.4 | 0.3 |
| Manufacturing | 23.2 | 19.6 | 17.4 | 14.2 | 13.9 | 12.4 |
| Transportation | 3.7 | 4.0 | 4.0 | 4.0 | 4.2 | 4.5 |
| Wholesale Trade | 2.3 | 2.2 | 2.7 | 2.8 | 2.7 | 3.0 |
| Retail Trade | 17.6 | 17.5 | 16.7 | 20.3 | 18.3 | 17.3 |
| Finance/Ins./Real Estate | 7.9 | 9.1 | 7.9 | 8.7 | 10.5 | 9.0 |
| Bus./Prof. Services | 28.0 | 29.2 | 33.7 | 36.4 | 37.1 | 40.9 |
| Personal Services | 9.8 | 11.2 | 11.5 | 6.6 | 5.8 | 5.7 |
| Public Admin. | 4.2 | 4.4 | 3.5 | 3.9 | 4.5 | 4.3 |

Sources: *Current Population Survey* computer tapes, 1984, 1988, 1992, from Edwin Meléndez, Francoise Carre, Evangelina Holvino, "Latinos Need Not Apply: The Effects of Industrial Change and Workplace Discrimination on Latino Employment," *New England Journal of Public Policy*, Special Issue, *Latinos in a Changing Society*, Part 1, Spring/Summer 1995, p. 98.

Accompanying the sectoral shift has been a decline in middle-wage jobs relative to high- and low-wage jobs (Table 3). In terms of employment shifts by race and gender, White males and White females experienced significant gains in the high-wage segment, while the concentration of Latinos and Latinas in the low-wage segment increased (Table 4).

### Table 3

### Employment Shares (%) by Industry/Occupation Wage Category, 1960 - 1990

|  | 1960 | 1970 | 1980 | 1990 |
|---|---|---|---|---|
| I.   High Wage | 24.6 | 25.5 | 28.2 | 32.9 |
| II.  Middle Wage | 40.2 | 39.6 | 38.2 | 34.4 |
| III. Low Wage | 35.1 | 35.0 | 33.6 | 32.6 |

Sources: U.S. Department of Commerce, Bureau of the Census, 1/1000 Public Use Sample, 1960, 1970, 1980; Current Population Survey, 1986, 1988, 1990, as cited in Carnoy (1994:96).

### B. Occupational Change

As the industrial base became more service-sector-dominant, the technological content of jobs increased, and the skill distribution of jobs became increasingly skewed. From the 1980s to the 1990s, the number of high-end professional and technical jobs grew. On the other hand, either relative or absolute job losses occurred in low-end jobs in precision production, operator positions, and farming. As seen in Table 5, among Latinos, the greatest amount of employment growth occurred in the low-end occupations requiring the least amount of skill and having the lowest wages.

## Table 4

## Employment Gains by Industry/Occupation Wage Category and Ethnic/Gender
## 1960 - 1990
## (thousands of additional jobs)

|  | 1970/60 | 1980/70 | 1990/80 |
|---|---|---|---|
| **White Males** |  |  |  |
| I.   High Wage | 1,600 | 2,900 | 4,600 |
| II.   Middle Wage | 500 | 1,100 | -2,200 |
| III.  Low Wage | 1,700 | 1,600 | 600 |
| **Latino Males** |  |  |  |
| I. | 150 | 250 | 300 |
| II. | 350 | 450 | 400 |
| III. | 300 | 600 | 1,400 |
| **White Females** |  |  |  |
| I. | 1,400 | 3,400 | 5,000 |
| II. | 2,700 | 3,500 | 1,300 |
| III. | 2,300 | 2,400 | 1,300 |
| **Latina Females** |  |  |  |
| I. | 50 | 200 | 350 |
| II. | 250 | 500 | 500 |
| III. | 150 | 550 | 500 |

Source: Table 5.1 percentages multiplied by civilian employment, by race and gender, from *Economic Report of the President,* January 1993, Table B-32. "White" figures corrected for Latinos currently in labor force from the proportion of Latinos in the all-worker sample in the Current Population Survey.  From Carnoy (1994:94).

## Table 5

## Occupational Distribution 1983, 1995

| Occupation | 1983 | | | 1995 | | |
|---|---|---|---|---|---|---|
| | Total (1,000) | % | % Latino | Total (1,000) | % | % Latino |
| **Total** | 100,834 | 100 | 5.3 | 124,900 | 100 | 8.9 |
| **Managerial/ Professional** | 23,592 | 23.4 | 2.6 | 35,318 | 28.3 | 4.4 |
| **Tech./Sales/ Administrative** | 31,265 | 31.0 | 4.3 | 37,417 | 30.0 | 7.3 |
| **Service Occup.** | 13,857 | 13.7 | 6.8 | 16,930 | 13.6 | 13.0 |
| **Precision Production/ Craft/Repair** | 12,328 | 12.2 | 6.2 | 13,524 | 10.8 | 10.6 |
| **Operators/Fabricators /Laborers** | 16,091 | 16.0 | 8.3 | 18,068 | 14.5 | 14.3 |
| **Farming/Forestry/ Fishing** | 3,700 | 3.4 | 8.2 | 3,642 | 2.9 | 18.1 |

Source: U.S. Bureau of Labor Statistics, *Employment and Earnings,* January issues.

Examination of the occupational distribution in greater detail reveals that Latino men and women are more likely to hold blue-collar jobs and lower-skilled jobs than are Whites; this is particularly true for Mexicans and Central and South Americans, and, to a lesser extent, for Puerto Ricans (Table 6).

## Table 6

## Occupational Distribution by Hispanic Origin and Sex, March 1992 (Thousands)

| | Total | White | Latino Total | | Latino Subgroups | | | | |
| --- | --- | --- | --- | --- | --- | --- | --- | --- | --- |
| | | | | Mexican | Puerto Rican | Cuban | Central & South Am. | Other |
| *Employed* | | | | | | | | |
| Males 16+ | 62,191 | 49,348 | 5,240 | 3,314 | 447 | 276 | 828 | 375 |
| *Percent* | | | | | | | | |
| Manag./Prof. | 26.0 | 28.6 | 11.4 | 9.3 | 10.9 | 21.3 | 13.6 | 18.3 |
| Tech./Sales/Admin. | 21.0 | 21.9 | 16.3 | 14.0 | 23.1 | 25.1 | 16.7 | 20.2 |
| Service Occup. | 10.8 | 9.0 | 17.7 | 16.6 | 22.4 | 12.4 | 22.2 | 15.5 |
| Farm./For./Fish. | 4.0 | 3.7 | 7.8 | 10.9 | 2.2 | 3.5 | 2.8 | 2.0 |
| Pr. Prod./Craft/Rep. | 18.2 | 18.8 | 19.4 | 20.0 | 18.0 | 14.7 | 17.6 | 22.4 |
| Op./Fab./Labor. | 19.9 | 18.0 | 27.5 | 29.2 | 23.5 | 22.9 | 27.1 | 21.7 |
| *Employed* | | | | | | | | |
| Females 16+ | 53,533 | 42,222 | 3,580 | 2,090 | 341 | 211 | 607 | 331 |
| *Percent* | | | | | | | | |
| Managerial/ Professional | 27.5 | 29.7 | 16.4 | 14.0 | 20.6 | 26.6 | 14.9 | 23.1 |
| Tech./Sales/Admin. | 10.8 | 9.0 | 17.7 | 16.6 | 22.4 | 12.4 | 22.2 | 15.5 |
| Service Occup. | 17.5 | 15.4 | 24.9 | 24.6 | 17.7 | 13.1 | 35.5 | 21.5 |
| Farm./For./Fish. | 0.8 | 0.9 | 1.7 | 2.8 | 0.0 | 0.0 | 0.3 | 0.4 |
| Pr. Prod./Craft/Rep. | 2.0 | 1.9 | 2.9 | 3.1 | 2.6 | 1.9 | 3.2 | 1.7 |
| Op./Fab./Labor. | 7.7 | 6.5 | 14.6 | 16.2 | 11.2 | 9.9 | 15.7 | 8.7 |

Source: *Current Population Survey* computer tapes, 1984, 1988, 1992, cited in Edwin Meléndez, et al., "Latinos Need Not Apply: The Effects of Industrial Change and Workplace Discrimination on Latino Employment" *New England Journal of Public Policy*, Special Issue, *Latinos in a Changing Society*, Part 1, Spring/Summer 1995, p. 94.

When grouped according to skill categories, in 1996, 73% of Latino men worked in services, and skilled and unskilled labor,* compared to 49% of Whites and 52% of the national total (Table 7). Among Latinos, the figures were highest for foreign-born (82%), Mexicans (77%), and Central and South Americans (71%). By contrast, only 27% of Latino men worked in professional, administrative, and sales occupations, compared to 48% of men as a whole, and 51% of Whites. Among Latinos, those most likely to hold higher-end positions were other Hispanics (45%), Cubans (44%), and those born in the U.S. (41%).

Women display a slightly different distribution (Table 7). A larger percentage of women in general, and Hispanic women in particular, are employed in professional, administrative, and sales occupations relative to men (with the bulk finding work in the latter two occupational categories). Although both Cubanas and those born in the U.S. follow the national patterns (72% each), a far smaller proportion of Latinas on the whole do (56%). This percent is smaller for Mexicans (55%), Central and South Americans (48%), and the foreign-born (40%).

## C. Labor Market Segmentation

Transformation of the U.S. employment base has been multidimensional. Not only has there been a shift of industries and occupations, but with these changes, the nature of the internal and external labor markets, or how people maneuver within and across jobs, has also been redefined. During the height of manufacturing dominance characterized by large, multinational firms, unionization was at its peak in the U.S., and blue-collar workers commonly bargained for stable, good-paying jobs with significant benefits. As U.S. industries experienced growing international competition, particularly during the 1970s and 1980s, they upgraded their process and product technology, and began shedding aspects of internalized production, or what is known as "vertical disintegration." The downsizing and increased reliance on external labor weakened the influence of unions, while spurring a rise in part-time and temporary work.

---

* The U.S. Department of Labor's Bureau of Labor Statistics collects data on the occupational distribution of workers according to the following categories: (a) Managerial/Professional Specialty; (b) Technical, Sales, and Administrative Support; (c) Service Occupations; (d) Precision Production, Craft, and Repair; (e) Operators, Fabricators, and Laborers; and (f) Farming, Forestry, and Fishing. The report from which these data were taken further grouped these categories into two sets of occupations: "Professional, Administrative, Sales" and "Service, Skilled/Unskilled Labor."

## Table 7
## Labor Force Characteristics by Race/Ethnicity and Gender, 1996

| Race/ Ethnic Group | Percent 16+ Unemployed Men | Women | Occupation of Employed 16+ Workers, by Percent — Men Prof., Admin., Sales | Service, Skilled/ Unskilled Labor | Women Prof., Admin., Sales | Service, Skilled/ Unskilled Labor |
|---|---|---|---|---|---|---|
| **Total** | 7 | 5 | 48 | 52 | 72 | 28 |
| **Non-Hispanic** | 6 | 5 | 50 | 50 | 74 | 26 |
| **White** | 5 | 4 | 51 | 49 | 76 | 24 |
| **Black** | 14 | 9 | 34 | 66 | 61 | 39 |
| **Other Non.** | 7 | 5 | 58 | 42 | 67 | 33 |
| **Hispanic** | 10 | 10 | 27 | 73 | 56 | 44 |
| **Mexican** | 10 | 10 | 23 | 77 | 55 | 45 |
| **Puerto Rican** | 10 | 11 | 37 | 63 | 64 | 36 |
| **Cuban** | 6 | 6 | 44 | 56 | 72 | 28 |
| **C./S. Am.** | 8 | 10 | 29 | 71 | 48 | 52 |
| **Other Hisp.** | 16 | 7 | 45 | 55 | 60 | 40 |
| **U.S.-Born** | 10 | 9 | 41 | 59 | 72 | 28 |
| **Foreign-Born** | 9 | 11 | 18 | 82 | 40 | 60 |

Source: March 1996, Current Population Survey, cited in Jorge del Pinal and Audrey Singer, *Generations of Diversity: Latinos in the United States, Population Bulletin,* vol. 52, no. 3, Washington DC: Population Reference Bureau, Inc., October 1997, p. 38.

From 1968 to 1994, the percentage of full-time work to total employment dropped from 85.9% to 81.0%, while part-time work was on the rise (DOL, 1995:152). Although a smaller percentage of Latinos reportedly work part-time relative to both the nation as a whole and Whites (in 1992, 18.9% of Latinos worked part-time, compared to 19.2% for the nation and 19.4% for Whites), a much larger percentage are employed part-time for economic reasons (9.3% as opposed to 5.4% for the nation and 5.1% for Whites) (Meléndez, et al., 1995). For many Latinos, part-time employment is not a choice, but the result of short work schedules and the seasonal fluctuations of jobs. This is large-ly attributable to their concentration in farm, laborer, service, clerical, and craft occu-pations that have a high incidence of part-time work.

In addition, the benefits normally associated with employment have diminished. Whereas in 1980, 10% of full-time employees participated in time-off plans, 97% in insurance plans, and 84% in retirement plans, by 1993 those figures had dropped to 9%, 82%, and 56%, respectively (DOL, 1995:198.). Some one-third of Latinos lack medical insurance, compared to one-fifth of Blacks and one-tenth of Whites (del Pinal and Singer, 1997; see also Santos and Seitz, Chapter 6, for a further discussion of these issues).

Seen as a whole, labor market segmentation in low-wage and low-skilled industries and occupations seems to be a persistent problem for a large number of Latinos. Although Latinos tend to exit and re-enter the labor market relatively rapidly, and despite their high labor force participation rates, they are circulating among poorly-paid jobs lack-ing benefits, security, or full-time employment (Boisjoly and Duncan, 1994). As such, they are considered to be among the "working poor."

## D. Labor Force Determinants

Although the economic position of Latinos can be attributed to multiple factors, the process of industrial transformation is widely acknowledged as having the greatest influence on their intransigent position at the occupational bottom (Weinberg, 1996). In an effort to determine which factors have shaped the labor market outcomes of Latinos during the manufacturing and post-manufacturing periods, Carnoy, et al. (1993) examined the four factors thought to contribute to income: the nature of work; relative education; wages paid; and immigration status. Using a simulation model in which the outcome for Latinos was compared to that for Whites, and to expected outcomes if their experiences had followed the paths of Whites, they found the following:

> Latino males' income rose relatively to [W]hite males in 1940-1970 for two
> main reasons: their shift in sectoral employment from agriculture to manu-
> facturing and their simultaneous increased education. It is difficult to sep-

arate these two effects. After a sharp drop in wage discrimination against Latinos in the 1940s, declines in discrimination were a smaller factor in explaining Latino advances in the 1950s and 1960s than sectoral employment shifts or increases in education. Latinas' income relative to white females' rose sharply in the 1940s from employment shifts in the 1950s and 1960s because of educational increases, and in the 1960s also due to a reduction in wage discrimination.

Since 1970, sectoral employment shifts and education were also foremost in shaping the decline in Latino relative incomes for both males and females. Although it appears that wage discrimination increased sharply in the 1970s and 1980s, this effect was probably mostly the result of the rising proportion of new immigrants in the Latino labor force. When we divide [Mexican Origin Labor] males into native- and foreign-born, our residual measure of wage discrimination is much higher for the foreign-born, and only rose slightly in the 1970s for the native-born. The higher residual for foreign-born, we argue, could well be a "limited English" effect rather than wage discrimination per se (Carnoy, et al., 1993: 47-48).

The conclusions of Carnoy, et al. mirror those of the U.S. Department of the Census (Weinberg, 1996), among others, that give primary emphasis to structural changes which in turn have penalized those lacking the necessary human capital to progress into higher-paying jobs.

## III. Spatial Dislocation

One dimension of the structural shifts has been the long-term dislocation of jobs. Entire regions, such as the Midwest and Northeast – the old industrial centers – were most negatively affected. Basic manufacturing centers suffered from plant closures, while newer regions grew on the basis of high technology, e.g., services and finances. The result was an eclipse of the "rust belt" by the "sun belt." Workers dependent on employment in heavy manufacturing experienced high rates of joblessness, often never fully to recover from the loss.

Within older industrial cities, such as New York, Chicago, and Boston, jobs in services- and goods-producing industries also migrated to the suburbs (Table 8). City centers were left with far fewer entry-level, low-skill or blue-collar jobs, and an emergence of managerial, professional, technical, and administrative jobs (Kasarda, 1989). For many inner-city residents, it is argued, this resulted in a spatial mismatch of jobs to the skill level of the workforce, with poorly-educated workers residing in urban areas having little or no access to employment. The selective out-migration of better-educated persons compounded the urban concentration of those least able to take advantage of the changing jobs patterns (Grier and Grier, 1988). As one illustration, in New York, blue-collar Puerto Ricans suffered disproportionately from a lack of comparable replacement jobs (Torres and Bonilla, 1993).

## Table 8

### Number of Job Changes for Selected Cities by Location and Occupation, 1970-1980

| Metropolitan Area | Managerial/ Professional | Technical/ Admin. | Clerical/ Sales | Blue Collar | Total |
|---|---|---|---|---|---|
| **Boston** | | | | | |
| Center city | 26,120 | 30,300 | -40,400 | -62,500 | -46,480 |
| Suburbs | 104,660 | 75,820 | 69,460 | 116,440 | 366,380 |
| **Chicago** | | | | | |
| Center city | 51,560 | 68,400 | -89,760 | -118,860 | -88,660 |
| Suburbs | 156,120 | 120,660 | 115,360 | 237,900 | 630,040 |
| **New York** | | | | | |
| Center city | 90,460 | 173,780 | -187,820 | -171,500 | -95,080 |
| Suburbs | 200,140 | 210,800 | 51,060 | 27,080 | 489,080 |

Source: U.S. Department of Commerce, Bureau of the Census, Machine Readable Public Use Microdata Sample File, 5% A Sample, 1980; Ibid; 15% County Group Sample, 1970, cited in John D. Kasarda (1989:29).

In yet other cities which benefited from the new growth economy, the issue was one of a bifurcated job structure and proliferation of low-wage jobs. Los Angeles provides one illustration. There, the urban core has been revitalized by the garment industry, warehousing, and other jobs that offer little employment security, few benefits, and extremely low wages, that are often dominated by Latino labor (Morales and Ong, 1993).

A close examination of Chicago illustrates the persistence of employment dislocation between the city and its surrounding suburbs (Ali, 1996).

Since World War II, the Chicago metropolitan area has experienced an employment shift to outlying counties. In 1947, 87% of all jobs were located in the city and 23% in the suburbs, but by 1994, 35% of all jobs (1.1 million) were located in the city and 65% (two million) in the suburbs (Schindler, Israilevich, and Hewings, 1995). Manufacturing moved out particularly fast; nearly 70% (438,000) of all metropolitan manufacturing jobs are currently located outside the city of Chicago (out of a total of 618,000).

Overall employment in the Chicago region has increased by approximately 50% since World War II, though employment in the central city has decreased by about 11%. Since 1980, 459,000 new jobs have been created, with 80% going to the northern and western outer-ring suburbs. Older inner-ring suburbs, on the other hand, have lost as much as 50% of their employment base (Orfield, 1996). Manufacturing jobs previously located in the city are being replaced by employment in government, services, finance, real estate, retail, and wholesale trade.

Although there has been recent job growth in the city (in 1994, jobs in the city grew by 6,000), it has been overshadowed by more than 24,000 jobs created in the suburbs. Nine suburbs experienced increases of over 2,000 jobs each, totaling more than 24,000 jobs, or four times the growth in the city of Chicago. Despite the suburban growth, only 12% of suburban jobs were held by city residents in 1994.

With the shift, a growing number of minority and immigrant groups have moved to the suburbs to follow the jobs. For example, in 1990, 51% of all Chicago metropolitan immigrants lived in the suburbs. Although immigrants constituted only 14% of the metropolitan labor force, they represented nearly 23% of all manufacturing workers. Nearly 44% of all Mexican immigrants worked in manufacturing.

From 1980 to 1990, although the suburban population grew among all races, the Latino population in the city of Chicago experienced a 50% increase (Table 9). In the city of

Chicago and the surrounding counties of Cook (excluding Chicago), DuPage, and Lake, Latinos made up 6% of the total labor force of 3.3 million persons (Table 10).

## Table 9

### Chicago City and Suburb Population by Race/Ethnicity, 1980 and 1990

|       | Latino | | Black | | White | |
|-------|---------|-----------|-----------|-----------|-----------|-----------|
|       | *Chicago* | *Suburbs\** | *Chicago* | *Suburbs\** | *Chicago* | *Suburbs\** |
| **1980** | 422,054 | 114,748 | 1,197,000 | 185,317 | 1,490,214 | 3,070,923 |
| **1990** | 535,315 | 232,016 | 1,086,389 | 280,991 | 1,265,953 | 3,104,565 |

\* Suburban Cook, DuPage, and Lake Counties.

Source: 1980 and 1990 Census.

## Table 10

### Employed Persons in Chicago Metropolitan Area, 1990

| *Residing In:* | *Latino* | *Black* | *White* | *Other* | *Total\*\** |
|----------------|----------|---------|---------|---------|-----------|
| **Chicago** | 140,490 (11%) | 439,107 (31%) | 686,238 (54%) | 57,294 (5%) | 1,323,129 (100%) |
| **Suburbs\*** | 47,751 (2%) | 143,190 (7%) | 1,754,526 (87%) | 72,438 (4%) | 2,017,905 (100%) |
| **Total** | 188,241 (6%) | 582,297 (17%) | 2,440,764 (73%) | 129,732 (4%) | 3,341,034 (100%) |

\* Suburban Cook, DuPage, and Lake Counties.
\*\* Includes rounding error.

Source: 1990 Census, PUMS.

Most Latinos who live in the city work there (Table 11), and most who live in the suburbs also work in the suburbs (Table 12). Whether Latinos live in the city of Chicago or in the suburbs, approximately one-quarter commute outside of or into the city for work.

### Table 11

### Place of Work of Chicago Residents, 1990

| Work in: | Latino | Black | White |
|---|---|---|---|
| **Chicago** | 87,507 (76%) | 279,795 (84%) | 448,617 (77%) |
| **Suburbs*** | 27,897 (24%) | 52,158 (16%) | 130,497 (23%) |
| **TOTAL:** | 115,404 (100%) | 331,953 (100%) | 579,114 (100%) |

\* Suburban Cook, DuPage, Lake Counties.

Source: 1990 Census, PUMS.

### Table 12

### Place of Work of Suburban Residents, 1990

| Work in: | Latino | Black | White |
|---|---|---|---|
| **Chicago** | 8,505 (27%) | 46,227 (40%) | 358,554 (24%) |
| **Suburbs*** | 31,881 (73%) | 69,093 (60%) | 1,115,226 (76%) |
| **TOTAL:** | 40,386 (100%) | 115,320 (100%) | 1,473,780 (100%) |

\* Suburban  Cook, DuPage, and Lake Counties.

Source: 1990 Census, PUMS.

The distribution of employment by industry and occupation is nearly identical in both the city and the suburbs, although the absolute numbers vary considerably. As a whole, Latinos tend to be over-represented in manufacturing and lower-skilled occupations, and under-represented in finance and professional services and higher-skilled occupations (Tables 13 and 14).

**Table 13**

**Employment in Selected Industries by Place of Residence, 1990**

| | *Latino* | | *White* | | *Black* | |
|---|---|---|---|---|---|---|
| | *Chicago* | *Suburbs\** | *Chicago* | *Suburbs\** | *Chicago* | *Suburbs\** |
| **Manufacturing** | 54,006 | 16,809 | 126,678 | 325,296 | 62,892 | 23,589 |
| | (38%) | (35%) | (19%) | (19%) | (14%) | (17%) |
| **Construction** | 6,807 | 3,630 | 29,748 | 99,981 | 12,069 | 3,336 |
| | (5%) | (8%) | (4%) | (6%) | (3%) | (2%) |
| **Retail Trade** | 24,144 | 8,856 | 107,988 | 307,086 | 72,024 | 20,121 |
| | (17%) | (19%) | (16%) | (18%) | (16%) | (14%) |
| **Finance** | 4,683 | 1,455 | 70,965 | 167,250 | 34,101 | 12,411 |
| | (4%) | (3%) | (10%) | (10%) | (7%) | (9%) |
| **Professional Services** | 1,989 | 1,863 | 158,874 | 38,940 | 109,296 | 35,097 |
| | (11%) | (9%) | (23%) | (2%) | (25%) | (25%) |
| **Public Administration** | 1,242 | 504 | 31,842 | 44,535 | 28,413 | 7,035 |
| | (2%) | (1%) | (5%) | (3%) | (7%) | (5%) |

\* Suburban Cook, DuPage, and Lake Counties. Percentages reflect workers by race and location.

Source: 1990 Census, PUMS.

The data reveal that although suburbanization of employment is occurring, the patterns of employment in the suburbs parallel those in the city, despite the geographic transformation taking place. That is, Latinos in the suburbs are no better off than those who live in the city. It suggests that the spatial mismatch triggered by metropolitan shifts is less significant than other structural, human capital, institutional, and discriminatory factors in determining employment outcomes.

### Table 14

### Employment in Selected Occupations by Place of Residence, 1990

| | *Latino* | | *White* | | *Black* | |
|---|---|---|---|---|---|---|
| | *Chicago* | *Suburbs\** | *Chicago* | *Suburbs\** | *Chicago* | *Suburbs\** |
| **Executive-Managerial** | 6,057 | 2,331 | 94,857 | 297,378 | 35,079 | 13,494 |
| | (4%) | (5%) | (14%) | (17%) | (8%) | (10%) |
| **Professionals** | 4,911 | 1,659 | 105,252 | 257,994 | 44,262 | 16,413 |
| | (4%) | (4%) | (16%) | (15%) | (10%) | (12%) |
| **Technicians** | 918 | 261 | 11,154 | 28,134 | 3,204 | 1,632 |
| | (1%) | (1%) | (2%) | (2%) | (1%) | (1%) |
| **Sales** | 10,059 | 2,946 | 79,722 | 255,630 | 41,901 | 13,170 |
| | (7%) | (6%) | (12%) | (15%) | (10%) | (10%) |
| **Administrative Support** | 19,125 | 5,658 | 130,461 | 342,798 | 107,049 | 33,759 |
| | (14%) | (12%) | (19%) | (20%) | (25%) | (25%) |
| **Machine Operators** | 34,089 | 10,374 | 47,394 | 74,460 | 34,167 | 10,323 |
| | (25%) | (22%) | (7%) | (4%) | (8%) | (8%) |
| **Precision Production** | 17,937 | 6,330 | 63,675 | 173,904 | 28,821 | 9,324 |
| | (13%) | (13%) | (9%) | (10%) | (7%) | (7%) |

\* Suburban Cook, DuPage, and Lake Counties.
Percentages reflect workers by race and location.

Source: 1990 Census, PUMS.

Across the nation, the employment of Latinos has been tied to the economy of urban areas. Compared to the nation as a whole, Latinos in 1990 had a far higher rate of urbanization (90% as opposed to 76%). The ten cities with the largest absolute Latino populations in 1990 housed nearly six million Latinos, or about 37% of the total population. In rank order, these cities were: New York, Los Angeles, Chicago, San Antonio, Houston, El Paso, San Diego, Miami, Dallas, and San Jose. Because the population of most cities spills over into adjacent communities, metropolitan areas (Consolidated Statistical Metropolitan Areas) provide an even broader picture of urban distribution. In 1996, nearly one-half of all Latinos lived in six metropolitan areas with more than one million Latinos each: Los Angeles, New York, Miami, San Francisco, Chicago, and Houston. More than one-fifth (6.1 million) of all Latinos lived in the Los Angeles metropolitan area alone in 1996.

Yet, in the past decade, Latinos have continued to contribute to the labor force of rural and suburban areas following the migration of manufacturing jobs, and provide an important source of labor for agriculture. Recent studies show that most nonmetropolitan Latinos are Mexican (77%), and tend to be less well-off socioeconomically relative to urban Latinos (del Pinal and Singer, 1997). Rural Hispanics are largely recent immigrants, poor, and speak little English (del Pinal and Singer, 1997). This dispersal is taking Latinos into a wide range of states, including such places as Tennessee, Wisconsin, Georgia, rural Illinois and New York, Michigan, and Washington.

## IV. Institutional Change

While industrial restructuring changes initiated a redefinition of jobs, institutional changes codified them. Throughout the recent period of economic transformation, employment has become less secure and unemployment more difficult to weather. The transformation of industry was complemented by a series of institutional changes aimed at improving the competitive position of U.S. firms. These included a dismantling of the social safety net, a virtual freeze of the minimum wage throughout the 1980s, and an erosion of labor, workplace environment, and training support legislation which, in the past, had improved the lives of workers both in and out of work, and had assured a livable wage. During the 1980s, federal social programs were cut by 55%, which had a significant impact on Latinos, who constituted between 9% and 17% of the beneficiaries of these programs (Center on Budget and Policy Priorities, 1988).

Minimum wage legislation, in particular, has had a negative effect on the wages of the working poor. In 1995, the minimum wage was set at $4.24. A person working full-time year-round and earning the minimum wage would have received a gross income of $8,500, well below the poverty level of $12,158 for a family of three or $15,569 for a family of four that year. Thus, working at low wages was insufficient to lift a family out of poverty.

Nonetheless, during the 1990s, social programs such as Aid to Families with Dependent Children, General Assistance, and Supplemental Security Income were specifically aimed at moving people off of welfare and into jobs, particularly low-wage jobs. Examination of the net effect of removing transfer income shows that while the poverty rate changes very little with the loss of cash assistance, that is, the same number of people remain poor, the extent of their poverty grows quite significantly, making it much harder for them to move out of poverty (Blank, 1997). Nevertheless, transfers have been less effective in the past in moving Latinos out of poverty, compared to their impact on the economic status of other groups (Enchautegui, 1995). In part, this is because Latinos have been significantly under-represented in federal anti-poverty and tax relief programs (NCLR, 1997, 1995).

In recent years, job training programs have also come under criticism for their apparent failure to prepare adequately both youths and adults for work. Such programs include job search assistance, education and training, and public sector employment. The effectiveness of the current shift in emphasis from training programs to job immersion is still to be determined. However, prior analysis shows that "when used in combination with cash assistance, job programs provide a complementary set of services that encourage work while still recognizing the reality of limited wages in low-income labor markets" (Blank, 1997:173).

Erosion of Affirmative Action, the policies which attempted to provide employment parity, especially in high-end or civil service employment, has significantly reduced other job opportunities and avenues for more-skilled Latino workers. Affirmative Action traditionally opened doors for Latinos, especially at the local, state, and national governmental levels.

Another recourse for improved wages and employment conditions that is diminishing is unionization. For years, unionization has been declining nationwide, but the decline has had a far more negative effect on Latinos than on other groups. In 1986, 20.0% of Latinos were unionized, compared to 19.1% of Whites and 26.7% of Blacks; by 1995, when 16.7% of all workers nationwide were represented by unions, the distribution was 15.9% of Whites, 22.3% of Blacks, and only 14.8% of Latinos (U.S. Bureau of Labor Statistics, *Employment and Earnings*, January 1995). Historically, unionized Latinos have earned 50% more than their unorganized counterparts (Torres, 1995).

Finally, recent changes in immigration legislation have also affected employment opportunities for Latinos. The Immigration Reform and Control Act of 1986 (IRCA) has as one of its primary objectives sanctions against employers who knowingly hire undocumented workers. Although IRCA was not intended to foster discrimination, audits of employment patterns demonstrate that implementation of IRCA has led to increased discrimination by employers against Latinos (Cross, et al., 1990).

Seen as a whole, these institutional changes have made it increasingly difficult for low-wage workers to progress out of poverty, and, in some instances, for Latinos even to enter into employment.

# V. The Impact of Employment Discrimination

Despite gains made through Affirmative Action and other programs, the issue of employment discrimination has remained an important factor in the new era. As the nation witnessed the structure of employment opportunities change, discrimination contributed to keeping Latinos locked into low-wage or insecure jobs in both the declining manufacturing and the emerging service sectors. Melendez, et al. (1995) point out that as internal labor markets and promotional ladders weakened, as hiring for mid- and upper-level positions increasingly came from the external labor market, and as the job pool was reduced along with weakened Equal Employment Opportunity (EEOC) standards, opportunities for advancement for Latino men and women declined.

Employment discrimination can occur in four principal ways: recruitment and hiring; job segregation and "tracking; mentoring; and representation in decision-making positions" (Melendez, et al., 1995:103).

Although studies of recruitment and hiring discrimination are hard to conduct, at least one report (Bendick, et al., 1991) based on a "controlled study comparing treatment among Latino and Anglo job applicants, found that discrimination was particularly prevalent for males and for city jobs that did not require a college degree and were not widely advertised" (Melendez, et al., 1995:103). Among the methods used to control recruitment and hiring include advertising in specific media to target particular applicants; adapting job qualifications to suit particular candidates; bias in the recruitment and promotion of selected employees; and demonstrating insensitivity to Latino concerns.

Job segregation occurs through the "tracking" or slotting of applicants into limited positions. Reyes and Halcon (1988) found such tracking to occur in educational institutions. Despite limited documentation, the practice is thought to be widespread. Mentoring, an informal means by which a person learns how to advance, is also widely acknowledged as lacking for Latinos (Knouse, 1992). Lastly, under-representation in positions of authority has been consistently monitored and reported by the Hispanic Association of Corporate Responsibility (HACR). In a 1993 study of public Fortune 500 corporations, HACR found that Hispanics hold fewer than 1% of director and executive positions (HACR, 1993).

In order to grasp the extent of discrimination in the hiring process, the Urban Institute conducted a series of audits across Chicago, Washington DC, and San Diego during the summer of 1989 (Cross, et al., 1990). The audits used matched pairs of individuals (Latino and non-Latino) with similar characteristics; however, the Latinos were specifically "Hispanic-looking" and had discernible accents. The purpose was to study the potential adverse impact of the employer sanctions provisions of IRCA on the job attainment of Latinos.

In the Chicago and San Diego Hispanic/Anglo employment audits, Hispanics were offered 34% fewer jobs than their teammates. By way of contrast, in the Chicago and Washington, DC Black/White audits, Blacks were offered 23% fewer jobs than their teammates (Fix and Struyk, 1992). Statistical tests* confirmed these results (Heckman and Siegelman, 1992). As reported, the audits showed discrimination exists against foreign-sounding/foreign-looking males in San Diego and Chicago. When disaggregated by cities versus suburbs, there were no significant differences in the hiring practices of firms. Specifically, the audits showed that "[B]lacks and Hispanics experience roughly equal treatment [as Whites] at the application stage; but at subsequent stages [e.g., interviews and job offers] [B]lack, and especially Hispanic, applicants are more likely to encounter unfavorable treatment" (Mincy, 1992:173). In addition, a 1990 survey by the General Accounting Office, which intended to determine whether there was a link between IRCA and discrimination against Latinos, confirmed widespread discrimination across industries of all sectors and sizes (GAO, 1990).

Despite these compelling results, a clear-cut interpretation is less definitive. In an audit of the Denver area (James and Del Castillo, 1991), the authors found almost no evidence of discrimination. The main difference is that the Denver study did not use auditors who were specifically "foreign-looking and foreign-sounding." Thus, the Urban Institute studies may have picked up the effect of being foreign as opposed to being Latino, as well as the effect of discrimination initiated by the changes in the immigration legislation. However, when seen as a whole, the audits suggest that

---

* The statistical tests performed included the sign test, large sample chi-squared test, and exact small-sample (binomial) test.

Latinos "experienced more unfavorable treatment when applying for jobs in management and service occupations, and in the manufacturing and construction industries . . . consistent with hypotheses that discrimination is more likely to occur in higher-paying or higher-status jobs and jobs with substantial amounts of customer contact" (Mincy, 1992:174-5).

Evidence of widespread discrimination is also apparent in the federal work force and within federal programs. In 1996, Latinos constituted 10.2% of the civilian labor force but only 6% of the federal workforce (MSPB, 1996). Ability even to enter into employment has been thwarted by under-representation in such job training programs as the Job Training Partnership Act (JTPA). In 1994, Latinos constituted 13.3% of the participants in Title II-A adult JTPA employment and training programs, compared to 50.8% for Whites and 30.6% for Blacks (NCLR, 1997). Thus, avenues for advancement for Latinos are limited, beginning with opportunities for training.

## VI. Summary of Findings

Despite a growth of jobs in the U.S. over the last decade, and the strong attachment of Latinos to the labor force, Latinos, as a whole, have been over-represented among the poor, especially the working poor, and among those falling furthest behind in the economy. But it was not always that way. During the post-World War II economic expansion, Latinos' incomes began to approximate that of Whites, due largely to the growth of urban manufacturing jobs and an increase in minority education (Carnoy, et al., 1993). However, the post-1973 economic recession and industrial restructuring had a greater negative impact on Latinos than on Whites. The employment shift adversely affected those with weak anchorage in the labor force, part-time workers, those who were furthest behind educationally, and the foreign-born (Carnoy, et al., 1993). Among those most negatively affected were Puerto Ricans and Mexican Americans, those who were unable to navigate a successful transition into higher-paying occupations, and recent immigrants thrust into low-paying jobs.

In addition, those workers who have been most dependent upon traditional routes for upward mobility in manufacturing and through unionized, blue-collar jobs have been adversely affected by the industrial restructuring. But while the restructuring of industries, occupations, and internal and external labor markets are most prominent in shaping the economic well-being of Latinos, the problem of discrimination persists, and remains vital for explaining their current situation.

As the process of industrial restructuring continues, manufacturing employment is expected to continue to decline, and be off-set by employment in retail trade and services. The jobs projected for further growth are in high-technology industries, such as medical equipment, electronic components, and high-technology services, each of which demands largely skilled labor (U.S. Department of Commerce, 1994). Thus, the economy is expected to maintain this skewed pattern of development in the future, which in the past has adversely affected Latinos (Reich, 1991).

The changes in incomes and earnings that have resulted from structural economic shifts have had a negative effect on income inequality nationwide. During the height of America's manufacturing prominence, from 1947 to 1968, family income inequality declined by 7.4%. But from 1968 to 1992, inequality grew by 16.1% and from 1992 to 1994, by 22.4%. By 1997, Latinos became the poorest racial/ethnic group in the country. Moreover, that year, Latinos constituted nearly one-quarter (24%) of the nation's poor, up eight percentage points since 1985 (Goldberg, 1997).

Seen as a whole, the structure of the contemporary labor market for Latinos as defined by their industrial and occupational opportunities, and further shaped by institutional parameters and employment discrimination, requires explicit policy interventions in order to reverse their sharply downward spiraling income and employment trends.

## VII. Research and Policy Implications

Despite a growth economy, continued trends toward increasing income inequality in the U.S., which affects all workers, creates not only a fragmented society but also signals that there is a misappropriation of the nation's resources. In order to address this problem and recreate the occupational ladders that once lifted people from lower-paying jobs into middle-income jobs, the nation would have to make income and employment policy a concerted goal. So far, the national focus has been primarily on absolute job generation, not on the creation of jobs that pay a living wage.

In addition, as the economy continues on the path of flexible production, the nation should strengthen networks of firms and promote the mobility of workers through external job ladders. This would respect current industrial trends while minimizing the burdens placed on workers.

These two considerations focus on structural conditions. Yet other policies should address institutional factors. For example, a third policy area concerns developing job training programs that reach hard-to-serve Latinos and making education and job-specific training primary national objectives.

Fourth, efforts to re-create the social safety net for the working poor and those attempting to improve their employment situation must be strengthened. Given that job mobility and part-time employment are on the rise, particular emphasis should be given to the portability of benefits across the course of a worker's career.

Fifth, in light of the importance of minimum-wage employment to a large number of working Latinos, sustained efforts should be made to raise the levels of the minimum wage with rising national productivity, income, and/or employment.

Sixth, vigorous enforcement of National Labor Relations legislation is necessary to protect the unionized status of Latinos.

Finally, efforts to reduce employment discrimination must continue to be a national priority. Here, the U.S. Department of Justice should use methods, such as employment audits, to enforce equal opportunity laws and regulations more effectively, and combat the persistent discrimination confronting Latinos.

Together, such a broad policy agenda, if adopted, would not only strengthen the path of upward mobility for Latinos, but would also result in a stronger national economy and society.

# 3

# Latino Unemployment: Current Issues and Future Concerns

**Jorge Chapa, Ph.D.**
*Indiana University*

**Craig Wacker, M.P. Aff.**
*Texas Center for Educational Research*

## Abstract

*This chapter examines Latino unemployment and related issues. After summarizing the arguments that Latinos are not attaining educational or economic parity with the general U.S. population, even after residing in the U.S. for several generations, the authors address the decreasing employment opportunities for workers with low levels of educational attainment. The combination of these two long-term trends with the short-term impacts of Proposition 187 and the 1994 devaluation of the Mexican peso is seen as resulting in a disproportionately high Latino unemployment rate. The chapter also examines Latino employment discrimination, underemployment, and the occupations with high concentrations of Latinos, which tend to be low-skilled and easily vulnerable to structural economic changes. It concludes with recommendations that could result in improved employment opportunities for Latinos.*

# Introduction

A significant segment of Latinos has not shared in the United States' past prosperity. The fact that Latinos have a substantially higher unemployment rate* than the majority population is part of the reason. Furthermore, the continuing difficulty that Latinos face in attaining higher levels of education, and the fear that the future holds the prospect of fewer jobs for workers with low levels of education, suggest that unemployment or even labor force participation may be bigger problems for Latinos in the future.

The experience of Latinos in the United States is one of mixed economic progress. Latinos are a diverse population comprised of Mexicans, Cubans, Puerto Ricans, Central-South Americans, and Dominicans. Within this group, Cubans have largely integrated into the mainstream economy, whereas a sizeable share of Mexican Americans, Puerto Ricans, and Dominican Americans have not (Chapa, 1990). As the latest Census information indicates, Latinos in aggregate have less schooling and lower salaries than the national average. Among some Latino groups, particularly Mexican Americans, the figures hint of serious skill shortages when a disproportionately youthful population comes of age. In other words, if current educational and occupational trends among the Latino population continue, today's Latino children may become tomorrow's under-skilled workforce. Such a course also has implications for the already-high Latino unemployment rate.

After setting the context for Latino economic progress, this chapter discusses several aspects of Latino unemployment, including a brief review of key data and trends, as well as a look at some of the major Latino worker groups disproportionately experiencing high unemployment. The chapter also assesses the factors associated with Latino unemployment, including the effects of Proposition 187 and the 1994 devaluation of the Mexican *peso* on the Latino workforce, and suggests that the restructuring of the U.S. economy has played a significant role in Latino unemployment. In addition, the authors review other relevant issues in the analysis of Latino unemployment trends, including underemployment and discrimination, and offer some recommendations that could result in improved employment opportunities for Latinos.

---

\* The unemployment rate is derived from a nationwide survey by the U.S. Bureau of Labor Statistics and reflects a measure of persons who did not have a job, but are available to work and have looked for work, in the month prior to the survey.

# Latino Employment and Economic Status: The Myth of Latino Progress

As the previous chapters in this volume describe, a combination of human capital and structural factors help to explain the economic status of Latinos in the U.S. They also have a role in the relatively high unemployment rate of the Latino workforce. Three issues are especially relevant: educational attainment levels, occupational distribution, and wages. A number of studies claim that Latinos, including Mexican Americans, the largest Latino subgroup, are closing the economic gap with the majority White population (Grebler, et al., 1970). Yet in order to claim this progress, according to Chapa, proponents of the assimilation paradigm must affirm three contentions. First, the educational attainment of Mexican Americans* must be similar to that of the White population. In other words, the average years that Mexican Americans attend school must be about the same as that of Anglo** residents of the same age. As the statistics show, this contention is currently false.[1] Chapa finds that third-generation Chicanos,*** a group slightly larger than first- and second-generation Mexican Americans, still have educational attainment levels far below those of the Anglo population (Chapa, 1990). For example, third-generation Mexican Americans attend school for an average of 10.4 years, whereas Anglos have an average of 12.5 years of schooling. The figures for recent Mexican immigrants present a bleaker picture. Many first-generation Mexican immigrants have less than an eighth grade education.[2]

In addition to the concern related to years of schooling, high school dropout rates are substantially higher for Latinos than for non-Latinos. The data further show that immigrant Latinos are especially not likely to graduate from high school. As a whole, compared to the non-Latino population, both immigrant and U.S.-born Latinos have lower levels of educational attainment and are disproportionately likely to leave high school without graduating, as Table 1 shows.

---

* Almost two-thirds of Latinos are Mexican Americans – the subgroup of reference used in Chapa's analysis and throughout this section of the chapter.
** The term "Anglo" refers to non-Hispanic Whites; it is used interchangeably with "White" in this chapter.
*** "Chicano" is used interchangeably with "Mexican American."

### Table 1

### Percent of status dropouts among 16- to 24-year-olds, by recentness of migration and ethnicity: November 1989

| Recentness of immigration | Total | Latino | Non-Latino |
|---|---|---|---|
| Total* | 12.5 | 31.0 | 10.3 |
| Born outside U.S. | 28.9 | 43.0 | 7.9 |
| First generation U.S.-born | 10.4 | 17.3 | 6.2 |
| Second or more generation born in U.S. | 11.2 | 23.7 | 10.7 |

* Total includes a small number for whom recentness of migration is unknown

Source: U.S. Dept. of Education, 1993.

Therefore, serious gaps remain between Latinos and their White counterparts in the education arena. Such deficiencies play a principal role in the labor market status of Latino workers, and specifically, in their likelihood of unemployment.

Second, in order to close the economic gap with the Anglo population, the distribution of employment among Mexican Americans should show the same cross-section as in the White population. That is, Mexican Americans should have a similar proportion of people in management, service, and low-skilled jobs, respectively, as the majority population. An analysis of current and past labor markets shows that this is not the case (see Chapter 1 for a detailed discussion of these issues). For example, Latinos are far less likely than other minorities (or Anglos) to fill management positions. Yet Latinos are also disproportionately placed in positions such as operator, fabricator, and laborer – positions which are especially likely to experience losses during times of economic uncertainty.

Finally, if Mexican Americans are indeed closing the economic gap with the majority population, then Mexican American wages should be comparable to those of Anglos and other ethnic groups. Unfortunately, this final indicator also reveals that Mexican Americans are not progressing toward wage parity with the rest of America, which Chapa asserts is an indication of economic stasis. As an example, Reimers found that both male and female U.S.-born Mexicans' wages in California declined in the 1980s, relative to U.S.-born Whites and Blacks.[3]   Another sign of the increasing wage gap among Latinos is that, from 1970 through 1990, median income increased substantially for White, Black, American Indian, and Asian male and female workers.  In sharp contrast, the median income for Latinos and Latinas decreased over this period.[4]

This brief overview of educational attainment, occupational distribution, and wages provides the backdrop for understanding Latino unemployment, and helps to explain both the disadvantaged position of Latinos in the U.S. labor force and their relatively high unemployment rates.

## Latino Unemployment

Notwithstanding Latinos' relatively disadvantaged human capital profile and the challenging structural factors at play in the current economy, the data show that Latinos are committed to work and are very active in the labor force.  Indeed, over the past decade, the Latino labor force in the U.S. has doubled; currently, one in ten American workers is Latino.  Further, Latino men have the highest labor force participation rate of all male worker groups.  Yet, as the discussion below shows, Latinos experience disproportionate unemployment relative to other American workers.

### Data and Trends in Latino Unemployment

A review of data since 1973, the first year that such statistics were collected for Latinos, indicates that Latinos have had higher unemployment rates than Anglos and a lower likelihood of being unemployed compared to African Americans.  For all groups, unemployment peaked in 1983-1984, a response to the severe economic recession that the nation experienced in the year prior.  By the late 1980s, unemployment for all groups was on a downward trend, although the gaps between the three major work groups persisted.  In particular, African Americans continued to have the highest level of unemployment, followed by Latinos.

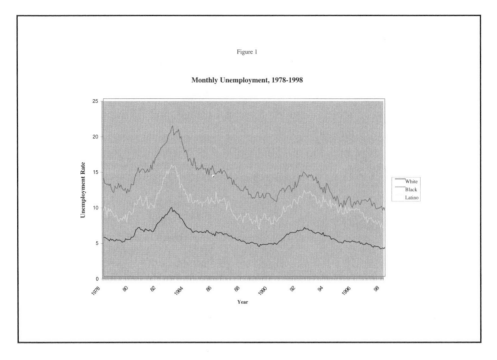

Figure 1

**Monthly Unemployment, 1978-1998**

In the early- to mid-1990s, unemployment rates began increasing for all worker groups (see Figure 1). In 1992 the national unemployment rate among Latinos was 11.5% – reflecting a significant rise from 1990, when 8% of Latinos were without jobs. That year, the Mexican American unemployment rate mirrored that of Latinos in the aggregate; 11.7% were unemployed. Although the Latino rate began to decline in the years that followed, the rate of decrease was not as great as that of their non-Latino counterparts. By January 1995, for the first time ever, Latinos and African Americans both had equally high rates of unemployment. Until then almost all of the monthly measures of unemployment for African Americans had reflected a rate about twice as high as the Anglo rate. The Latino unemployment rate would typically be in the middle. In January 1995, however, the gap narrowed and 10.2% of both worker groups were unemployed. By contrast, the Anglo rate was 4.9%. Moreover, in 1994, 1995, and 1996, Latinos were twice as likely as Anglos to experience unemployment; the ratio of Latino to Anglo unemployment was 2.06:1, 2.11:1, and 2.12:1, respectively (NCLR, October 1997).

By mid-1997, this ratio had once again declined slightly, but Latinos were still one-and-a-half times as likely to be unemployed than the labor force as a whole. That year, 7.0%

of all Latino men 16 years and over were unemployed; the rate for their female counterparts was 8.9%. Despite recent declines in the Latino unemployment rate, due in
large part to their strong attachment to the labor force and a vibrant economy, there continues to be a significant gap between their levels of unemployment and those of White
workers.

## Latino Worker Groups and Unemployment

Unemployment has had a differential impact on select segments of the Latino labor
force. In particular, women and young Latinos are especially likely to experience job
loss. Latino unemployment also varies by subgroup.

Across all ages, Latinas are more likely than Latino men to be unemployed; in 1996, for
instance, among workers 16 years and over, 7.9% of Latino men were unemployed,
compared to 10.2% of Latinas. Among women workers, Latinas were twice as likely to
be unemployed than Anglo women (10.2% vs. 4.1%) and had a slightly higher unemployment rate than Black women (9.0%) in 1996. Subgroup data show that Mexican
American women had the highest unemployment rate (11%), while Cuban women had
the lowest unemployment rate (8.3%) – although even this rate was twice that of Anglo
women in 1996.

In a study that focused principally on the economic and emotional stress that accom-
panies job loss, Gloria Romero, Felipe Castro, and Richard Cervantes followed a group
of Latinas who had been employed at a Starkist Tuna cannery in Wilmington, California but lost their jobs (Romero, et al., 1988). The plant closed in October 1984, releas-
ing 3,000 employees, 900 of whom were Latinas, primarily of Mexican descent. Of the
114 women surveyed, 25% served as the heads of households, and all had been laid off
for at least 18 months at the time of the study. The issues of primary concern for these
women were discrimination, economic hardship, and length of unemployment. Many
women felt that securing another job was more difficult because of their Latina status.
Further, the women laid off from the Starkist plant were searching for new work in a
climate in which unemployment periods tended to be significantly longer for Latinos
and African Americans. The typical length of unemployment for Whites during this
period was 12 weeks, whereas Latinos typically needed 16 weeks and African Americans 21 weeks to locate new employment.

Another group that is disproportionately affected by unemployment is Latino youth.

## Table 2

## Employment status of the Hispanic-origin population by age or sex, 1997

| Age and sex | Percent population in labor force | Percent population not in labor force | Percent workers employed in agriculture | Unemployment rate |
|---|---|---|---|---|
| **Men and Women** | | | | |
| 16 years and over | 67.9% | 32.1% | 5.2% | 7.7% |
| 16 to 17 years | 28.9% | 71.1% | 3.1% | 27.7% |
| 18 to 19 years | 57.7% | 42.3% | 5.1% | 18.4% |
| 20 to 24 years | 76.4% | 23.6% | 5.8% | 10.3% |
| 25 to 54 years | 79.1% | 20.9% | 5.1% | 6.1% |
| 55 to 64 years | 53.8% | 46.2% | 5.2% | 6.5% |
| 65 years and over | 11.9% | 88.1% | 4.6% | 6.8% |
| **Men** | | | | |
| 16 years and over | 80.1% | 19.9% | 7.4% | 7.0% |
| 16 to 17 years | 30.2% | 69.8% | 4.6% | 26.5% |
| 18 to 19 years | 66.3% | 33.7% | 7.2% | 17.9% |
| 20 to 24 years | 88.1% | 11.9% | 8.4% | 9.8% |
| 25 to 54 years | 91.8% | 8.2% | 7.2% | 5.2% |
| 55 to 64 years | 68.4% | 31.6% | 7.8% | 6.8% |
| 65 years and over | 17.3% | 82.7% | 6.7% | 7.2% |
| **Women** | | | | |
| 16 years and over | 55.1% | 44.9% | 1.8% | 8.9% |
| 16 to 17 years | 27.5% | 72.5% | 1.0% | 29.2% |
| 18 to 19 years | 48.5% | 51.5% | 2.6% | 19.1% |
| 20 to 24 years | 62.3% | 37.7% | 1.2% | 11.0% |
| 25 to 54 years | 65.7% | 34.3% | 1.9% | 7.4% |
| 55 to 64 years | 40.6% | 59.4% | 1.3% | 6.1% |
| 65 years and over | 8.1% | 91.9% | 1.4% | 6.0% |

Source: Calculated from data presented at Bureau of Labor Statistics WWW-site (http://stats.bls.gov/ Table AA4).

Overall, Latinos are a young population. One-third are less than 18 years of age and almost half are under 25. Therefore, the continued rapid increase in the number of young Latinos, especially among those entering the labor force, might add an age component to higher Latino unemployment; i.e., Latino youth could have an especially high rate of unemployment that combines the employment problems of being Latino with those of being young. Table 2 shows that young Latinos do indeed have very high rates of unemployment. In 1997, the unemployment rate for Latino young men aged 18 to 19 – which would include those right out of high school – was 17.9%. Even among those 20 to 24 years old, unemployment was high, at 9.8%. Similarly, almost one in five (19.1%) young Latinas aged 18 to 19 years old was unemployed.

**Table 3**

**Labor force participation rates and unemployment rates of total population age 16 and older: native and foreign-born, also, Latinos by nativity, U.S., 1990**

|  | Labor Force Participation Rates | Unemployment Rates |
|---|---|---|
| Total Native | 65.4 | 6.2 |
| Total Foreign | 64.3 | 7.8 |
| Not Latino Native | 65.3 | 6.0 |
| Not Latino Foreign | 60.9 | 5.9 |
| Latino Native | 65.6 | 10.4 |
| Latino Foreign | 69.7 | 10.4 |
| Mexican Native | 67.2 | 10.1 |
| Mexican Foreign | 69.7 | 11.3 |
| Puerto Rican Native | 60.4 | 12.4 |
| Puerto Rican Commonwealth | 62.5 | 11.5 |
| Cuban Native | 70.7 | 7.5 |
| Cuban Foreign | 63.8 | 6.8 |

Source: 1990 Census CP-3-3, Table 4.

In the context of continued, massive educational failure for Latino children and youth across the nation, as alluded to in the earlier section of this chapter, these figures are worrisome. As Table 1 above indicates, both U.S.-born and foreign-born Latinos have, by far, the largest proportion of adults with less than a high school education. In addition, the recent drastic decrease in earnings and employment (Brauer and Hickok, 1995) for high school dropouts suggests that unemployment is one of several challenges that Latino youth and young adults face in the labor market.

Latino immigrants also have high unemployment levels, but these rates do not differ as much from those of their native-born counterparts. Table 3 shows that, in 1990 (the most recent year for which such data are available that allow for this comparison), both U.S.-born and foreign-born Latinos had the same rate of unemployment, 10.4%. Note that this level is indeed much higher than the 6% level of unemployment experienced by the non-Latino U.S.-born population. Moreover, as the table shows, 12.4% of Puerto Ricans born on the U.S. mainland were unemployed – a rate higher than that of both their island-born counterparts and of foreign-born Mexicans. Similarly, foreign-born Cubans have a slightly lower unemployment rate than U.S.-born Cubans (6.8% vs. 7.5%).

## Factors Associated with High Unemployment

A number of factors contribute to the high unemployment rates of Latino workers. From a human capital perspective, given their educational profile and relative youthfulness, Latino workers are often at a disadvantage in the labor market. Specifically, low levels of education influence occupational placement; the employment options of those workers without high school diplomas or college degrees are often constrained to unstable industries. Additionally, young workers have not been able to accumulate either sufficient work experience, which limits their attractiveness to employers, or an employment network that would facilitate their movement in the labor force.

A consequence of this is that Latinos are especially likely to be susceptible to job loss – and to face barriers to re-entry into the workforce. Overall, most Latino unemployment, as unemployment for the population as a whole, results from job loss; few unemployed Latinos leave their jobs voluntarily. According to unpublished data from the March 1996 Current Population Survey[5], the primary cause of unemployment for Latinos was job loss or completion of temporary work (48%). While only 8% of Latinos had left their jobs voluntarily, 11.4% of Whites and 8.6% of Blacks had left their jobs of their own accord (NCLR, October 1997). Johanne Boisjoly and Greg J. Duncan posit that the relative youth, low skills, and low educational attainment of Latinos place them in peripheral industries that are more prone to job loss. Job loss data from the 1992 recession reflect this vulnerability.

According to Boisjoly and Duncan (1994), during the period 1987-1992, the Latino job loss rate was 11.8%, a percentage much greater than the 8.8% experienced by African Americans and 7.9% suffered by Whites. These authors studied the dynamics of Latino job retention with a spring 1990 survey of Latino workers who had worked at least 12 months at their current jobs, had worked 1,000 hours in 1989, were not self-employed, and were between the ages of 25 and 59. A year after the first administration of the survey, respondents were re-interviewed to determine whether they had retained their positions, or lost them for reasons like "company folded" and "laid off, fired." The Boisjoly and Duncan study showed significantly higher job displacement and lower job retention among Latinos, with immigrants, Mexican Americans, and Puerto Ricans faring the worst.

Further, the types of industries in which Latinos worked were particularly susceptible to the economic downturn in the early 1990s. Specifically, Latinos have worked precisely in those industries that have suffered losses in the past two decades. According to the U.S. Bureau of Labor Statistics, in 1995 and 1996, unemployment was highest in construction, apparel manufacturing, and agriculture – Latinos represented approximately 10% of construction workers, one-quarter of apparel workers, and 18% of the agricultural workforce in 1996.

In the Boisjoly and Duncan study, respondents who were employed in low-skill jobs, construction, or extraction were the most likely to be displaced. Conversely, those with professional or government positions had a much lower likelihood of displacement.

Geographic differences also affect, to some degree, the Latino unemployment rate. For example, the states with the highest concentration of Latinos in 1995 all had employment declines higher than the national average in the mid-1990s. Further, Latinos in western states suffered far more from the 1992 recession than did their eastern U.S. counterparts. Another factor which has greatly affected Latino unemployment in the past decade is their concentration in urban areas – which have been disproportionately affected by a loss of manufacturing jobs and the shift from this type of employment to service work. The study of the Wilmington Starkist plant discussed above found that over 80% of Latinas live in cities, where available jobs are often tied to industries that are particularly susceptible to job loss. Indeed, the overall trend of deindustrialization, which hurts cities more than other areas, is especially damaging to jobs that employ Latinas. Overall, 25% of Latinas work in unstable "laborer" positions, compared to 11% of all U.S. women. The combination of high unemployment and jobs in unstable sectors leads Romero, et al. to conclude that Latinas are greatly affected by fluctuations in labor markets. This is especially important since Latinas provide the primary income for at least 25% of the overall Latino population (Romero, et al., 1988).

To be sure, youthfulness, insufficient schooling, insufficient labor market experience, lack of transferable skills, and residence in high unemployment areas contribute to the precarious position of Latinos in the workforce. These factors also exacerbate the displacement issue; Latino workers with such characteristics may have a difficult time regaining employment. Boisjoly and Duncan found that among native and immigrant populations, Latino workers had the hardest time finding work after being released from positions. To corroborate this further, a recent analysis of Latino unemployment by the National Council of La Raza found that recovery from displacement was harder for Latinos than for Anglos between 1993 and 1996. Latinos were less likely than Anglos to be re-employed following displacement (NCLR, October 1997).

The high Latino unemployment rate is, undoubtedly, tied to both their human capital characteristics and the impact of economic changes on those industries and areas in which Latinos tend to work and live. But two other short-term factors have influenced the rise of Latino unemployment during the 1990s.

### Short-Term Factors: Proposition 187* and the *Peso* Devaluation

The two events that may well have had a great and sudden impact on Latino unemployment are Proposition 187 and the *peso* devaluation. While Proposition 187 was targeted against undocumented immigrants, there can be no doubt that it could have an impact on Latinos who are citizens or documented residents as well. *New York Times* reporter Robert Hershey observed that:

> *Many Latino workers are held back by outmoded skills, job inexperience and weaker educational credentials. But these days they are also finding themselves*

---

* As described by the National Immigration Forum, Proposition 187, which California voters passed in 1994, sought to obligate public agencies, such as schools, health care facilities, and social service providers, to determine the immigration status of those they serve, deny services to those they suspect are undocumented, and report them to the Immigration and Naturalization Service.

*increasingly subject to intense suspicion, resentment and, in many cases, outright discrimination. (Hershey, 1995, p. C-1)*

He goes on to quote Juan Vargas, Deputy Mayor of San Diego:

*There's no doubt that discrimination has increased against Latinos. Proposition 187 has created almost a crisis in the Latino community. It has employers panicked. (Hershey, 1995, p. C-6)*

While Proposition 187 was aimed at health care, social services, education, and law enforcement, its effects have been far-reaching, as the quote above suggests. After the passage of this measure, discrimination against Latinos was manifested in many ways. Latinos were insulted, assaulted, physically attacked, pelted with rocks, illegally refused service, and denied employment opportunities.[6] The proposition resulted in a more hostile climate for Latinos in California, and this has almost certainly had a negative impact on Latino employment opportunities in the state, since the measure intended to target anyone who is "reasonably suspected" of violating federal immigration laws. Moreover, the potential discrimination stemming from Proposition 187 builds on the anti-immigrant and anti-Latino effects of the 1986 "employer sanctions" immigration law.[7] Given that California has almost one-third of the Latino population in the U.S., the state proposition could easily have had a national impact on the overall status of Latinos. In addition, other states have considered adoption of similar initiatives.

The impact of the *peso* devaluation on Latino unemployment could also have an immediate, localized effect that could conceivably be reflected in the national statistics, especially in areas with high Latino concentration. With the formalization of the North American Free Trade Agreement (NAFTA) and an over-valued *peso*, Mexico went on a sustained shopping spree in the U.S., particularly in Texas border cities. The population and the labor force in many of these cities are predominantly Latino. The *peso* devaluation stopped the spree overnight. The headline, "*Peso's* drop hurts South Texas business," considered along with the predominantly Latino demographic composition of South Texas, can point directly to another factor leading to increased Latino unemployment locally and nationally. The immediate employment impacts of the *peso* devaluation can be seen in the fact that unemployment along the Texas border increased from December 1994 to January 1995. In Brownsville, unemployment went up from 12.8% to 14.7% in January 1995 and rose to 16.8% in June of that year. El Paso unemployment went from 8.3% in December 1994 to 10.8% in June 1995. In Laredo, where trade with Mexico is the major part of the economy, unemployment jumped from 8.8% in December 1994 to 12.0% in January 1995 and increased to 18.0% by June 1995. During the same period, unemployment in Dallas and Houston increased and decreased slightly from month to month.[8]

A number of short-term factors have clearly affected Latino unemployment. The remaining question is how much of this convergence reflects the long-term trends that are reshaping the U.S. economy, including the fact that workers with low skills and educational levels have had decreasing wages and diminishing opportunities for employment since the mid-1970s. The future employment prospects of workers with low levels of education are even bleaker than those of the recent past.

## Long-Term Factors in the Restructuring in the U.S. Economy
While there is widespread consensus on the characteristics of the major changes in the U.S. economy, there is an extensive debate on the reasons or causes for this economic restructuring. The relevant economic literature lists a number of possible causes of the economic losses. Among these are increased international trade, technological change, widespread computerization, industrial decline, increased immigration, increased inconsistency in the quality of education, skill restructuring, use of computers, and the decreasing influence of unions, labor laws, and other wage-setting institutions.[9]

The connection between economic restructuring and the decreasing quantity and quality of jobs available to Latinos can be found in the type of jobs that were lost as U.S. corporations restructured themselves to compete in a global economy. The biggest and earliest job losses occurred in manufacturing. The higher the pay, the more likely the job would be exported. Before restructuring, many Americans – including Latinos – with relatively low levels of education could support themselves and their families with high-wage manufacturing jobs. In the late 1970s, Latino workers were highly concentrated in manufacturing jobs (Chapa 1990). The globalization of these jobs formerly based in the U.S. greatly decreased the number and wages of jobs available to all workers who had a high school education or less.[10] DeFreitas' research (1991) confirms that deindustrialization and the dramatic shift away from manufacturing industries is a major cause of high rates of Puerto Rican unemployment.

These deeper structural trends occurring in the U.S. economy have meant that workers with low levels of education have a much harder time finding jobs that pay well; further, when the economy is not booming, they will have a harder time finding jobs at all. At this writing, the U.S. economy has just recorded its longest period of growth ever and unemployment rates for all groups, including Latinos, are at historic lows. However, when a recession occurs, recent experience (see the Boisjoly and Duncan discussion above) supports the contention that low-skilled workers with low levels of education will be those most likely to lose their jobs. More and more, the workers who fit this description are Latinos. That Latino unemployment rates are more sensitive to changing economic conditions, like economic recessions and layoffs, than Anglo unemployment rates is also supported by DeFreitas' analysis which shows that Latino unemployment rises rapidly during recessions and decreases rapidly during recoveries.

It is clear from the literature that there is no one factor that will explain all of the economic changes in all of the sectors over the post-boom period. It is also clear that whether they are a cause or a consequence, all of these factors are implicated in the increased internationalization of the U.S. economy and the decreased opportunities – and increased unemployment – for Latinos with low levels of education.

## Discrimination

Another issue that merits attention in the discussion of the employment status of Latinos and their high unemployment rate is discrimination, which is undoubtedly a factor in the earnings and employment disparities experienced by minorities relative to Whites. Genevieve Kenney and Douglas A. Wissoker designed a study to map the types of discrimination faced by young Latino job-seekers in several parts of the country (Kenney and Wissoker, 1994). Over 350 "audits" were executed to help ascertain the rate of successful job application, interview callback, and job offers among young Latino men. Latino auditors, who had to be fluent in English and Spanish, physically identifiable as Latino, and with a Spanish surname, were paired with Anglo auditors of similar educational background. For some auditors, educational background and work history were fabricated to match the requirements for the jobs sought. Auditors then applied for jobs, and reported the results to Kenney and Wissoker.

Not surprisingly, Anglo job applicants had higher success rates in every category of the employment search. For example, Anglos had a 95% success rate in filing job applications, whereas Latinos successfully submitted applications 91% of the time. At the interview stage, Anglos were 30% more likely than Latinos to receive interviews. Finally, Latinos had a job offer rate 52% lower than that of Anglos, perhaps revealing that official discrimination (i.e., restrictions upon filing an application) gives way to more subtle discrimination in the final steps of job application. A similar trend involved the geographic placement of job offers. Anglos were much more likely to be offered positions in high-income areas, possibly revealing a client "taste" for Anglo employees. Small, local companies were especially likely to hire Anglos. Kenney and Wissoker stress that small companies often operate outside of the non-discrimination guidelines followed by larger firms. The differential treatment experienced by Latino job applicants, argue Kenney and Wissoker, indicates that discrimination is still a powerful force in minority labor market participation.

Various theories of labor market discrimination exist, many of which focus on the "taste" of employers and clients for employees of certain ethnic/racial groups (Hirsch and Schumacher, 1992). Under what is known as the "taste model," employers, due to discriminatory preferences, will pay higher wages to employ Anglos. Among employees, the taste model posits that some majority-population workers will demand higher wages to work in a primarily minority labor market. Other models, such as the statistical discrimination model, explore other facets of workforce discrimination. Under statistical discrimination, employers use statistics covering items like educational attainment and household income to make generalizations about the employability of minorities. Similar to statistical discrimination is "quality sorting," a process wherein racial stereotypes are used to allocate employment. Finally, "racial crowding" is a term relating to the concentration of minorities in low-skill, low-paying jobs. Among these models, Hirsch and Schumacher maintain that no evidence exists for taste or statistical discrimination, but that quality sorting, racial crowding, and language discrimination are applied to the minority population.

Given that these studies on the impact of employment discrimination on Latino workers were focused on job seekers, there is a connection to the role that such bias plays in maintaining a higher-than-average Latino unemployment rate.

## Latino Underemployment

Unemployment is a vexing and widely studied subject. A problem that is equally disturbing, yet receives much less attention, is underemployment. For example, the fact that the Mexican American population in the United States is disproportionately represented among the ranks of the unemployed is widely accepted. Unemployment rates one-and-a-half to two times greater than that of the Anglo population are alarming, but they mask the number of individuals who are discouraged, working part-time involuntarily, employed intermittently, or working full-time, yet still earning wages below the poverty line.

Discouraged workers, according to the U.S. Bureau of Labor Statistics, are those who simply "give up" looking for a job, in part because they do not believe their prospects are bright. Many have searched extensively for a job but cannot find one (De Anda, 1994). Typically, these potential workers are not counted among the unemployed. Similarly, those involuntarily working part-time would like to get work with longer hours, but often cannot find it. Intermittent workers, those who work on short-term projects that have a high turnover rate, are also frustrated in their search for stable employment. For intermittent workers, the challenge is even greater, since they are sometimes seen as indolent or unreliable because of the short tenure of their work. Lastly, the working poor have perhaps the worst situation. They have obtained full-time employment, but cannot win a wage high enough to bring themselves and their families above the poverty line. Together, these groups form what DeAnda calls the "underemployed."

DeAnda studied the incidence of underemployment among Latinos using the Labor Utilization Framework (LUF) created by Clogg, et al. The LUF measures the "quantity and quality" of employment by rating measures such as hours worked and wages. All of the individuals included in DeAnda's study worked at least 35 hours per week and held a job commensurate with their level of education. These guidelines were included to ensure that the study was tracking people who had full-time labor market participation. After applying the LUF index to the labor participation of Mexican Americans, DeAnda found that 47.3% of Mexican American women and 42% of Mexican American men were underemployed. These rates are near double that of the Anglo male population and more than 1.5 times that of the Anglo female population. Mexican Americans fare especially poorly in two subcategories of underemployment. The rate of Mexican American men who work part-time involuntarily is 1.5 times that of Anglo men. The rate of involuntary part-time work for Latinas is even greater, at 1.8 times the Anglo female rate. Overall, Latinos are overrepresented among the working poor. The number of working poor Latino men is more than twice the number of work-ing poor Anglo men.

The distribution of underemployment among the Latino population is influenced by age. Within the 16-24 age bracket, two-thirds of Latinas and 61% of Latino men are underemployed. The Anglo population in this age bracket experiences 50% underemployment. DeAnda suggests a combination of factors to explain the disproportionate underemployment suffered by young Latinos. Influences such as low educational attainment and employment in low-skill periphery industries place young Latinos at a substantial risk of underemployment. Latino youth, however, are not the only age group at risk of underemployment. DeAnda found that Latino men aged 35-54 – who represent a significant share of workers in their prime employment age and who are heads of households – were 2.4 times as likely to be underemployed as their Anglo counterparts.

Deficiencies in education, according to DeAnda, also explain the high incidence of underemployment among Latinos. High school graduation, for example, pays dividends to Latino workers. Almost half (49.9%) of Mexican American men who failed to graduate from high school experienced underemployment, compared to slightly more than one-third (36.9%) of those who gain a high school diploma. The difference is even greater among Latinas. Latinas without a high school diploma encounter underemployment at a rate of 60.2%, whereas those with a diploma experience underemployment at a rate of 44.7%. Generally, as the level of education among Mexican American workers increases, their likelihood of being included among the ranks of the underemployed decreases.

As in wages, employment, and unemployment, the type of work pursued by Latinos influences their rate of underemployment. In the peripheral sector that DeAnda outlines, the rate of Mexican American underemployment is 14.5%, whereas the rate for Anglos is 8%.

DeAnda concludes that traditional reliance on unemployment figures alone threatens to obscure the problem of underemployment. Unemployment, by DeAnda's calculation, represents only one-third of total underemployment among Mexican Americans. As the magnitude of DeAnda's numbers suggest, underemployment is a serious problem for the Latino population in the U.S., especially among Mexican Americans. Within the Mexican American population, young people and women suffer the most.

Another factor that plays a large role in explaining employment outcomes for some Latinos is the period during which those who are immigrants arrived in the U.S.

Recent Mexican immigrants, for example, typically earn 20-25% less than earlier generations. At the same time, even those who arrived up to 15 years before the current wave of Latino immigrants have yet to enjoy the benefits of economic assimilation. Borjas maintains that assimilation does not pay adequate dividends in the first 15 years of residence in the U.S., but may do so afterwards. The immigrant experience also heavily influences the employment path of new U.S. residents. According to Borjas, "political refugees" often face an initial labor market disadvantage. Similarly, the refugee experience often favors the types of human capital enhancement that immigrants seek, thereby influencing their labor force participation (Borjas, 1981).

The combination of high unemployment and underemployment undermines the strong attachment of Latinos to the labor force. It also greatly affects their overall economic progress. In particular, education levels and poor occupational placement need to be improved. Such issues are especially critical to address in the context of globalization, economic competitiveness, the changing demographics of the U.S. workforce, and the increasing influence of Latino workers.

## Future Prospects for Low-Skilled Workers

The Hudson's Institute's report, *Workforce 2000*, created a stir by asking if the future U.S. workforce would have the skills necessary to be economically competitive. The authors argued that the following trends would have a great impact on America's economic future: 1) the continuing growth of service employment and continuing decline in manufacturing; 2) an increasing demand for more-highly-educated workers; 3) a larger share of future labor force entrants who are women and minorities as the population ages; 4) inadequate child care and other support systems, which limit the potential productivity of women; and 5) ineffective educational institutions, which limit the potential productivity of minorities. One major possible consequence of the interaction of these trends is a future shortage of well-educated workers in comparison to the requirements of newly-created jobs (Johnston and Packer, 1987).

How do these considerations apply to future employment opportunities for Latinos? To get a sense of this, Table 4 shows that Latinos are concentrated in occupations requiring low levels of skills and severely underrepresented in managerial and professional occupations. The table also shows the average language, math, and total skill rating scores used in the Hudson Institute reports. These ratings are based on the

## Table 4

## Latinos as a percentage of employees in occupational categories and the skill ratings associated with those categories, 1997

|  | Latinos as % of occupational category | Language Skill Rating | Math Skill Rating | Total Skill Rating |
|---|---|---|---|---|
| **Manager or Administrator**<br>Officials and administrators<br>Management-related occupations | 5.2% | 4.4 | 4.2 | 8.6 |
| **Professional or Technical**<br>Other technicians<br>Health technicians | 5.9% | 4.0 | 3.9 | 7.9 |
| **Sales**<br>Cashiers<br>Sales workers<br>Sales supervisors | 7.7% | 3.6 | 3.3 | 6.9 |
| **Clerical**<br>Secretaries and typists<br>Administrative support<br>Office machine operators | 8.6% | 2.9 | 2.7 | 5.6 |
| **Protective services**<br>Police, sheriffs and corrections<br>Firefighters<br>Guards, excluding crossing guards | 13.8% | 4.0 | 3.2 | 7.2 |
| **Service workers**<br>Cleaning and building services<br>Food preparation<br>Health service occupations | 14.9% | 2.6 | 2.2 | 4.8 |
| **Craft workers**<br>Carpenters, electricians<br>Equipment repairers<br>Vehicle mechanics | 12.2% | 2.9 | 2.8 | 5.7 |
| **Operators and laborers**<br>Bus drivers<br>Truck drivers<br>Construction laborers | 15.6% | 1.6 | 1.5 | 3.1 |
| **Agricultural & related** | 22.8% | – | – | – |
| **WEIGHTED AVERAGE**<br>(excluding Agriculture) | 100% | 2.8 | 2.6 | 5.4 |

Source: Latino percentages calculated from data presented on Bureau of Labor Statistics website (http://stats.bls.gov/ Table AA11). Skill ratings from *Civil Service 2000*, pp. 11-15.

General Education Development Score used by the U.S. Department of Labor to measure math, language, and reasoning skills on a scale from one through six. A job with a math rating of six, the top score, would require the ability to use calculus, econometrics, or other highly-developed mathematical abilities. A job at the bottom of the scale would have a score of one and only require the ability to add and subtract two-digit numbers. The opposite extremes of the language scale also reflect large differences in ability. Jobs with high language skill scores require employees with the ability to read and write scientific, technical, financial, or legal publications and documents. Occupations with the lowest language skill ratings require the ability to read or deliver simple messages, follow oral instructions, fill out forms, etc. In Table 4, typical job titles are listed below each category in order to give a sense of what types of jobs are covered by these categories. In sum, Table 4 shows that Latinos are concentrated in jobs that have relatively low skill ratings and low educational levels. If the economy is requiring an increasing supply of highly-trained and skilled workers, does this mean that the skill requirements of all jobs will likewise increase?

Some of the apparent differences between the projected supply and demand for highly-educated workers in the future workforce come from comparing the needs of jobs with the fastest growth rates to current levels of educational attainment. Even if many or most of the newly-created jobs of the future will indeed require highly-educated workers, this does not mean that many or most of all jobs will have such requirements. Even though many new jobs, including those in state and local government, for example, do require highly-educated workers, the foreseeable future includes a need for the services of many nonprofessional and paraprofessional state employees. Even if there were a steady trend that acted to increase the proportion of professionals and to decrease the proportion of nonprofessionals in state and local government, it would take a long time for such a trend to reduce the 79% share of nonprofessional state-local employees to an insignificant figure.

The report of the National Center on Education and the Economy, *America's Choice: High Skills or Low Wages*, provides a very helpful complement to *Workforce 2000*. The fact that the new jobs created by economic growth and change generally do require higher educational levels, as *Workforce 2000* indicates, does not mean that the skill requirements for existing jobs are increasing. The authors of *America's Choice* argue that these new jobs stand on the stable strata of the large majority of jobs with low formal educational requirements and no indication of a demand for change. In their analysis, America's workforce is composed of three groups of approximately similar sizes. The first consists of jobs that require no more than an eighth-grade-level com-petency in math and language, the requisite physical ability to do the work, and an agreeable personality. The service workers and operatives and laborers listed in Table 4 are examples of this group. The second workforce group is comprised of jobs that require specialized training beyond basic literacy and numeracy, but not a four-year college degree. Many of the clerical and craft occupations from Table 4 are examples of these jobs. The third category encompasses the occupations that do require college degrees and thus are not of direct concern here. The skill shortage, which was identi-fied in *America's Choice*, consisted of shortages or deficiencies in interpersonal skills, reliability, communications ability, and other work-related attitudes and manners (National Center on Education and the Economy, 1990). *America's Choice* emphasizes that our present and future workforce needs good training, but it does not need a work-force exclusively composed of Ph.D.s or other very highly-trained workers. A large proportion of jobs in the future will require workers with basic cognitive and work skills.

## Conclusions and Recommendations

This chapter earlier presented evidence that suggested that employment opportunities for Latinos with low skill and educational levels are diminishing. While the evidence is far from conclusive, this may indeed be true. However, even if it is, the weight of the arguments presented in *America's Choice* is that there are still many low-skill jobs available. The increases in Latino unemployment discussed earlier may simply have been the temporary consequence of two simultaneous shocks to those economic sectors which are heavily Latino. However, it is also possible that the decrease of Latino unem-ployment compared to Black unemployment since 1995 may also be a temporary con-sequence of our current economic boom. The true test of a possible convergence will be how similar the rates are during the next national recession. Furthermore, even if Latino rates never again become as high as those experienced by African Americans, the goal of any policy must be to make them as low as possible.

A large proportion of jobs in the future will require workers with basic cognitive and work skills. There are two great problems in our public high schools. One is the extremely high rate at which Latinos drop out. The other is the schools' failure to pro-vide high school students and graduates with an institutionalized connection with employers. One approach that is more consistent with the thinking presented in *Amer-ica's Choice* is to make high school course work more "relevant" to employers. Another one of the key points of *America's Choice* is that education should be available over the life course. For instance, the authors of *America's Choice* call for a flexible education structure that imparts basic workforce skills to all students at a very early age, and then permits every individual to tailor the combination of education and work experience that would meet his or her needs and abilities (The National Center on Education and the Economy, 1990). In this sense, American students would not have to choose between finishing high school or never holding an adequate job.

As national wage and employment data continue to show, Latinos are not progressing rapidly toward economic parity with the majority Anglo population. The average wages earned by Latinos are well under those of the non-Latino population, and the occupational distribution for Latinos is skewed toward positions that require few skills and offer few opportunities for advancement. Further, even though Latinos often occupy well-paying blue-collar positions, such as carpenter or builder, these jobs are often subject to market fluctuations. Unemployment is thus an added barrier to adequate Latino labor market participation and success. Yet unemployment figures alone often mask the equally disturbing problem of underemployment. Many Latinos are unable to locate positions that offer them dependable, full-time work.

The troublesome portrait of Latino labor market participation revealed by labor statistics can be explained in a variety of ways. Human capital theory, which attaches monetary values to knowledge and skills, explains wage inequity through measures like educational attainment. The lower educational attainment of Latinos would, therefore, explain their lower wages and occupational status. Other theories, however, focus on the labor market barriers that Latinos face. Segmented labor market theory, for example, maintains that numerous individual labor markets exist, each with a distinct set of wages and occupations. The simplest form of segmented labor market theory posits that two unequal markets exist. In dual labor market theory, the first market sector is characterized by high-skill, high-paying positions that have good prospects for advancement. The second sector, conversely, is characterized by low-skill, low-paying positions that have very limited prospects for career growth. Both of these theories are valuable in assessing the labor market participation of Latinos, yet neither fully explains the employment experiences of the Latino population. In order to get a comprehensive picture of the workforce participation of Latinos, social factors must be considered.

"Concentration" is a term that refers to communities that are densely populated with minority populations. Most Latinos in the U.S. live in such communities, thus the employment dynamics that result from concentration are important to understand in the consideration of Latino labor market inclusion. Overall, the effects of minority concentration are disputed. Some scholars maintain that Latinos can take advantage of minority business and social contacts in such communities. Others, however, point to the sometimes discriminatory structures that exist in labor markets where most workers are minorities. Indeed, discrimination is another social factor that shapes Latino employment. Lower wages, a skewed occupational distribution, and high unemployment can in part be attributed to the discriminatory practices of employers. Discrimination is especially strong in determining the labor market outcomes of Latino immigrants, individuals who often lack the social and linguistic ties to the United States necessary for career advancement.

The experiences of Latinos once they enter the workforce are strong determinants of their ultimate occupational attainment. However, education plays a strong role in channeling Latino workers before they enter the adult work force. High dropout rates, low enrollment in institutions of higher education, and limited transfers from community to four-year colleges limit the career potential of Latino students, and often relegate them to lower-skilled and lower-paying positions.

There seem to be large and effective factions active in American politics today which work to exclude Latinos from full participation in the U.S. economy and the means of obtaining prosperity. This is particularly true in California. Recent initiatives, court cases, and laws are likely to restrict further Latino rights with an evident vengeance. The first of these is California's Proposition 187, passed in 1994, which intends to deny government services to undocumented immigrants. While Proposition 187 was targeted against undocumented immigrants, there can be no doubt that it has implications for Latinos who are citizens or legal residents. The startling increase in Latino unemployment, to equal the African American rate, followed by a few months the ratification of Proposition 187.

California has also led the way in obstructing access to higher education for Latinos and other minorities. This occurred first in the decision of the University of California Regents to end their affirmative action programs, followed by the passage of Proposition 209, which ended affirmative action programs in all state institutions. Finally, the very recent passage of Proposition 227 – which would replace today's range of bilingual programs with a one-year immersion in English instruction for those with limited proficiency – will very likely result in decreasing educational opportunities for almost one-third of all Latinos in the U.S..

These initiatives and continued discrimination against Latinos would be unwelcome news in any context. However, they are especially tragic given that, even with the enhanced opportunities offered by affirmative action, Latinos – including those who have been in this country for many generations – are not attaining educational, economic, or occupational parity with Anglos. Any movement to share prosperity with Latinos has to begin by countering these and other efforts to relegate Latinos to the bottom of the economy and society. Specifically, strategies should be pursued to:

1.  **Lower the Latino Unemployment Rate:** Latinos are disproportionately represented in industries like construction and assembly that are prone to high unemployment rates. Perennial unemployment not only hurts the earning potential of Latino workers, but also can lead to problems of long-term underemployment. While Latino unemployment cannot solely be addressed by public policy, strategies that aim to diversify the Latino workforce, such as workforce development programs and assistance to reintegrate displaced workers into the labor force, can help create a buffer against the market forces that have traditionally steered Latino economic participation.

2.  **Study the Issue of Latino Underemployment:** Underemployment appears to be a significant characteristic of the Latino employment picture. Yet, not enough is known regarding the degree to which underemployment is rising or falling, or the effects the nation's continued economic restructuring has on underemployed Latinos. Furthermore, the socioeconomic consequences of underemployment on Latino economic progress should be examined and addressed.

3.  **Reinforce Affirmative Action Programs in the Workplace:** The American workforce has a dearth of Latino managers, and the overall occupational distribution of Latino workers accounts for their disproportionate propensity to be affected by economic shifts. A variety of explanations accounts for the inability of Latinos to reach the highest levels of occupational status. One of the most compelling is that Latinos are discriminated against in their efforts to seek a variety of jobs, and to climb corporate and other workforce ladders to management or economically stable and promising positions. Additionally, employment discrimination appears to play a role in the unemployment rate of Latinos. Moreover, the absence of Latinos

in such positions reinforces the hopelessness of those who have high economic aspirations, yet are faced with limited employment prospects.

4.  **Strengthen the School-to-Work Transition of Latino Youth:** Young Latino job-seekers have weaker employment networks than their non-Latino counterparts, a fact that influences the high youth unemployment rate among Latinos. Better School-to-Work programs could help find stable, well-paying jobs for Latinos who are not bound for college. Further, such programs could help to reallocate workers into positions less prone to labor market fluctuations.

5.  **Support Existing, Effective Workforce Development Programs:** Like their young counterparts, many adult Latinos benefit from programs that provide them with marketable job skills. Some programs even link workers with existing jobs to guarantee employment to all individuals who enroll. Such efforts should be made available to those geographic areas with high concentrations of Latino workers.

6.  **Support Programs that Meet the Specific Language Needs of Different Latino Populations:** English proficiency often determines the labor market outcomes of Latinos. Most native-born Latinos are English-proficient, yet many of their immigrant counterparts are not. Immigrants who lack strong English skills are often relegated to low-status jobs with little hope of advancement – and vulnerability to unemployment. Language programs that concentrate on the needs of adult immigrants as well as of children would improve the human capital characteristics – and employment options – of Latino workers.

7.  **Expand Existing Programs to Bolster Latino Business Enterprise:** Government policies concerning the awarding of contracts to minority-owned businesses should be fostered, especially since Latino entrepreneurs are isolated in a few industries. Expansion into traditionally non-Latino industries, like banking and real estate, should provide a wider base of support for Latino entrepreneurial ventures. Such efforts would expand the labor market alternatives of Latino workers, and allow for the creation of jobs for Latino and other workers with limited prospects in the workforce.

# NOTES

1.  Chapa concentrates his analysis on third-generation Mexican Americans because, while the participation of Mexican immigrants in the U.S. economy has been widely studied, the fate of Chicanos often receives less attention from scholars.

2.  Assimilationists would argue that the higher educational attainment figure proves that Mexican Americans benefit through residence in the United States. Chapa rejects this argument by reinforcing the idea that the demographic profile of immigrants can change over time. The fact that current Mexican immigrants have a lower educational attainment level than long-term U.S. residents does not necessarily prove that long-term residents have improved their schooling. In order to bolster this argument, Chapa turns to statistics on Asian American immigrants. Asian Americans, sometimes mistakenly portrayed as an immigrant group without hardship, actually experienced a relative drop in the educational attainment of third-generation American residents. That is, recent Asian American immigrants have a higher level of educational attainment than their long-term American counterparts. Chapa argues that this is not a reflection of the decline in Asian American assimilation, but rather of the changing profile in Asian immigration to the United States.

3.  Reimers, Cordelia W., "Caught in the Widening Skill Differential: Native-Born Mexican American Wages in California in the 1980s," Hunter College, Department of Economics, December 1993, Revised June 1994.

4.  Harrison, Roderick and Claudette Bennett in Reynolds Farley (ed.), *State of the Union: America in the 1990s,* Vol.1: Economic Trends, Russell Sage: New York, 1995.

5.  Cited in National Council of La Raza, "Unemployment Issue Brief," Washington, DC: 1996.

6.  National Immigration Forum, Fax Memorandum, "Proposition 187 – Update of Abuses in California, Status of Lawsuits, Developments Around the Country," February 17, 1985.

7.  As the General Accounting Office documented in 1990, 10% of 4.6 million employers surveyed admitted to one or more acts of national origin discrimination, in part because they feared hiring undocumented immigrants. Additionally, 52% more job offers, in matched pair testing, went to those applicants who did not look or sound "foreign."

8.  Data extracted from Bureau of Labor Statistics web-site ftp://ftp.bls.gov/pub/time. series/la/la_data-51.Texas.

9.  A review of this literature and analysis of the relative importance of these factors can be found in Grubb, Norton W. and Robert Wilson, "Trends in Wages and Salary Inequality, 1967-1988," *Monthly Labor Review*, September, 1993, vol. 115, No. 6, p. 23; Howell, David R. and Susan S. Weiler, "Trends in Computerization, Skill Composition and Low Earnings: Implications for Education and Training Policy," paper presented at the Association for Public Policy Analysis and Management Meetings, Chicago, IL, October 1994; Lawrence, Robert Z., "U.S. Wage Trends in the 1980s: the Role of International Factors," *Federal Reserve Bank of New York Economic Policy Review*, January, Vol.1, No. 1, p. 18, 1995; and Brauer, David A. and Susan Hickok, "Explaining the Growing Inequality Across Skill Levels," *Federal Reserve Bank of New York Economic Policy Review*, January, Vol.1, No.1, p. 65, 1995.

10. For details on the direct connection between the loss of manufacturing jobs and decreased opportunities for Latino workers, see Morales, Rebecca and Frank Bonilla (eds.), *Latinos in a Changing U.S. Economy, Comparative Perspectives on Growing Inequality*, Newbury Park, CA: Sage Publications, 1993.

# Latino Immigrants in the Labor Force:
# Trends and Labor Market Issues

**Guillermo J. Grenier, Ph.D.**
**Peter Cattan, Ph.D.**
*Center for Labor Research and Studies*
*Florida International University*

## Abstract

*This chapter examines three questions occasioned by the recent influx, from Latin America and the Caribbean, of immigrants with low levels of educational attainment. First, how do they compare with native-born Hispanics in terms of key socioeconomic indicators? Second, will the low levels of educational attainment of these recent arrivals prevent them from thriving in their new country? Third, do they undercut the employment and wages of native-born workers? We address the first question in a statistical profile of the socioeconomic status of Hispanic immigrants, noting that they have high rates of employment and an incidence of poverty that is not markedly different from that of native-born Hispanics. With regard to the second question, a marked gap between entry wages of immigrants and the wages of non-Hispanic Whites is cause for concern, but we reject the contention that recent immigrants are destined to remain at the bottom of the socioeconomic ladder. Although there is no dearth of research addressing the third question, findings concerning key issues are often contradictory. We find little evidence that low-skill immigrants are a major source of the economic problems of native workers. We conclude with a set of policy recommendations to address the labor market problems of both native and immigrant workers.*

# I. Overview

Approaching the record set at the turn of this century, the United States has admitted almost 13 million immigrants over the past 15 years. In contrast to the early 1900s, when most immigrants came from Europe, a large component of recent immigrants have come from Latin America and the Caribbean. In fact, Latinos accounted for approximately one of every three immigrants between 1980 and 1995. A heterogeneous population, Latino immigrants represent many nationalities, including Mexicans, Cubans, persons from 15 Central and South American countries, Spain, and the Dominican Republic. With three million immigrants over the past 15 years, Mexico has been the single largest source of immigration. For the same time period, there was a combined total of 1.5 million immigrants from Central and South America, and 470,000 from the Dominican Republic, a dramatic increase for both from previous decades. Cuban immigration has averaged a relatively small, but steady, stream of approximately 14,000 persons per year since 1980.

As the tabulation below indicates, six states accounted for approximately two of every five immigrants in the nation in 1990:

### Table 1

### Percent distribution of immigrants by state, 1990

| State | Percent of Nation's Immigrants (%) |
|---|---|
| California | 12 |
| New York | 7 |
| Texas | 7 |
| Florida | 5 |
| New Jersey | 3 |
| Illinois | 5 |
| Other states | 61 |

Source: National Research Council (1997:59), derived from U.S. Bureau of the Census (1993a).

As will be noted below, Latino immigrants are particularly concentrated in California, Texas, New York, Florida, and Illinois. In contrast, New Jersey's immigrant population is more diversified (Espenshade, 1997).

The objective of this chapter is to profile the socioeconomic status of Hispanic immigrants nationwide and in key states, with a particular emphasis on their education, employment, and poverty status. We use data from the 1990 Census to address the question, "How much of Hispanic poverty did immigration explain in the 1980s?" This is followed by a section addressing specific major debates concerning immigrants in the workforce.

Our focus on poverty updates an earlier analysis by Valenzuela (1991), who mobilized evidence from the 1970 and 1980 Censuses that the relatively high incidence of poverty among Hispanics cannot be solely attributed to immigrants. We disaggregate persons by nativity in order to determine the extent to which poverty and other indicators of economic problems continue to characterize persons born in the U.S. as well as those born abroad. In addition, we examine the contention that immigrants are "destined for the bottom of the socioeconomic ladder" (see Jensen, 1991 for a critique); and that they negatively affect socioeconomic indicators for Hispanics overall (downgrading the socioeconomic levels of earlier, established Hispanic immigrant groups and perhaps reinforcing negative public perceptions and stereotypes of all Hispanic immigrants and Hispanics in general).

By combining our findings for 1990 with those of Valenzuela, we show that the "ethnic gap" – the ratio of Hispanic immigrant to non-Hispanic White poverty rates – has edged up over the past two decades. We also find that the gap has widened between native-born Hispanics and non-Hispanics as well. In fact, the incidence of poverty among immigrants does not explain why the average poverty rate for Hispanics is high. As will become clear, our findings for 1990 complement earlier patterns documented by Valenzuela, NCLR (1989), and Chapa and Jahn (1993). Subsequently, we critically assess existing literature concerning the socioeconomic fate of recent immigrants and immigration's effects on jobs and wages.

Because a large number of persons emigrated from the Dominican Republic and Central and South American countries during the 1980-90 decade, we are able to examine national origin groups in some detail for the nation as a whole and for five large states. As illustrated below, these indicators vary greatly across the states. Analyses which

## Table 2

### The distribution of immigrants for the total United States by Hispanic origin, 1990

|  | United States, total | | |
|---|---|---|---|
|  | Total | Percent | Arrived 1980-90 (%) |
| Total population | 248,709,873 | 100.00% | 3.5% |
| Total U.S.-born | 228,942,557 | 92.05 | N/A |
| Total foreign-born | 19,767,316 | 7.95 | 43.9 |
| Foreign-born Latinos | 7,841,650 | 3.15 | 51.3 |
| Mexican | 4,459,837 | 1.79 | 48.9 |
| Cuban | 754,716 | 0.30 | 25.8 |
| Dominican | 367,073 | 0.15 | 53.4 |
| Central American | 1,046,099 | 0.42 | 69.8 |
| Guatemalan | 215,996 | 0.09 | 69.0 |
| Nicaraguan | 164,295 | 0.07 | 74.4 |
| Salvadoran | 458,676 | 0.18 | 75.4 |
| Other Central | 207,132 | 0.08 | 54.6 |
| South American | 776,036 | 0.31 | 51.1 |
| Colombian | 281,069 | 0.11 | 51.8 |
| Ecuadorian | 141,339 | 0.06 | 43.7 |
| Peruvian | 134,505 | 0.05 | 22.8 |
| Other South | 219,123 | 0.09 | 33.3 |
| Other Latino | 437,889 | 0.18 | 37.5 |

Source:   U.S. Bureau of the Census (1993b).

focus exclusively on data for the nation as a whole, therefore, obscure the diversity of the immigrant experience. This cautions against overgeneralizing with respect to the processes affecting the socioeconomic standing of Hispanic immigrants.

## II. National Profiles: Education, Employment, and Poverty

Based on U.S. Department of Commerce tabulations of the 1990 Census – the largest, most recent source of detailed demographics currently available for immigration research – Table 2 shows that Central and South Americans and Dominicans are the newest Hispanic immigrants to the U.S., with the largest proportion having arrived during the decade just prior to the 1990 Census.

Table 3 provides an overview of selected socioeconomic characteristics. The top half of this table provides an overview of aggregate trends, while the bottom half provides a profile of trends for women. Examining the top half first, it is clear that **Hispanic immigrants were much less likely than native-born Hispanics to have graduated from high school or beyond in 1990**. Nevertheless, **immigrants were at least as likely as native-born Hispanics to be employed in 1990**. As one might expect, the occupational distribution of immigrants tended to be less favorable, as **a lower percentage of immigrants were employed as managers and professionals than was true for their native-born counterparts.** The native- versus foreign-born gap in these top-level occupations was particularly large among Central Americans and rather small for Cubans, testimony perhaps to the disadvantages imposed by low levels of educational attainment for Central American immigrants, on the one hand, and the special benefits provided by the large concentration of Cubans in Miami (the "enclave") on the other.

**In 1990, the average poverty rate for Hispanic immigrants was only 0.7 percentage points higher than that for native-born persons (25.7% vs. 25.0%).** This is rather similar to the situation that existed in 1970 and 1980 (Valenzuela, 1991; NCLR, 1989). Table 3 shows that, with a handful of exceptions, differences in poverty rates for native- and foreign-born nationalities tended to be slight or, in the case of Dominicans and Ecuadorians, to favor immigrants, since data indicate that native-born Latinos in those groups have higher poverty rates than their foreign-born counterparts.

With a few interesting exceptions, the trends for women (Table 3A) are similar to the aggregate patterns. Note, however, that the poverty rates for single-headed households are exceedingly high, regardless of nativity. This is particularly true for single-headed Dominican households, over half of which live below the poverty line.

In addition, regardless of ethnicity, U.S.-born women are consistently more likely to work than their foreign-born co-ethnics. The differential is particularly pronounced for

## Table 3

### Percentage distributions of persons for selected categories of educational attainment, labor force status, occupational employment, and poverty status by nativity and Hispanic origin

| United States, both sexes | High school or beyond[1] U.S.-born | High school or beyond[1] Foreign-born | Employment-to-population[2] U.S.-born | Employment-to-population[2] Foreign-born | Manager and professional[2] U.S.-born | Manager and professional[2] Foreign-born | Poverty rates[3] U.S.-born | Poverty rates[3] Foreign-born |
|---|---|---|---|---|---|---|---|---|
| Hispanic, total | 60.8% | 38.4% | 57.7% | 62.2% | 17.7% | 10.2% | 25.0% | 25.7% |
| Mexican | 60.7 | 24.7 | 59.5 | 61.6 | 16.5 | 5.8 | 24.5 | 29.8 |
| Cuban | 81.4 | 53.6 | 64.0 | 59.3 | 26.0 | 22.6 | 13.5 | 14.9 |
| Dominican | 65.5 | 41.1 | 48.2 | 53.5 | 16.2 | 10.5 | 39.2 | 30.5 |
| Central American | 80.6 | 43.6 | 62.9 | 66.5 | 23.9 | 8.7 | 20.5 | 24.6 |
| Guatemalan | 69.8 | 63.2 | 59.9 | 67.9 | 21.3 | 6.9 | 22.3 | 26.0 |
| Nicaraguan | 85.6 | 58.8 | 65.7 | 65.9 | 26.6 | 11.3 | 16.7 | 24.4 |
| Salvadoran | 69.2 | 67.5 | 61.6 | 68.0 | 18.2 | 5.8 | 23.6 | 25.1 |
| South American | 84.5 | 69.7 | 61.8 | 68.1 | 24.7 | 19.6 | 13.7 | 14.6 |
| Colombian | 86.1 | 66.2 | 61.1 | 67.2 | 22.8 | 16.4 | 14.5 | 15.4 |
| Ecuadorian | 79.9 | 59.9 | 59.0 | 66.8 | 20.2 | 13.9 | 17.8 | 15.3 |
| Peruvian | 86.6 | 78.6 | 64.0 | 70.2 | 26.0 | 17.9 | 11.5 | 14.8 |
| Non-Hispanic | | | | | | | | |
| White | 79.8 | 67.8 | 63.4 | 52.1 | 26.2 | 30.3 | 9.2 | 10.1 |
| Black | 62.9 | 69.9 | 55.6 | 69.1 | 15.6 | 19.4 | 25.1 | 15.2 |

1. Persons age 25 years and over.
2. Persons age 16 years and over.
3. All ages.

Source: U.S. Bureau of the Census (1993b) and Rumbaut (1997: 35).

## Table 3A

### Percentage distributions of women for selected categories of educational attainment, labor force status, occupational employment, and poverty status by nativity, and Hispanic origin

| United States, women | High school or beyond | | Employment-to-population | | Manager and professional | | Female householder poverty rates* | |
|---|---|---|---|---|---|---|---|---|
| | U.S.-born | Foreign-born | U.S.-born | Foreign-born | U.S.-born | Foreign-born | U.S.-born | Foreign-born |
| Hispanic, total | 59.9% | 38.8% | 51.3% | 47.4% | 20.7% | 12.1% | 48.3% | 41.5% |
| Mexican | 59.4 | 24.6 | 53.1 | 42.5 | 19.4 | 7.7 | 44.3 | 47.2 |
| Cuban | 81.7 | 52.8 | 63.0 | 49.3 | 28.3 | 23.0 | 30.0 | 25.6 |
| Dominican | 65.9 | 39.5 | 47.8 | 43.6 | 18.2 | 11.4 | 51.8 | 56.0 |
| Central American | 81.7 | 43.0 | 61.0 | 55.8 | 24.0 | 9.3 | 30.5 | 37.7 |
| Guatemalan | 71.4 | 36.1 | 57.0 | 55.4 | 22.4 | 7.8 | 26.4 | 38.1 |
| Nicaraguan | 84.9 | 55.1 | 63.0 | 56.3 | 28.0 | 10.0 | 32.3 | 32.9 |
| Salvadoran | 67.3 | 31.8 | 58.1 | 56.9 | 20.0 | 6.3 | 35.6 | 39.9 |
| South American | 84.6 | 67.6 | 60.0 | 56.9 | 26.0 | 18.7 | 28.3 | 27.9 |
| Colombian | 81.5 | 63.6 | 58.8 | 57.1 | 24.8 | 15.6 | 30.6 | 27.2 |
| Ecuadorian | 80.2 | 58.6 | 60.9 | 54.5 | 22.5 | 14.7 | 33.6 | 34.4 |
| Peruvian | 85.4 | 75.8 | 60.8 | 58.1 | 25.9 | 16.8 | 27.9 | 25.8 |
| Non-Hispanic | 77.3 | 67.1 | 53.5 | 47.9 | 28.3 | 27.4 | 30.0 | 20.5 |
| White | 79.5 | 65.6 | 55.1 | 41.8 | 27.0 | 26.9 | 20.6 | 19.2 |
| Black | 63.8 | 69.1 | 52.3 | 65.0 | 18.3 | 20.3 | 43.0 | 24.9 |

* Female-headed households, no husband present, 16 years and over

Source: U.S. Bureau of the Census (1993b).

Mexicans and Cubans. A variety of demographic factors probably helps account for this gap, including differences by nativity in average ages, levels of educational attainment, and child care responsibilities.

A comparison of the percent of women employed as managers and professionals with the aggregate trend in the upper half of Table 3 shows that, for most Hispanic ethnic groups, the likelihood of native-born women to be employed as managers and professionals slightly exceeds the aggregate. In other words, Hispanic women born in the U.S. are somewhat *more* likely than Hispanic men born in the U.S. to work as managers and professionals.

The data presented in Table 4 combine statistics for earlier decades from Valenzuela and Bean and Tienda (1987) to provide a time series of poverty rates. Poverty rates for the total Hispanic population fluctuated slightly over the 1970-to-1990 decades, edging down from 24.8% in 1970 to 23.2% in 1980, with a subsequent rebound to 25.3% in 1990. The incidence of poverty among Hispanic immigrants rose slightly over the two decades, while that for Hispanic natives fluctuated within a very narrow range. These differences in patterns for Hispanic foreign- and native-born populations are subtle, however, particularly in light of the *similarity* in poverty rates for the two Hispanic groups. In contrast, as the data for ethnic gaps show, both sets of Hispanic rates were consistently more than double the rates for White non-Hispanics. Moreover, both sets of gaps widened over the two decades. With few exceptions, similar trends characterize the detailed Hispanic ethnicities. At least for the nation as a whole, then, the data continue to contradict the contention that immigrants distort the aggregate Hispanic poverty profile. These findings complement earlier trends identified by Valenzuela, NCLR (1989), and Chapa and Jahn (1993).

## III. Employment and Poverty Patterns in 1990 for Key States

The large number of Hispanic immigrants in the 1980s makes it possible to analyze at a rather detailed level statistics on the economic well-being of national-origin groups for five large states in 1990, namely, California, New York, Texas, Illinois, and Florida. Table 5 shows that these states accounted for most Hispanic immigrants that year. For example, almost three of five Guatemalan and Salvadoran immigrants lived in California. Similarly, while Colombians were concentrated in New York and Florida, most Mexican immigrants resided in California and Texas. Approximately 70% of Cuban immigrants made Florida their home, while a similar proportion of Dominican immigrants lived in New York.

## Table 4

## Incidence of poverty and ethnic gaps, total United States, 1970-1990

| Ethnicity and nativity | Poverty rates | | | Ethnic gaps* | | |
|---|---|---|---|---|---|---|
| | 1970 | 1980 | 1990 | 1970 | 1980 | 1990 |
| *All persons* | | | | | | |
| Hispanic, total | 24.8% | 23.2% | 25.3% | 2.3 | 2.5 | 2.8 |
|   Mexican | 27.5 | 22.9 | 26.3 | 2.5 | 2.4 | 2.9 |
|   Cuban | 13.5 | 12.7 | 14.6 | 1.3 | 1.4 | 1.6 |
|   Central/South American | 16.0 | 20.3 | 20.9 | 1.5 | 2.2 | 2.3 |
|   Other | 21.3 | 17.2 | 21.2 | 2.0 | 1.8 | 2.3 |
| *Non-Hispanic* | | | | | | |
|   White | 10.8 | 9.4 | 9.2 | 1.0 | 1.0 | 1.0 |
|   Black | 34.6 | 29.9 | 31.3 | 3.2 | 3.2 | 3.4 |
| *Foreign-born* | | | | | | |
| Hispanic, total | 23.4 | 25.2 | 25.7 | 2.2 | 2.7 | 2.8 |
|   Mexican | 28.8 | 26.5 | 29.8 | 2.7 | 2.8 | 3.2 |
|   Cuban | 13.5 | 12.9 | 14.9 | 1.3 | 1.4 | 1.6 |
|   Central/South American | 17.0 | 20.0 | 21.3 | 1.6 | 2.1 | 2.3 |
|   Other | 21.7 | 17.2 | 21.8 | 2.0 | 1.8 | 2.4 |
| *Native-born* | | | | | | |
| Hispanic, total | 25.3 | 22.4 | 25.0 | 2.3 | 2.4 | 2.7 |
|   Mexican | 27.2 | 21.6 | 24.5 | 2.5 | 2.3 | 2.7 |
|   Cuban | 13.4 | 11.9 | 13.5 | 1.2 | 1.3 | 1.5 |
|   Central/South American | 13.8 | 21.7 | 18.0 | 1.3 | 2.3 | 2.0 |
|   Other | 21.1 | 17.2 | 20.6 | 2.0 | 1.8 | 2.2 |

* The ethnic gap is derived by dividing the Hispanic or Black poverty rate by that for non-Hispanic Whites.

Source: Bean and Tienda (1987); U.S. Bureau of the Census (1993b); Rumbaut (1997:35).

## Table 5

## Percent distribution of Hispanic immigrants by state, 1990

| National origin | Total | CA | TX | NY | FL | IL | Other |
|---|---|---|---|---|---|---|---|
| Mexican | 100.0% | 59.4% | 21.8% | 1.1% | 1.7% | 6.4% | 9.6% |
| Cuban | 100.0 | 6.8 | 1.5 | 6.9 | 68.2 | 1.6 | 15.0 |
| Dominican | 100.0 | 0.8 | 0.5 | 70.5 | 7.2 | 0.3 | 20.7 |
| Central American | 100.0 | 47.4 | 8.2 | 10.1 | 12.0 | 2.2 | 20.1 |
| Guatemalan | 100.0 | 58.8 | 5.3 | 8.7 | 5.7 | 5.3 | 16.2 |
| Nicaraguan | 100.0 | 36.6 | 4.5 | 4.2 | 43.4 | 0.8 | 10.5 |
| Salvadoran | 100.0 | 56.4 | 11.3 | 7.6 | 1.9 | 1.5 | 21.3 |
| South American | 100.0 | 17.6 | 3.6 | 28.8 | 18.5 | 3.1 | 28.4 |
| Colombian | 100.0 | 8.8 | 3.7 | 29.6 | 27.1 | 2.7 | 28.1 |
| Ecuadorian | 100.0 | 15.6 | 1.1 | 55.7 | 6.8 | 4.7 | 16.1 |
| Peruvian | 100.0 | 28.9 | 3.8 | 18.0 | 12.7 | 3.0 | 33.6 |

Source: Tabulations by the U.S. Bureau of the Census, Population Division.

Because averages for the nation as a whole do not always reflect the profiles of individual states, it is important to compare information at both geographic levels. We derived our statistics for this analysis from the 1/100 Public Use Microdata Sample of the 1990 Census data for each state.* Table 6 provides percentages employed in managerial and professional positions and poverty rates by nativity for each of the five states.** The column labeled "Total minus native-born" shows the "immigrant effect," which identifies the extent to which immigrants raised (or lowered) the overall statistic. For example, the proportion of all Mexicans in California who were employed as managers and professionals was approximately 5.4 percentage points lower than that

* We thank Katherine Condon of Florida International University's Southeast Florida Center on Aging for deriving these detailed statistics. This version of the Public Use Microdata Samples (PUMS) is a part of a much larger data set known as the University of Minnesota IPUMS (Integrated Public Use Microdata Sample), Version 2, prepared by Steven Ruggles and Matthew Sobek of the Minnesota Historical Census Projects, University of Minnesota, 1997. For additional information and to download, visit http://www.ipums.umn.edu.
** Cells in these tables are left blank wherever the sample yielded zero cases. Based on exploratory tabulations, we decided not to disaggregate these analyses by gender because it would result in an impractically large number of blank cells.

## Table 6A

## Immigrant effects on occupational composition and poverty rates: *California*

| | Percent manager and professional | | | | Percentage of persons living in poverty | | | |
|---|---|---|---|---|---|---|---|---|
| California | Total | Foreign-born | Native-born | Total minus Native-born | Total | Foreign-born | Native-born | Total minus Native-born |
| *Latino* | | | | | | | | |
| Mexican | 9.59% | 5.70% | 14.94% | -5.35* | 20.84% | 24.64% | 15.65% | 5.19* |
| Cuban | 24.46 | 23.79 | 26.96 | -2.50 | 12.37 | 11.57 | 16.75 | -3.38 |
| Dominican | 13.48 | 9.09 | 27.78 | -14.30 | 9.19 | 9.48 | 8.20 | 0.99 |
| Cntrl. American | 7.58 | 6.65 | 21.63 | -14.05 | 23.25 | 23.77 | 15.05 | 8.21 |
| Guatemalan | 6.71 | 6.11 | 19.29 | -12.57 | 26.35 | 26.94 | 14.01 | 12.33 |
| Nicaraguan | 11.30 | 9.89 | 19.88 | -8.57 | 20.27 | 21.67 | 10.54 | 9.73 |
| Salvadoran | 5.28 | 4.91 | 14.09 | -8.81 | 22.54 | 22.50 | 23.29 | -0.75 |
| Other | 15.64 | 12.84 | 37.40 | -21.77 | 22.67 | 24.46 | 6.53 | 16.14 |
| So. American | 24.59 | 24.88 | 22.84 | 1.75 | 13.08 | 13.42 | 10.91 | 2.17 |
| Colombian | 21.54 | 23.04 | 13.65 | 7.89 | 23.54 | 26.19 | 8.11 | 15.43 |
| Ecuadorian | 25.33 | 27.13 | 17.29 | 8.03 | 9.83 | 9.23 | 12.77 | -2.95 |
| Peruvian | 21.18 | 20.98 | 22.76 | -1.58 | 10.96 | 10.71 | 13.18 | -2.21 |
| Other | 21.46 | 20.27 | 31.17 | -9.71 | 10.99 | 11.12 | 10.14 | 0.85 |
| *Non-Latino* | | | | | | | | |
| Black | 20.13 | 25.05 | 19.86 | 0.27 | 21.56 | 14.65 | 21.91 | -0.34 |
| White | 33.17 | 45.16 | 32.35 | 0.82 | 8.94 | 11.32 | 8.70 | 0.23 |
| Asian | 26.82 | 25.07 | 33.27 | -6.45 | 14.30 | 15.38 | 9.78 | 4.52 |
| Other | 19.23 | 13.19 | 19.92 | 0.70 | 16.62 | 16.82 | 16.59 | 0.02 |

*Percentage points.

Source: Ruggles and Sobek (1997).

for U.S.-born Mexicans. The poverty rate for all Mexicans in California was approximately 5.2 points higher than that for U.S.-born Mexicans.

In general, the patterns for occupational employment are similar to the national averages. Thus, native-born Hispanics were more likely to be employed as managers and professionals than immigrants, with the important exception of foreign-born South Americans. In contrast, for non-Hispanics, there is virtually no difference in occupational distribution by nativity.

Not surprisingly, native-born persons were less likely to be poor than immigrants. There are numerous exceptions, however. For example, several South American immigrant nationalities in California and Florida were less likely to be poor than their native-born counterparts. While a systematic examination of these exceptional cases is beyond the scope of this study, we hypothesize that the relatively low incidence of poverty for these groups may be a function of their disproportionate concentration in well-paying jobs. These South Americans – Colombians, Ecuadorians, and Peruvians in particular – have relatively high proportions of persons who have college educations (between one-quarter and one-third), are fluent English speakers (above three-quarters), and work as managers or professionals. In contrast, there was little difference in the incidence of poverty for native and foreign-born Dominicans in New York, while Salvadoran immigrants in Texas were better off than native-born Salvadorans. More importantly, poverty rates for these groups were particularly high, regardless of nativity. These exceptions suggest that the mechanisms affecting the incidence of immigrant and native poverty vary by state and ethnicity. Generalizations by nativity based on figures for the nation as a whole present an overly simplified picture of the correlation of poverty with nativity.

Tables 6 A-E can also be used to examine the contention that, at the state level, the socioeconomic standing of U.S.-born Hispanics is similar to that of non-Hispanic Whites. In fact, the levels are quite different. On average, U.S.-born Hispanics are approximately six-tenths as likely as their White counterparts to be managers and two-to-three times as likely to be poor. These data confirm the earlier finding that, with few exceptions, U.S.-born Hispanics are much less likely than non-Hispanic Whites to be managers and professionals and much more likely than non-Hispanic Whites to be poor. Moreover, native-born African Americans were three-to-four times as likely as non-Hispanic Whites to be poor. As Table 4 shows, these patterns are very similar to those found by Valenzuela for 1970 and 1980. The well-documented obstacles to ethnic/racial equality among native-born Hispanics have been remarkably recalcitrant.

## Table 6B

## Immigrant effects on occupational composition and poverty rates: *New York*

| New York | Percent manager and professional | | | | Percentage of persons living in poverty | | | |
|---|---|---|---|---|---|---|---|---|
| | Total | Foreign-born | Native-born | Total minus Native-born | Total | Foreign-born | Native-born | Total minus Native-born |
| *Latino* | | | | | | | | |
| Mexican | 11.72% | 5.46% | 27.25% | -15.53* | 17.23% | 19.02% | 12.89% | 4.34* |
| Cuban | 31.64 | 30.89 | 34.02 | -2.38 | 13.93 | 14.36 | 12.41 | 1.52 |
| Dominican | 9.76 | 9.17 | 16.89 | -7.13 | 31.25 | 31.16 | 32.35 | -1.10 |
| Cntrl. American | 8.64 | 8.78 | 6.67 | 1.98 | 16.77 | 16.97 | 13.47 | 3.30 |
| Guatemalan | 7.07 | 7.49 | ** | ** | 14.88 | 15.51 | ** | ** |
| Nicaraguan | 13.03 | 13.03 | ** | ** | 6.90 | 7.11 | ** | ** |
| Salvadoran | 5.89 | 5.21 | 26.42 | -20.52 | 20.06 | 19.90 | 27.66 | -7.60 |
| Other | 10.91 | 11.74 | 3.33 | 7.57 | 16.51 | 16.74 | 14.18 | 2.33 |
| So. American | 12.80 | 12.33 | 19.15 | -6.35 | 16.79 | 17.26 | 10.37 | 6.42 |
| Colombian | 11.68 | 11.19 | 20.50 | -8.82 | 14.87 | 15.46 | 4.41 | 10.46 |
| Ecuadorian | 8.23 | 7.72 | 14.45 | -6.23 | 19.36 | 19.65 | 15.60 | 3.76 |
| Peruvian | 12.74 | 12.67 | 14.63 | -1.89 | 20.73 | 20.74 | 20.59 | 0.14 |
| Other | 22.36 | 23.22 | 24.52 | -1.16 | 13.08 | 13.80 | 6.72 | 6.36 |
| *Non-Latino* | | | | | | | | |
| Black | 21.95 | 21.54 | 22.13 | -0.18 | 19.91 | 13.12 | 22.24 | -2.33 |
| White | 33.25 | 31.17 | 33.44 | -0.19 | 7.00 | 10.31 | 6.60 | 0.41 |
| Asian | 30.54 | 29.46 | 43.03 | -12.49 | 13.61 | 14.09 | 7.59 | 6.02 |
| Other | 26.01 | 28.20 | 24.95 | 1.06 | 17.37 | 17.22 | 17.43 | -0.06 |

*Percentage points.
**Sample yielded no cases for these cells.

Source: Ruggles and Sobek (1997).

# Table 6C

## Immigrant effects on occupational composition and poverty rates: *Texas*

| | Percent manager and professional | | | | Percentage of persons living in poverty | | | |
|---|---|---|---|---|---|---|---|---|
| *Texas* | Total | Foreign-born | Native-born | Total minus Native-born | Total | Foreign-born | Native-born | Total minus Native-born |
| *Latino* | | | | | | | | |
| Mexican | 8.20% | 4.14% | 10.23% | -2.03* | 29.56 | 37.68 | 25.47 | 4.09* |
| Cuban | 17.80 | 21.14 | 8.08 | 9.72 | 11.23 | 12.40 | 7.87 | 3.36 |
| Dominican | 18.88 | 17.95 | 23.08 | -4.20 | 4.20 | 5.13 | ** | ** |
| Cntrl. American | 7.73 | 7.11 | 22.32 | -14.59 | 33.08 | 33.70 | 18.43 | 14.65 |
| Guatemalan | 11.63 | 9.76 | ** | ** | 28.04 | 29.12 | ** | ** |
| Nicaraguan | 9.77 | 9.98 | ** | ** | 29.18 | 29.82 | ** | ** |
| Salvadoran | 5.76 | 5.33 | 30.36 | -24.59 | 36.96 | 36.76 | 48.21 | -11.25 |
| Other | 9.99 | 9.67 | 12.21 | -2.22 | 26.56 | 28.76 | 10.46 | 16.07 |
| So. American | 21.77 | 22.14 | 18.91 | 2.86 | 15.80 | 16.37 | 11.26 | 4.54 |
| Colombian | 16.69 | 14.66 | 32.93 | -16.24 | 12.57 | 13.23 | 6.67 | 5.90 |
| Ecuadorian | 18.45 | 18.45 | ** | ** | 5.83 | 5.83 | ** | ** |
| Peruvian | 28.73 | 31.33 | 5.41 | 23.32 | 25.20 | 25.90 | 18.92 | 6.28 |
| Other | 23.51 | 25.10 | 13.45 | 10.06 | 15.74 | 16.38 | 11.76 | 3.98 |
| *Non-Latino* | | | | | | | | |
| Black | 11.62 | 22.65 | 11.33 | 0.29 | 28.04 | 15.84 | 28.37 | -0.34 |
| White | 23.26 | 25.29 | 23.2 | 0.06 | 9.25 | 11.23 | 9.19 | 0.06 |
| Asian | 24.70 | 24.38 | 28.1 | -3.39 | 16.68 | 16.52 | 18.52 | - 1.84 |
| Other | 14.51 | 10.58 | 15.07 | -0.56 | 22.20 | 24.05 | 21.94 | 0.26 |

*Percentage points.
**Sample yielded no cases for these cells.

Source:   Ruggles and Sobek (1997).

# Table 6D

## Immigrant effects on occupational composition and poverty rates: *Florida*

| Florida | Percent manager and professional | | | | Percentage of persons living in poverty | | | |
|---|---|---|---|---|---|---|---|---|
| | Total | Foreign-born | Native-born | Total minus Native-born | Total | Foreign-born | Native-born | Total minus Native-born |
| **Latino** | | | | | | | | |
| Mexican | 10.04% | 5.72% | 15.43% | -5.39* | 23.31% | 26.69% | 19.44% | 3.87* |
| Cuban | 21.48 | 20.77 | 26.60 | -5.12 | 15.55 | 16.16 | 10.65 | 4.90 |
| Dominican | 18.24 | 18.25 | 18.18 | 0.06 | 25.58 | 27.63 | 10.00 | 15.58 |
| Cntrl. American | 11.75 | 11.25 | 25.00 | -13.25 | 25.10 | 25.26 | 20.00 | 5.10 |
| Guatemalan | 11.94 | 9.52 | ** | ** | 19.59 | 19.78 | 16.67 | 2.92 |
| Nicaraguan | 10.99 | 10.83 | 25.00 | -14.01 | 27.67 | 27.55 | 40.00 | -12.33 |
| Salvadoran | 3.85 | 3.85 | ** | ** | 30.67 | 29.73 | ** | ** |
| Other | 17.37 | 17.24 | 18.75 | -1.38 | 21.10 | 21.72 | 11.11 | 9.99 |
| So. American | 20.07 | 20.91 | 10.29 | 9.78 | 17.17 | 17.45 | 13.86 | 3.31 |
| Colombian | 19.91 | 20.57 | 12.82 | 7.09 | 16.13 | 15.90 | 18.64 | -2.51 |
| Ecuadorian | 14.52 | 16.67 | ** | ** | 12.24 | 11.90 | 14.29 | -2.04 |
| Peruvian | 17.31 | 18.95 | ** | ** | 26.51 | 25.83 | ** | ** |
| Other | 23.08 | 23.42 | 16.67 | 6.41 | 17.28 | 17.96 | 5.26 | 12.02 |
| **Non-Latino** | | | | | | | | |
| Black | 15.72 | 14.75 | 15.91 | -0.19 | 27.94 | 25.51 | 28.35 | -0.41 |
| White | 27.87 | 31.66 | 27.67 | 0.20 | 7.53 | 8.76 | 7.45 | 0.08 |
| Asian | 29.32 | 28.26 | 37.08 | -7.75 | 13.12 | 13.54 | 10.22 | 2.90 |
| Other | 13.28 | 14.29 | 13.15 | 0.13 | 19.08 | 2.94 | 20.61 | -1.53 |

*Percentage points.
**Sample yielded no cases for these cells.

Source: Ruggles and Sobek (1997).

## Table 6E

## Immigrant effects on occupational composition and poverty rates: *Illinois*

| Illinois | Percent manager and professional | | | | Percentage of persons living in poverty | | | |
|---|---|---|---|---|---|---|---|---|
| | Total | Foreign-born | Native-born | Total minus Native-born | Total | Foreign-born | Native-born | Total minus Native-born |
| **Latino** | | | | | | | | |
| Mexican | 7.70 | 4.50 | 13.80 | -6.10 | -14.60 | 15.50 | 12.90 | -1.70* |
| Cuban | 30.50 | 29.20 | 34.80 | -4.30 | 10.30 | 11.60 | 4.80 | -5.50 |
| Dominican | 50.00 | 40.00 | ** | ** | 36.40 | 40.00 | ** | ** |
| Cntrl. American | 11.10 | 7.87 | 35.30 | -24.20 | 12.10 | 13.40 | ** | ** |
| Guatemalan | 9.20 | 9.80 | ** | ** | 13.10 | 13.90 | ** | ** |
| Nicaraguan | 30.80 | 22.20 | ** | ** | ** | ** | ** | ** |
| Salvadoran | 5.60 | 2.90 | ** | ** | 12.80 | 13.20 | ** | ** |
| Other | 13.30 | 4.35 | ** | ** | ** | ** | ** | ** |
| So. American | 26.10 | 25.20 | 38.50 | -12.40 | 7.80 | 7.00 | 16.70 | 8.90 |
| Colombian | 28.10 | 22.90 | ** | ** | 12.30 | 11.10 | 18.20 | 5.90 |
| Ecuadorian | 15.50 | 16.10 | ** | ** | 7.70 | 6.50 | 33.30 | 25.60 |
| Peruvian | 40.70 | 42.30 | ** | ** | 8.80 | 9.40 | ** | ** |
| Other | 14.70 | 30.30 | ** | ** | ** | ** | ** | ** |
| **Non-Latino** | | | | | | | | |
| Black | 16.10 | 18.50 | 16.10 | 0.00 | 25.30 | 16.10 | 25.40 | -.10 |
| White | 24.90 | 22.70 | 25.00 | -0.10 | 7.00 | 7.80 | 6.90 | .10 |
| Asian | 34.50 | 34.80 | 32.20 | 2.30 | 9.80 | 9.90 | 8.60 | 1.20 |
| Other | 18.20 | 11.10 | 18.70 | -0.50 | 13.00 | 10.00 | 13.40 | -.40 |

*Percentage points.
**Sample yielded no cases for these cells.

Source: Ruggles and Sobek (1997).

## Table 7

### "Ethnic Gaps": Poverty rate of U.S.-born Latinos and others divided by the poverty rate for U.S.-born Whites by Hispanic origin and race, for five large states, 1990

|  | California | New York | Texas | Florida | Illinois |
|---|---|---|---|---|---|
| **U.S.-born Latino** | | | | | |
| Mexican | 1.80 | 1.95 | 2.77 | 2.61 | 1.86 |
| Cuban | 1.81 | 1.88 | 0.86 | 1.43 | 0.69 |
| Dominican | * | 4.90 | * | 1.34 | * |
| Central American | 1.73 | 2.04 | 2.01 | 2.68 | * |
| Guatemalan | 1.61 | * | * | * | * |
| Nicaraguan | 1.21 | * | * | * | * |
| Salvadoran | 2.68 | * | * | * | * |
| Other | 0.75 | * | * | * | * |
| South American | 1.25 | 1.57 | 1.22 | 1.86 | * |
| Colombian | 0.93 | 0.67 | * | 2.50 | * |
| Ecuadorian | 1.47 | 2.36 | * | * | * |
| Peruvian | 1.51 | * | 2.06 | * | * |
| Other | 1.17 | 1.44 | * | 0.38 | * |
| **U.S.-born non-Latino** | 1.17 | 1.22 | 1.31 | 1.32 | 1.33 |
| Black | 2.52 | 3.37 | 3.09 | 3.81 | 3.66 |
| White | 1.00 | 1.00 | 1.00 | 1.00 | 1.00 |
| Asian and Pacific Islander | 1.12 | 0.72 | 2.02 | 1.37 | 1.24 |
| Other | 1.91 | 2.64 | 2.39 | 2.77 | 1.92 |

*Identifies cells where sample sizes for U.S.-born Latinos were too small to analyze.

Source: Table 6.

Table 7 applies the data in Table 6 to provide an overview of the ethnic gaps in poverty rates between U.S.-born minorities and non-Hispanic Whites. Clearly, native-born Dominican New Yorkers and Blacks are at the greatest disadvantage. Other ratios vary widely, but there are numerous native-born Latino groups with poverty rates twice that of their non-Hispanic White counterparts. On the other hand, as Table 7 also illustrates, there are several U.S.-born Latino groups whose incidence of poverty barely exceeds, or falls below, that of non-Hispanic Whites. These include Cuban Americans in Texas and Illinois and persons of South American origin in California and Texas. Clearly, additional research is warranted concerning the incidence of Latino poverty among the five large states, with a special focus on Latino groups with relatively favorable poverty profiles.

## IV. Key Employment and Labor Market Issues

Two prominent labor force issues with regard to U.S. immigration are:

- The socioeconomic fate of recent immigrants to the U.S.
- Immigration's effects on jobs and wages.

The following discussion presents these issues in more detail.

### The Socioeconomic Fate of Recent Immigrants to the U.S.

As noted earlier, recent immigrants are disproportionately represented in low-skill, low-paying occupations. Throughout the decades, this recurring pattern in U.S. history has consistently raised questions concerning the socioeconomic fate of recent immigrants. Are immigrants destined to remain at the bottom of the socioeconomic hierarchy? Alternatively, do the earnings of immigrants eventually catch up with those of natives? Two decades ago, the evidence seemed clear. It appeared that the more time immigrants spent in the U.S., the more their socioeconomic status approximated that of natives. More recently, this perspective has been seriously challenged by a less optimistic scenario. Of special concern are recent immigrants from Latin America and the Spanish-speaking Caribbean, who seem particularly concentrated in low-skill, low-paying jobs.

### Overview of Research

Recent immigrants are disproportionately represented among persons who hold low-wage jobs, as indicated by recent tabulations from the Current Population Survey (CPS).

As the data on median weekly earnings show, relative to more recent arrivals, immigrants who have been here for ten years or more tend to be better off than more recent

**Table 8**

**Percent employed in "low-skill jobs" (as service workers, operators, fabricators, and laborers) and median weekly earnings of all workers by nativity and year of arrival**
**Annual averages for 1997**

| Nativity and Year of Arrival | Percent Employed in Low-skill Jobs | Median Weekly Earnings |
|---|---|---|
| U.S.-born | 28.9% | $516 |
| Foreign-born, all years | 42.9 | 389 |
| 1993-97 | 52.0 | 317 |
| 1989-92 | 52.7 | 322 |
| 1982-88 | 44.7 | 371 |
| 1975-81 | 41.6 | 405 |
| 1965-74 | 33.9 | 499 |
| Before 1975 | 28.2 | 610 |

Source: Unpublished tabulations of 1997 annual averages from the Current Population Survey, U.S. Department of Labor, Bureau of Labor Statistics.

arrivals. In fact, as the above tabulations also show, the longer the time spent in the U.S., the more closely immigrants approximate the socioeconomic patterns of natives. It would be tempting to conclude that, with time, the employment and earnings patterns of the most recent immigrants will converge with those of natives. And, in fact, this was the thesis of an entire tradition of immigration research in the early decades of the century. (For a highly readable critique of the sociological literature, see Portes and Stepick, 1993.)

### Chiswick's Research

A more recent version of this "assimilationist" view – that the wages of immigrants improve rapidly – is exemplified by the research of Barry Chiswick (1978). Using data similar to those above, Chiswick asserted that, as recent immigrants gained work experience in the U.S., their earnings would rise to the level of natives' earnings. Subsequent research, described below, criticized Chiswick's methodology of using data for one point in time – a "snapshot" or "cross-sectional" analysis – to make an argument about processes that occur over time (a "longitudinal" approach). Before summarizing the issues and evidence on both sides, it is worth noting that data for tracking the progress of immigrants over time are limited (see box).

---

### Limitations to Longitudinal Immigration Research

It may seem self-evident that to track the progress of immigrants across time, researchers would need panel data, i.e., a survey which follows the same individuals over time with the objective of comparing changes in the socioeconomic well-being of recent and early immigrants and native-born persons at different points in time. However, there are no such data because most longitudinal data sets are severely limited for this purpose, containing very few immigrants.* Instead, most studies follow chronologically-designated aggregations of immigrants across the decennial Censuses (Borjas, 1994). Although the public discussion of labor force issues is generally focused on changes experienced by immigrant individuals, most studies are limited to discussing trends in terms of changes in the aggregate characteristics of specific immigration waves. The disjuncture between policy discussions and existing data is a perennial problem for this literature.

---

\* In 1990, a sample of Latino households was added to the University of Michigan's Panel Study of Income Dynamics (PSID), providing several years of longitudinal data for Mexican, Cuban, and Puerto Rican households, many of them migrants. More recently, a representative sample of Latino and non-Latino immigrant households was added to the PSID. Website information is available at http://www.isr.umich.edu/src/psid/.

---

### Borjas' Challenge

In a now-classic article published in 1985, George Borjas questioned the logic of using a snapshot of immigrant earnings to make inferences about longitudinal processes. In so doing, Borjas challenged Chiswick's assumption that the entry wages of recent immigrants would rise to the level of earlier immigrants' current wages. Convergence is especially doubtful if the entry wages of recent immigrants are dramatically lower than were those of their predecessors. In this case, it is unlikely that the wages of recent immigrants will grow rapidly enough to catch up with the current wages of their immigrant predecessors or of native-born workers. Convergence is also doubtful if wage growth for recent arrivals is sluggish.

Borjas offered two sets of empirical findings that challenge Chiswick's view. First, Borjas provided evidence that the entry wages of recent immigrants are far below the entry wages of earlier immigrants. Second, Borjas showed that the gap between the wages of recent immigrants and native-born workers is wide and has shown few signs of narrowing. In other words, as Borjas reveals, relative to wages of native-born workers, those of recent immigrants grow very sluggishly.

**Entry wages.** In a detailed examination of data from the 1970 and 1980 decennial Censuses, Borjas (1985) showed that entry wages for recent immigrants in the 1980 Census were much lower than those for recent immigrants in the 1970 Census. Later, an analysis of recent immigrants in the 1990 Census showed that their entry earnings were even lower than those of their predecessors in the 1980 Census (Borjas 1992). Further analysis suggested that the decline in entry earnings characterizes immigrant cohorts, even controlling for education and age.

**The wage gap.** Borjas compared the average wages for recent immigrants to those for native-born workers (the "wage gap"). As the data in Table 9 illustrate, the wage gap has widened over the decades. While the average wage for newcomers has always been substantially below the average wage for native workers, the fact that this gap has widened means that successive waves of immigrant men are increasingly disadvantaged in the U.S. labor market. For example, the first column shows that recently-arrived 25-to-34-year-olds in 1990 were approximately twice as disadvantaged as their counterparts in 1970 (24.5/11.2).

As the second column shows, the wage gap for women tended to be somewhat smaller than that for men. Rather than reflecting a more privileged situation for immigrant women, this narrower gap probably reflects the rather high concentration of all women – native- and foreign-born alike – in low-paying jobs. More importantly, as was the case for men, the immigrant vs. native gap widens for women as well, indicating that recently-arrived immigrant women were also at an increasing disadvantage in the labor market.

**Wage growth.** As Borjas' tabulations show, entry wages for recently-immigrated men and immigrants from Mexico – regardless of gender – are markedly below those of native workers. It seems plausible to suggest that, because wage growth is so sluggish, the wage gap for these groups will not disappear over the upcoming two decades (see Table 10).

**Table 9**

**Comparison #1: Percentage wage differential between immigrants who arrived one to five years prior to each decennial Census (1970, 1980, and 1990) and natives, at the time of the Census, by gender and country of origin**

|  | Men | | | Women | | |
|---|---|---|---|---|---|---|
|  | All Countries | Mexico | Other Countries | All Countries | Mexico | Other Countries |
| 25-34 in 1970 | -11.2% | -39.8% | -7.5% | -7.5% | -31.0% | -5.1% |
| 25-34 in 1980 | -21.9 | -51.1 | -17.6 | -13.7 | -33.3 | -10.5 |
| 25-34 in 1990 | -24.5 | -44.7 | -15.8 | -16.9 | -40.9 | -11.9 |
| 35-44 in 1970 | -17.3 | -52.2 | -14.0 | -10.9 | -36.1 | -9.1 |
| 35-44 in 1980 | -24.3 | -53.6 | -24.4 | -13.8 | -32.4 | -11.6 |
| 35-44 in 1990 | -29.8 | -55.1 | -22.5 | -24.8 | -42.8 | -22.6 |
| 45-54 in 1970 | -23.7 | -49.0 | -20.4 | -20.4 | -33.5 | -18.0 |
| 45-54 in 1980 | -29.8 | N/A | -21.6 | -21.6 | -34.9 | -20.9 |
| 45-54 in 1990 | -35.8 | -62.1 | -29.2 | -28.9 | -46.9 | -26.8 |

Source: National Research Council (1997): 199, 200, 203, 204, 249, and 250.

Trends for non-Mexican women present a fairly optimistic scenario. For Mexican women, however, the starting wage is so much lower than that for native-born women that the pessimistic scenario of no convergence is indeed plausible.

In sum, the trends Borjas has identified are troubling. Wages of recent immigrants are increasingly far below those of native-born workers. The failure of the gap to narrow as the newcomers age means their relegation to low-paying jobs appears to be permanent. The pessimistic trends are especially pronounced for Mexican immigrants, who make up the largest proportion of Hispanic immigrants.

In general, Borjas follows the human capital tradition of economics, which posits that the earnings of individuals are a function of their skills and productivity. Thus, Borjas

## Table 10

### Comparison #2: Do wages converge as cohorts age?
### Percentage wage differential between immigrants and natives

| Immigrants from Mexico | Men | | | Women | | |
|---|---|---|---|---|---|---|
| | 1970 | 1980 | 1990 | 1970 | 1980 | 1990 |
| *1965-69 Arrival* | | | | | | |
| 25-34 in 1970 | -39.8% | -31.9% | -39.5% | -31.0% | -21.0% | -29.4% |
| 35-44 in 1970 | -52.2 | -38.2 | -44.7 | -36.1 | -23.6 | -28.3 |
| 45-54 in 1970 | -49.0 | -36.7 | N/A | -33.5 | -23.1 | N/A |
| *1975-79 Arrival* | | | | | | |
| 25-34 in 1970 | | -51.1 | -52.7 | | -32.4 | -40.9 |
| 35-44 in 1970 | | -53.6 | -54.5 | | -34.9 | -37.7 |
| 45-54 in 1970 | | N/A | N/A | | N/A | N/A |
| *1985-89 Arrival* | | | | | | |
| 25-34 in 1970 | | | -44.7 | | | -40.9 |
| 35-44 in 1970 | | | -55.1 | | | -42.8 |
| 45-54 in 1970 | | | -62.1 | | | -46.9 |

| Immigrants from Countries other than Mexico | Men | | | Women | | |
|---|---|---|---|---|---|---|
| | 1970 | 1980 | 1990 | 1970 | 1980 | 1990 |
| *1965-69 Arrival* | | | | | | |
| 25-34 in 1970 | -7.5 | 0.2 | 6.5 | -5.1 | 8.5 | 8.1 |
| 35-44 in 1970 | -14.0 | -12.9 | -4.1 | -9.1 | -3.4 | 0.3 |
| 45-54 in 1970 | -20.7 | -19.6 | N/A | -18.0 | -8.7 | N/A |
| *1975-79 Arrival* | | | | | | |
| 25-34 in 1970 | | -17.6 | -14.4 | | -11.6 | -6.2 |
| 35-44 in 1970 | | -24.4 | -20.1 | | -20.9 | -9.6 |
| 45-54 in 1970 | | N/A | N/A | | N/A | N/A |
| *1985-89 Arrival* | | | | | | |
| 25-34 in 1970 | | | -15.8 | | | -11.9 |
| 35-44 in 1970 | | | -22.5 | | | -22.6 |
| 45-54 in 1970 | | | -29.2 | | | -26.8 |

Source: National Research Council (1997): 199, 200, 203, 204, 249, and 250.

interprets the decline in entry wages for recent immigrants as reflecting a decline in their skills and productivity. He hypothesizes that this could be attributable to several possible factors, including a shift in the countries of origin, which has resulted in a preponderance of immigrants with skills that are not immediately transferable. Also, changes implemented in 1965 to the official criteria for admitting immigrants now place greater emphasis on family ties than was true earlier, and may have "generated a less-skilled immigrant flow" (1996).*

## Challenges to Borjas
### 1. From within the human capital tradition:

Two challenges to Borjas' interpretation come from studies by Duleep and Regets. The first mobilizes longitudinal data to track wage growth over the course of a year for native and recent immigrant respondents (Duleep and Regets, 1997). The findings suggest that among workers with similar levels of educational attainment and work experience, the rate of wage growth for immigrants exceeds that for natives. Of course, a one-year time span is rather limited and does not necessarily reflect the average growth rate over a worker's career.

In "The Elusive Concept of Immigrant Quality," Duleep and Regets (1996) examine median wages for 96 groups of recent immigrants in the 1970 Census, defined according to country, age, and educational attainment categories, and track growth in this median across the subsequent two Censuses. The authors find a striking inverse correlation between entry wage and wage growth from 1970 to 1990. This means that, as a rule, for these groups, the lower the median entry wage, the more rapid the wage growth.

This finding does not negate the fact that immigrant educational attainment is increasingly below that of native workers, however, which is a problem in itself (Borjas, 1998b). As a result, while immigrants who lack a high school diploma can expect eventually to attain – or surpass – the wages of their native counterparts, the majority probably will not attain the average wage of native high school graduates, who are far more typical of the U.S. work force. On the other hand, the finding that the earnings of low-skill immigrants rise rapidly is a corrective to the image of a low-paid work force whose

---

* Tabulations by Cohen, et al. (1997) indicate that mean years of schooling for immigrant men declined from 1970 to 1982, but – as a result of increased migration from many Asian countries – rose markedly during the 1982-1988 period.

wages are stagnant. Also, many immigrants arrive with math skills superior to those of native workers (Rivera-Batiz, 1996), which warns against placing undue emphasis on more limited measures of educational attainment. Finally, more recent data suggest that some of the negative patterns which Borjas identified may have reversed; educational attainment and wage growth among recent immigrants appear to exceed those which Borjas identified (Duleep and Regets 1997b; Sorensen and Enchautegui 1994; Funkhouser and Trejo 1995).

Other findings from human-capital-based immigration research provide additional perspectives. These include:

- Downturns in the business cycle severely affect wage growth of low-skilled workers and immigrants in particular. Because they are based on Census data (separated by ten-year intervals), Borjas' results do not reflect the potentially rapid annual growth in immigrant wages during economic upturns (Lalonde and Topel, 1991; McDonald and Worswick, 1998; Reimers, 1998, 1997).

- Much of the wage gap between immigrants and native workers might be attributable to immigrants' shorter length of time on the job. While information on job tenure is unfortunately unavailable from the U.S. Census, suggestive research using Canadian data suggests that the immigrant/native wage gap is markedly reduced when comparisons are made for workers with similar lengths of job tenure (McDonald and Worswick, 1998).

- The preoccupation with the educational attainment and abilities of individuals may be misplaced with regard to immigrants, whose achievements frequently rely more on family and community support. For example, by pooling the incomes of multiple earners, recently-immigrated households greatly increase their household income and mitigate poverty (Perez, 1986; Jensen, 1991). Another example is derived from evidence that many so-called low-skilled individuals are extremely productive in the labor markets of their ethnic communities or in immigrant-dominated firms (Portes, 1995; Waldinger, 1996).

## 2. From outside the human capital tradition:

- To some extent, the low entry wages and low wage growth of immigrants can be attributed to the crowding of immigrants into "immigrant jobs" (DeFreitas, 1988,

1991; Waldinger, 1996; Tienda, 1998; Reimers, 1998, 1997; Hsueh and Tienda, 1996, 1995). The abundant supply of labor keeps wages low and is a disincentive for employers to provide job training and upward mobility (Piore, 1979). This "segmentation of labor" perspective places greater emphasis on employer practices and less emphasis on worker abilities in explaining low wages and slow wage growth among low-skilled workers.

- Immigrants' low levels of educational attainment may be used by employers as a basis to discriminate against immigrants rather than as an indicator of level of ability. A strong correlation between low entry wages and recentness of arrival might in this case reflect an increase in discriminatory practices rather than a decline in ability.

- The social context within which individuals find themselves helps determine what they are able to achieve. The nature of the historical epoch, the state of the economy, and governmental policies towards immigrants all provide the "filter" through which individual abilities operate. Thus, the fact that the wage gap identified by Borjas increased dramatically in the 1970s may reflect a fundamental "structural" effect, i.e., the restructuring in the economy, whereby all low-wage workers, whether native or immigrant, lost ground (Hinojosa-Ojeda, et al., 1991). Recent work by Myers and Cranford (1998) provides a promising means for distinguishing between individual, cohort, and structural effects on individual achievement.

## Immigration's Impact on Jobs and Wages

A major issue in immigration policy debates is whether the influx of immigrants creates an overabundance of low-skilled workers, thereby driving wages down for similarly low-skilled native-born workers. (For several takes on the literature, see National Research Council, 1997; Camarota, 1998; Center for Immigration Studies, 1998; Borjas, 1994; Tienda and Liang, 1992). In his influential 1994 article, Borjas noted that the literature has been fraught with "a number of conceptual problems . . . As a result, the accumulated empirical evidence has little to say about the underlying questions." Thus, although much of this literature is policy-driven, the methodologically complex nature of the issues and the ambiguities in the results do not readily lend themselves to policy proscriptions.

In this section, we review the major findings of this literature. We group the studies according to the geographic area they analyze, that is, the nation as a whole versus smaller labor markets. After briefly reviewing the findings, we provide a summary of important policy implications.

## National Studies

The review of this literature by the National Research Council (NRC) concluded that, in general, immigration has had a positive effect on the wages and employment of native-born workers. Immigrant workers increased the U.S. supply of workers by an estimated 4% in the 1980s, and thus exerted a beneficial impact on the American economy. Immigrants helped counterbalance the nation's declining rate of labor force growth – the result of an aging workforce and a pattern of increasingly early retirement among men (Simon, 1991, 1989).

In addition, by providing relatively cheap labor, **immigrants have lowered the prices of many commodities, enabling higher levels of consumption and demand which, in turn, stimulates demand for workers and raises wages.** While it is probably impossible to estimate the effect with precision, the analysis by the NRC suggests that immigrants raised the average aggregate level of income for native-born workers by a range of $1 billion to possibly as high as $10 billion annually (Borjas and Freeman, 1997; NRC, 1997).

**The positive wage and employment effects accrue primarily to higher-skilled workers, that is, workers with high school diplomas, and, especially, college graduates.** In general, these workers hold different types of jobs – higher-skilled and higher-paying – than most recent arrivals seek. Because they do different types of work, these two groups of workers – educated natives and under-educated immigrants – are said to "complement" each other in the work force. This is in contrast to natives and immigrants who lack a high school diploma, whom economists portray as competing for similar jobs and who therefore are said to be potential "substitutes" for each other.

**Most economic analyses of lower-skilled, native-born workers view this group as competitors for jobs sought by many recent arrivals.** As such, economic theory anticipates that lower-skilled, native workers form the group most likely to be penalized by immigration, in contrast to higher-skilled native workers, who are more likely to benefit from the presence of low-skilled immigrants.

Most studies identify "lower-skilled" workers as high school dropouts (fully 8% of all native-born workers aged 25 years and over). Some researchers also include high school graduates within this "lower-skilled" category. Because minority groups – especially African Americans and Hispanics (some of whom are themselves immigrants) – generally have lower average levels of educational attainment than native-born Whites, it seems plausible to suggest that the negative impact of immigration may be particularly pronounced for minorities and may be a factor exacerbating racial/ethnic inequalities.

For the nation as a whole, then, does immigration have a detrimental impact on the wages and employment of native-born workers who lack a high school degree? Most studies at the national level, including those reviewed by the NRC, find little effect on employment. Estimates of wage effects vary depending on how the impact is measured. On the whole, the NRC takes a rather optimistic stance. Extrapolating from economic studies of labor demand (based on Hamermesh, 1993), the NRC:

> suggests that a 10 percent increase in the size of the labor force will reduce the wages of competing workers by about 3 percent of that change. During the 1980s, immigration increased the supply of all workers about 4 percent. Therefore, immigration may reduce the wages of competing native workers by only about 1.2 percent (NRC 1997).

The size and complexity of the U.S. economy are said to buffer low-skilled native workers from the potentially negative effects of the influx of low-skilled immigrants (NRC, 1997: 220).

Another finding cited by the NRC seems to contradict this optimistic position, however. Apparently, immigration accounts for a portion of the wage gap between native high school dropouts and other native workers (Borjas et al., 1992, 1997; cited in NRC 1997: 227). This gap increased a total of 11% between 1980 and 1994. According to Borjas et al., immigration was responsible for 4.8% of this 11% increase, that is, 44% of the total wage gap increase (4.8%/11%). Wage gaps for workers in other categories of educational attainment were not found to be substantially affected by immigration.

Using a similar methodology, Jaeger (1995) obtained very similar results for high school dropouts. In contrast to the studies by Borjas et al., Jaeger found surprisingly strong, positive effects of immigration on the wages of college graduates, a finding in accordance with the notion that immigrants and native college graduates are complements in the labor market.

Despite the serious implications of a link between immigration and wage inequality among native-born workers (as Borjas and Freeman emphasized in a letter to the *New York Times*, 1997), the NRC emphasizes the more benign view of immigration's wage effects summarized above. In part, this may reflect NRC's recognition that estimates concerning wage gaps are based on highly tentative assumptions. "As a result," the NRC notes, "if the economic model used in the simulations does not accord with the real-world labor markets, the validity of the conclusions comes into question" (1997:227; also see a similar critique by DiNardo, 1997). We describe some of the assumptions below.

The NRC notes that **there is little evidence that immigration has negatively impacted the employment and earnings of African Americans,** at least when examined at the level of the nation as a whole. To a large extent, this is attributable to the living patterns of the two groups; most African Americans live in areas with relatively few immigrants, while immigrants tend to congregate geographically. Recent theoretical work by Borjas (1998a) suggests the NRC may be overly optimistic on this score. His calculations hinge, in part, on the observation that many of the benefits from immigration accrue to the owners of firms and, in addition, that a very small percentage of Blacks own firms. Depending on which set of assumptions is used, then, Borjas' "back of the envelope" estimates suggest immigration accounts for African American losses of $80 to $400 per person per year. Conceivably, the losses might be exacerbated for those African Americans who live in areas of high immigration, though the evidence on this score is somewhat mixed, as will be discussed below.

In contrast to other population groups, **immigrants from earlier waves may be the group most adversely impacted by recent immigration.** A 10% increase in the number of immigrants is estimated to reduce the wages of earlier immigrants by at least 4% (NRC 1997: 223).

Most recently, "The Wages of Immigration," by Steven Camarota (1998; Center for Immigration Studies, 1998) hypothesized that the processes by which immigrants exert negative effects on the wages of minority and other low-skilled native workers take place within occupations. That is, an oversupply of immigrants in a given occupation will lower the wages of native-born workers there. Using cross-sectional data based on the June 1991 CPS, Camarota found that workers in occupations with high percentages of immigrants earned less than their counterparts in occupations with fewer (or no) immigrants, a finding which cannot be attributed to other characteristics of occupations or demographic differences among workers. The strongest relationship was for natives employed in jobs where the average level of educational attainment was only a high school degree or less ("low-skilled occupations"). In low-skilled occupations with work forces that were 15% immigrant, Camarota found that native workers earned, on average, 12% less than similar workers in occupations with no immigrants.

Many of Camarota's findings are in accord with a hypothesis derived from the "segmentation" literature, namely, that low-paid immigrants are disproportionately hired in low-paying jobs where other low-paid natives, especially minorities, are also employed. However, Camarota interprets his findings in *longitudinal* terms, that is, that an influx of immigrants lowers the wages of natives. While Camarota's reliance on cross-sectional data is deliberate (he rejects using longitudinal data for several good reasons), his argument actually involves a causal ordering of variables that can only be tested with longitudinal data – namely, that an influx of immigrants into an occupation is followed by a decline in wages. We agree with Camarota that there are severe, and possibly insurmountable, methodological problems in using longitudinal data to test this hypothesis. On the other hand, the disjuncture between data and interpretation is likely to leave skeptical readers unconvinced that the negative correlation between the percent of immigrant workers in an occupation and wages is *entirely* attributable to the influx of immigrants. While it seems plausible to argue that *some* of the relationship between immigrant composition and wages is due to immigrant underbidding, we are left with the original question, "How much?"

The evidence concerning the impact of immigrants on the wages of low-skilled natives has prompted some researchers to call for drastic changes in immigration policies (for a comprehensive discussion of the issues, see the volume by Duleep and Wunnawa 1996; also, Center for Immigration Studies 1998). However, the extent to which these findings are meaningful hinges on the extent to which the assumptions used to derive them are tenable. (For a note on the assumptions used, see box next page.)

## Questionable Assumptions Underlie Some Immigration Findings

As the NRC noted, estimating the impact of immigrants on the wages of natives in these studies is greatly dependent on estimating the extent to which immigrants and natives are substitutes. These estimates, in turn, are based on the assumption that immigrants and natives of similar ages and levels of educational attainment are substitutes in the labor market. In reality, immigrants' wages and the determination of where immigrants are employed are affected by non-economic variables, such as employer preferences and informal hiring networks, or ethnic economies (Portes 1995; Enchautegui 1997, 1995). In addition, most economic models posit that the effects of an influx of foreign low-skilled workers are similar to an increase in the supply of low-skilled natives. However, it is difficult to determine how similar those effects really are. Moreover, few analyses take immigrant homogeneity into account. For example, immigrants often are more productive than native workers, bringing with them their own sources of capital, creating employment for fellow ethnics, and transforming neighborhoods into viable centers of economic activity. Finally, the extent to which all of these factors affect native workers probably varies according to local labor market conditions and employer hiring practices. In sum, while the studies described above provide tangible numbers with which to judge the impact of immigration, it is important to keep in mind that they are based on simplifying assumptions, many of which do not accord with important real-world complexities.

The restrictionist argument generally entails the notion that "immigrants and natives compete for an ever-dwindling supply of low-skill jobs." In fact, this image may be overdrawn, as more than 7.2 million job openings over the next ten years will be in low-skill jobs – truck drivers, child care workers, maintenance repairers, food counter workers, guards, waiters, cooks, and home care aides, among others – while the proportion of native workers with some college education or beyond is expected to increase (Silvestri, 1997).

### Labor Market Studies

The studies of the nation as a whole, reviewed above, were at least partly intended to inform debates regarding immigration policy. After all, federal policy makers want to know what the overall effects of immigration are for the U.S. However, findings at the national level can often obscure important differences among regions, states, or metropolitan areas. For example, where immigration is found not to have a strong, negative impact on native workers for the entire country, it may have a significant impact in metropolitan areas. In fact, recent studies of these areas have found evidence of substantial negative impacts from immigration. These include:

- Negative impacts on the wages of high school dropouts (Jaeger, 1995; Reimers, 1998).
- Increased unemployment among minorities and high school dropouts (Kposowa, 1995; Schoeni, 1997).

Reimer's labor market analysis (1998) found that the negative wage effects of immigration were particularly concentrated among higher-paid high school dropouts. This finding calls into question the traditional assumption that low-skill immigrants compete with all high school dropouts.

There are some inconsistencies in the findings of these studies. For example, in contrast to Jaeger, Kposowa and Schoeni found no effects on wages. More importantly, other studies have failed to find substantial negative effects. On the contrary, a recent comparison of metropolitan areas around the nation concluded that immigrants created large numbers of jobs between 1980 and 1990, thereby offsetting potentially negative effects on wages and employment occasioned by an increased supply of low-skill workers (Enchautegui, 1997). In addition, there is evidence that, on the whole, wages for the lowest-paid African American workers rose much faster for those living in areas of high immigration than was the case for their counterparts in other parts of the country (Enchautegui, 1995).

Similarly, a recent case study of New Jersey found immigrants to have a generally favorable effect on the economic well-being of residents there, including lower-skilled workers. A particularly striking finding is that the wages of native-born high school dropouts are markedly higher in industries with high proportions of immigrants (Butcher and Piehl, 1997). This finding suggests that further research is warranted to test the following hypothesis: in some labor markets and in some industries, immigrants may actually improve the economic situation of native-born workers. The authors suggest several plausible reasons why this might be so, including:

- Immigrants may help low-skill industries survive, thrive, and ultimately increase their wage structure.
- Industries with higher proportions of immigrants may be experiencing increases in demand.
- As low-paid natives leave low-skill industries for higher-paying positions, immigrants replace them (a pattern described by Waldinger [1996] for New York).

**While there are good reasons to believe that many low-skilled workers are at a particular disadvantage in labor markets with large influxes of low-skilled immigrants, there is no reason to believe that the negative impact is uniform across labor markets.** Particularly given the sensitivity of estimates to assumptions, it seems commonsensical to reject attempts to generalize across labor markets. Instead, it seems much more plausible to suggest that the impact will vary by individual market, particularly given the diversity of both states and cities, as well as of local economies, around the country. A surprisingly large number of studies fail to find an immigration impact at the local level, however, leading some economists to view the national level as the logical unit of analysis (NRC: 221-226). Borjas suggests that the local labor market impact of immigration is difficult to identify because:

- Native workers move to other labor markets when their jobs or wages are threatened by an influx of immigrants.
- Firms also move in response to labor movements.
- Immigrants tend not to go where jobs are in short supply.

On the other hand, as DiNardo has noted, it is conceivable that studies fail to identify a large, negative immigrant effect because one does not exist, at least not uniformly across labor markets (1997). This debate is not likely to be resolved any time soon.

# V. Policy Implications

The policy discussions in much of this literature hinge – correctly, we feel – on the implications of immigration for low-skilled native workers. The restrictionists argue that a necessary step for improving the economic well-being of low-skilled native workers is to implement a change in immigration policy that would reduce the influx of low-skilled immigrants. In particular, much of this discussion argues in favor of a shift in immigration policy from an emphasis on family re-unification to a more skills-oriented policy, which would increase the proportion of immigrants with higher levels of educational attainment. Based on our reading of existing studies, we believe low-skilled immigrants are a relatively minor source of the economic problems of low-skilled native workers and, in this regard, a focus on low-skilled immigrants and immigration policy diverts attention from the larger, more pertinent issues, including:

1. **Low-skilled native workers should not be faced with a choice of competing over jobs paying poverty-level wages or not working at all.**

That low-skill jobs pay poverty-level wages in areas with high, as well as low, rates of immigration belies the notion that immigration caused the poverty-level wages. It is simply implausible to suggest that low-skilled native workers migrate out of high-immigrant cities to low-immigrant areas in such large numbers as to lower wages significantly. Similarly, the economic obstacles faced by African Americans in areas with little or no immigration are testimony of more complex societal failures. In this sense, undue emphasis on immigrants as the source of the economic problems of other minorities amounts to scapegoating. Instead, the roots of low-paid work must be found in:

- The relative abundance of low-skilled native-born workers available to perform this work, which is generated, at least in part, by the failure of schools to dramatically reduce the rate of high school dropouts in low-income communities.
- The failure of unions and other employee associations to incorporate low-skilled workers (immigrants and natives alike).
- The failure of the political system to implement demand-side incentives to encourage employers to pay living wages and provide benefits, training, and upwardly-mobile career paths.

2. **The U.S. government should promote assistance programs for recent immigrants seeking to become fully-participating members of U.S. society.**

The federal government denies much assistance to adult immigrants that it provides to many political refugees. This assistance helps account for much of the ability of refugees to integrate successfully into the U.S. labor market. Such assistance includes the provision of educational programs to facilitate acculturation, including English proficiency; resettlement assistance, including assistance with job and home searches; and low-interest loans to purchase homes and start up new businesses.

In *Warmth of the Welcome: The Social Causes of Economic Success for Immigrants* (1998), Jeffrey Reitz compares the treatment of immigrants in the United States to that of immigrants in Canada. He concludes that part of the immigrant success story in Canada is attributable to governmental policies there that enhance the likelihood of economic success among recent arrivals. In contrast, the U.S. emphasis on individualism and the general "hands-off" policy of the government contribute to higher poverty rates among immigrants here. To some extent, the Canadian experience could be replicated by extending the "warmth of the welcome" accorded refugees to all other immigrants.*

There can also be more public-private partnerships to promote the socioeconomic well-being of immigrant communities. It is certainly congruent with the objectives of most businesses, unions, and private non-profit organizations to help facilitate immigrant education and the processes that lead to naturalization. As noted in the 1997 report to the U.S. Congress by the Commission on Immigration Reform, some of these efforts can supplement an overburdened Immigration and Naturalization Service. Unfortunately, while models of this type of private sector involvement exist (see National Council of La Raza, 1991), they are still the exception rather than the rule.

3.   **The federal government, in conjunction with unions, corporations, and private nonprofit organizations, should develop strategies to reduce the perceived conflicts of interest between low-income native communities and immigrants.**

The effective assistance provided refugees by the federal government could be used as a model and extended to low-income communities. Public-private partnerships could be implemented to encourage cooperative business ventures between low-income native and immigrant entrepreneurs in low-income communities. Such efforts would go a long way toward reducing tensions between these groups. In addition, federal grants should be awarded those cities serving as immigrant gateways to help promote immigrant adjustment. Finally, strategies that increase business ownership among native workers with low levels of education will help reduce their economic competition with immigrants.

---

* Reitz argues compellingly against the belief that the Canadian occupationally-based immigration policy results in a higher-caliber immigrant workforce than that of the U.S. "Census data on immigrants shows that in virtually every origin category common to the three countries, the United States out-competes . . . Canada . . . for highly skilled immigrants . . . Immigrants to the United States from most specific [countries] are in fact better educated than those in Canada" (1998: 22).

**4. Governmental efforts must be stepped up to reduce discriminatory practices against immigrants and other minorities.**

This includes strict prohibition of raids by the Immigration and Naturalization Service (INS) that result in prejudiced actions against legal immigrants, often those Hispanic or Asian and native-born Americans who, because of appearance, accent, or surname, are perceived to be "immigrant." In addition, governmental efforts must be reinvigorated to monitor discriminatory hiring practices (Lowell, Teachman, and Jing, 1995).

**5. An emphasis on family reunification in immigrant admissions has positive economic effects on immigrant families.**

"Are immigrants admitted for their special skills truly more productive than immigrants admitted for their family ties?" (Lowell, 1996). In an argument against abandoning the current emphasis on family reunification, Lowell's answer to the above question is "No." Many restrictionists assume that a shift in immigrant admissions criteria away from family reunification and toward a greater emphasis on skills would be beneficial. It is true that family-based-admissions immigrants tend to have lower levels of education than immigrants admitted on the basis of skills. However, there are many reasons to believe that family-based admissions is a more effective system in the long run. For example:

- The family is a source of information regarding housing and jobs, particularly those in co-ethnic enterprises, which are often important sources of job training.
- The family is a source of moral and financial support, which includes income pooling to pay for housing and establish small businesses or support entrepreneurial ventures.
- The family provides child care and labor for family-run businesses.

Lowell concludes that "a completely skill-based system would violate the humane principle of family reunification, disregard the complexity of immigrant adjustment, and weaken the richness of ethnic communities that provide transitional frameworks for immigrants" (1996: 367).

# V. Conclusion

In this chapter we have addressed three questions occasioned by the recent influx of Hispanic immigrants: 1) How does the incidence of poverty among these recent arrivals compare with that for native-born Hispanics? 2) Will the low levels of educational attainment of recent immigrants prevent them from thriving here? 3) Do they displace native-born workers and undercut their wages? The answer to the first question is clear. Although foreign-born Hispanics are less likely than native Hispanics to have completed high school or beyond, immigrants do not have a markedly higher incidence of poverty. There is no clear-cut answer to the second question. On the one hand, the average wage gap between recent Hispanic immigrants and native-born workers is wide and probably will not be eliminated over the next several decades. On the other hand, the data for immigrant and native workers who have similar levels of education suggest that immigrant wages do in fact rise rapidly. Third, we find little evidence to support the contention that immigrants are a major source of job loss and wage stagnation among native-born workers.

Other findings merit further research. First, there is a surprising amount of diversity among the five immigrant-gateway states. In fact, there are numerous instances in which the socioeconomic profile of immigrants is at least as favorable as that of natives. Second, immigrants are not overrepresented at the extreme bottom of the wage distribution or in the least desirable jobs, a finding which complements the view that recent immigrants probably do not compete with natives at the lowest end of the skills distribution. Finally, in light of calls for overhauling U.S. immigration policy, additional research is warranted concerning the implications of a skills-based admissions system, with a tallying of the undesirable as well as the desirable consequences. Most importantly, however, a focus on immigration reform should not divert policy makers' attention from other, more pressing needs of low-skilled workers.

# 5

# Compensation for the Latino Worker

**Cordelia W. Reimers, Ph.D.**
*Hunter College and the Graduate School of CUNY*

## Abstract

*This chapter describes what has happened to the full-time weekly wages of Hispanic men and women since 1990, as revealed by monthly data from the Current Population Survey, and examines the differences by age and education, by occupation, by nativity, by national origin, and among married and single parents. The trend in Latinos' inflation-adjusted wages is compared with the trends in wages earned by Black and White non-Hispanics. Overall, Latinos' wages are lower than those of White or Black non-Hispanics. Differences among these ethnic groups in terms of age, education, proportion of foreign-born, geographic location, and industrial and occupational concentration help explain these wage gaps. Moreover, like the pay of other less-educated groups, Latinos' inflation-adjusted wages declined more than those of White non-Hispanics between 1990 and 1996, so that the wage gap between Whites and Latinos widened over this period. Young Latino college graduates were the exception; their wages rose, while young Black and White college graduates' wages declined, so that Latina college graduates earned more than comparable Whites or Blacks in 1996.*

## I. Introduction

A family's standard of living rests on several supports: earnings, unearned income from assets and government transfers, and "in-kind" income such as homeownership, local public services, Medicaid, and fringe benefits. The most important is the earnings of family members, which depend on how many adults are present, whether or not each one has a job outside the home, whether they work full- or part-time, and their wage rates. Thus, differences in wages are one of the important reasons for differences in family economic well-being.

Most of the published research on Latinos' wages has used Census data from 1990 and earlier years; thus, the latest year included is 1989. There has been very little in-depth analysis of Latinos'* wages using post-1990 data. Reports issued annually by the Census Bureau provide data from the monthly Current Population Survey (CPS) on the mean and median incomes of Hispanic, Black, and White year-round full-time workers, by gender. These income figures include unearned income as well as earnings. Since 1995, these reports have also tabulated mean and median earnings for year-round, full-time workers, which comes closer to measuring wage rates. They show that Hispanics' wages are lower than Blacks' and Whites'. In 1996, the median earnings of Hispanic male full-time workers were $21,056, up just $75 from 1995, after adjusting for inflation. The median earnings of Black men were $26,404 (up $1,255), and the median earnings of White men were $32,996 ($126 lower than in 1995). The median earnings of Hispanic women were only $18,665 (up $980 from 1995); the median earnings of Black women were $21,473 (up $198); and the median earnings of White women were $24,160 (up $572).[1]

The published reports do not tabulate earnings for more detailed classifications of Hispanics by nativity, ethnicity, age, education, or occupation. In order to examine wages for young Mexican male dropouts in 1996, for example, it is necessary to tabulate the unpublished CPS data. This chapter describes what has happened to the wages of Hispanic men and women since 1990, and examines the differences by age and education, by occupation, by nativity, by national origin, and among married and single parents. The trend in Latinos' wages is compared with the trends in wages earned by Black and White non-Hispanics. Overall, Latinos' wages are lower than those of White or Black non-Hispanics. Moreover, their wages declined more than those of White non-Hispanics between 1990 and 1996, so that the wage gap between Whites and Latinos widened. Young Latino college graduates were the exception; their wages rose, while young Black and White college graduates' wages declined, so that young Latina college graduates earned more than comparable Whites or Blacks in 1996.

---

\* In this chapter, "Hispanic" is used when referring to the Census Bureau classification, to conform to Census terminology. Otherwise, "Hispanic" and "Latino" (or "Latina") are used interchangeably. White and Black non-Hispanics are sometimes referred to simply as "Whites" and "Blacks" for the sake of brevity. Hispanics may be of any race.

## II. Data and Methods

Most of the data for this chapter come from the National Bureau of Economic Research (NBER) "Labor Extracts" of the CPS monthly microdata files for 1990 to 1996. Each month the CPS surveys about 50,000 randomly-chosen households in the U.S. to collect information about current labor market activity (such as employment, unemployment, hours worked, occupation, industry) and basic demographic characteristics (including race, Hispanic origin group,* gender, age, education, occupation, marital status, and relationship to household head). In addition, 25% of the CPS sample (the "outgoing rotation groups") are asked about earnings, hours worked, and other characteristics of their current main job. Since January 1994, the entire sample has been asked about their birthplace, date of entry to the U.S., citizenship, and parents' birthplace. The NBER has compiled ready-to-use files containing 50 variables from these outgoing rotation group files for each month from 1979 through 1996. The variables selected pertain to employment, earnings, and background characteristics. In this chapter, the data for each year consist of the 12 monthly files combined.

Because the NBER's CPS Labor Extracts do not include information on the presence of children, the wages of married vs. single female family heads with children under 18 are based on the March CPS microdata file for each year. In March, additional questions are asked about income and its sources, weeks worked, and usual hours worked per week in the previous year. The March sample is also expanded to increase the representation of Latino households. Since data on current-job earnings are available for fewer than 25% of the individuals in the March sample, while annual earnings and weeks worked in the previous year are available for the entire March sample, the latter were used to compute wages for family heads for 1990 and 1996. Thus, the wages of family heads are measured as annual wage and salary income last year, divided by weeks worked last year, for full-time workers aged 16-64 (that is, those who usually worked 35 or more hours a week).

In the other tables in this chapter, wages are measured as usual weekly earnings on the current job, for full-time workers aged 16-64. Part-time workers are not included, and

---

* Origin or descent is identified in the CPS questionnaire as "Mexican American," "Chicano," "Mexican," "Puerto Rican," "Cuban," "Central/South American," and "Other Spanish" (in 1990-1993) or "Other Hispanic" (in 1994-1996).

differences in weekly hours worked above 35 show up as wage differences.* Despite these drawbacks, full-time weekly earnings are used in most analyses of wages because they are reported directly in the data, whereas the hourly wages of salaried workers have to be calculated by dividing weekly earnings by hours worked. Therefore, the hourly wage is subject to more measurement and reporting errors, which can produce implausibly large or small wage values.

In order to focus on changes in purchasing power, real wages in constant 1996 dollars are reported, where nominal wages are adjusted for inflation using the Consumer Price Index-Urban (CPI-U) for 1996 and the year when the wages were earned (i.e., the year of the surveys for the monthly outgoing rotation groups, or the year before the March survey). The appropriate sample weights are used throughout this chapter, so that the tables report estimated median real wages for the relevant adult non-institutionalized population aged 16-64.

## III. Results: Trends for Latinos, Comparison with Black and White Non-Hispanics

### A. Men and Women (see Tables 1 & 2)

Hispanic men and women receive lower wages than Black and White non-Hispanics, and the White-Latino wage gap has widened somewhat since 1990.

### Men

The median real wage of Hispanic men declined by 6% between 1990 and 1996, from $384 to $360 per week in 1996 dollars. Most of this drop occurred between 1992 and 1994. Meanwhile, the median real wage of Black non-Hispanic men declined by 7%, from $432 in 1990 to $403 in 1996; and the median real wage of White non-Hispanic men stagnated at $600 per week. Thus, Hispanic men earned 89% as much as Black men in both 1990 and 1996. However, Latinos earned only 60% as much as White non-Hispanic men in 1996, whereas in 1990 they had earned 64% as much.

---

* If some groups have more overtime than others, or if overtime varies by occupation, age, or education, this will affect the comparisons of median wages reported here. Nevertheless, insofar as the trends in part-time and full-time wages are similar and the amount of overtime work has remained the same, these data depict the overall trend in Latinos' hourly pay. And insofar as changes in part-time vs. full-time or in overtime are similar across groups, they cancel out when making inter-group comparisons.

## Table 1

## Median Real Full-time Weekly Earnings of Males
## by Race/Ethnicity, Education, & Age (1996 $)

| Year, Race, and Age | Education | | | |
|---|---|---|---|---|
| | No Diploma | 12–15 | >= BA | Total |
| **1990** | | | | |
| *Hispanic* | | | | |
| 16-34 | 288 | 384 | 600 | 336 |
| 35-64 | 367 | 553 | 810 | 480 |
| Total | 312 | 456 | 720 | 384 |
| *Black NH* | | | | |
| 16-34 | 300 | 360 | 600 | 372 |
| 35-64 | 384 | 480 | 720 | 480 |
| Total | 360 | 425 | 660 | 432 |
| *White NH* | | | | |
| 16-34 | 360 | 480 | 720 | 490 |
| 35-64 | 509 | 660 | 989 | 720 |
| Total | 432 | 570 | 900 | 600 |
| **1996** | | | | |
| *Hispanic* | | | | |
| 16-34 | 260 | 350 | 634 | 320 |
| 35-64 | 320 | 500 | 782 | 410 |
| Total | 288 | 400 | 692 | 360 |
| *Black NH* | | | | |
| 16-34 | 260 | 340 | 550 | 346 |
| 35-64 | 350 | 480 | 769 | 480 |
| Total | 319 | 400 | 692 | 403 |
| *White NH* | | | | |
| 16-34 | 315 | 438 | 663 | 471 |
| 35-64 | 450 | 640 | 1000 | 705 |
| Total | 384 | 550 | 876 | 600 |

Source: Author's tabulations of weighted data on current weekly earnings of full-time workers in Current Population Survey Merged Outgoing Rotation Groups microdata files.

## Table 2

### Median Real Full-time Weekly Earnings of Females
### by Race/Ethnicity, Education, & Age (1996 $)

| Year, Race, and Age | Education | | | |
| --- | --- | --- | --- | --- |
| | No Diploma | 12–15 | >= BA | Total |
| **1990** | | | | |
| *Hispanic* | | | | |
| 16-34 | 240 | 331 | 540 | 300 |
| 35-64 | 264 | 406 | 612 | 360 |
| Total | 240 | 360 | 582 | 330 |
| *Black NH* | | | | |
| 16-34 | 240 | 312 | 495 | 330 |
| 35-64 | 288 | 396 | 630 | 413 |
| Total | 264 | 360 | 600 | 360 |
| *White NH* | | | | |
| 16-34 | 250 | 360 | 576 | 384 |
| 35-64 | 300 | 420 | 693 | 465 |
| Total | 288 | 384 | 618 | 421 |
| **1996** | | | | |
| *Hispanic* | | | | |
| 16-34 | 230 | 310 | 565 | 300 |
| 35-64 | 244 | 376 | 692 | 336 |
| Total | 240 | 340 | 600 | 320 |
| *Black NH* | | | | |
| 16-34 | 213 | 300 | 461 | 316 |
| 35-64 | 280 | 375 | 638 | 400 |
| Total | 252 | 340 | 576 | 360 |
| *White NH* | | | | |
| 16-34 | 226 | 340 | 548 | 384 |
| 35-64 | 290 | 423 | 730 | 480 |
| Total | 260 | 386 | 653 | 442 |

Source: Author's tabulations of weighted data on current weekly earnings of full-time workers in Current Population Survey Merged Outgoing Rotation Groups microdata files.

## Women

During the same period, the median real wage of Hispanic women declined by 3%, from $330 to $320 per week in 1996 dollars, with most of the drop again occurring between 1992 and 1994. Meanwhile, the median real wage of Black non-Hispanic women stagnated at $360; and the median real wage of White non-Hispanic women rose by 5%, from $421 to $442. In 1996, Latinas earned only 72% as much as White non-Hispanic women and 89% as much as Black women; whereas in 1990, they had earned 78% as much as White women and 92% as much as Black women.

## B. Parents with Children under 18, by Marital Status (see Table 3)

The wage gaps between Latino and White and Black parents have generally increased as the earnings of Latino married men with children and single mothers have declined since 1990.

### Married men with children

The median wage of Hispanic married men with children was higher than for all Latino men, but it also declined, from $462 in 1990 to $440 in 1996 (a 5% decline). Meanwhile, the wages of Black and White non-Hispanic married men with children were rising slightly, from $531 to $538 for Blacks and from $739 to $750 for Whites. Therefore, the gap between Hispanic and Black married men with children increased from 13% to 18%, and the Latino-White gap increased from 37% to 41%.

### Married women with children

The median wage of Hispanic married women with children is similar to that of all Latinas, and it hardly changed between 1990 ($323) and 1996 ($327). During this period, wages of Black non-Hispanic married women with children fell by 2% (from $409 to $400), and of White non-Hispanic married women with children rose by 9% (from $425 to $462). Thus, the wage gap between Hispanic and Black married women with children narrowed from 21% to 18%, while the Latina-White gap widened from 24% to 29%.

### Single female family heads

The median wage of Latina single female family heads was also similar to that of all Latinas in 1990 ($332), but by 1996 it had dropped by 16%, to $279. At the same time, the median wage of Black non-Hispanic single female family heads declined by 8% (from $347 to $320), while the median wage of White non-Hispanic single female family heads rose by 2% (from $395 to $404). Thus, the gap between Hispanic and Black single female family heads increased from 4% to 13%, and the Latina-White gap almost doubled, from 16% to 31%.

**Table 3**

**Median Real Full-time Weekly Earnings of Parents with Children Under 18 (1996 $)**

| Year and Race/ Ethnicity | Family Relationship | | | |
| --- | --- | --- | --- | --- |
| | Husband | Wife | Single Female Head | Total |
| **1990** | | | | |
| Hispanic | 462 | 323 | 332 | 397 |
| Black NH | 531 | 409 | 347 | 439 |
| White NH | 739 | 425 | 395 | 594 |
| Total | 693 | 416 | 369 | 554 |
| **1996** | | | | |
| Hispanic | 440 | 327 | 279 | 385 |
| Black NH | 538 | 400 | 320 | 423 |
| White NH | 750 | 462 | 404 | 606 |
| Total | 673 | 442 | 365 | 558 |

Source: Author's tabulations of weighted data on average weekly earnings in Current Population Survey microdata files for March of the following year.

## C. By Age and Education (see Tables 1 & 2)

Differences in average education and age may help to explain the wage differences among Hispanics, Blacks, and White non-Hispanics. It is useful, therefore, to examine wages within age-education groups.

### Payoffs to education for Hispanics

In general, better-educated workers earn more than less-educated ones of the same age, and the payoff to education increased dramatically during the 1980s.

- **Young Hispanics (age 16-34).** In 1996, the median earnings of young Hispanic men with at least a Bachelor of Arts (BA) degree were $634 per week, 1.8 times the median for young Hispanic male high school graduates who did not finish college ($350), and 2.4 times the median for high school dropouts ($260). These percentage payoffs to education were the same for young women as young men, although young Hispanic women earned only 89% as much as men with the same education.

- **Mature Hispanics (age 35-64).** The payoff to a college degree was slightly lower for mature Hispanic men than for young men. In 1996, the median earnings of mature Latinos with a BA or higher degree were $782, 1.6 times the median for mature Latino high school graduates who did not finish college ($500), and 2.4 times the median for high school dropouts ($320). The payoffs to education were somewhat higher for mature Hispanic women than men. In 1996, those with a BA or higher degree earned 1.8 times the median for high school graduates, and 2.8 times the median for high school dropouts. While mature Latinas with a BA earned 88% as much as men, those with less than a college degree earned only 75% as much as men in the same age and education group.

The premium for a BA has grown since 1990, when young Latinos and Latinas with a BA earned 1.6 times as much as high school graduates and 2.1-2.25 times as much as dropouts, and mature Latinos and Latinas with a BA earned 1.5 times as much as high school graduates and 2.2-2.3 times as much as dropouts. The premium for high school graduation remained the same, with young Latino/a graduates earning about 1.3 times as much as dropouts and mature Latino/a graduates earning 1.5 times as much as dropouts.

## Payoffs to experience for Hispanics

Because of greater work experience, on-the-job training, and seniority, mature workers earn more than young ones with the same education.

- **Dropouts.** Among Hispanic high school dropouts in 1996, mature men (age 35-64) earned 23% more than young men aged 16-34, but mature women earned just 6% more than young women. The payoffs to experience were slightly lower than in 1990, when they were 27% for men and 10% for women.

- **High school graduates.** Among high school graduates without a BA, mature men earned 43% more than young men in 1996, and mature women earned 21% more than young women. The payoffs to experience were almost the same as in 1990 (when they were 44% for men and 23% for women).

- **College graduates.** Among college graduates, mature men and women both earned 23% more than young persons of the same gender. The payoff to experience had declined sharply for men since 1990 (from 35%) and risen sharply for women (from 13%).

## Young dropouts (under age 35)

The median real weekly wage of all groups of high school dropouts declined from 1990 to 1996, but for young Hispanics the decline was less than for young non-Hispanic Whites and Blacks of the same gender. Among young Hispanics who did not finish high school, men's wages declined by 10% (from $288 to $260), while women's declined by 4% (from $240 to $230). Meanwhile, the median wage of young Black and White male dropouts both declined by 13% (from $300 to $260 and $360 to $315, respectively), while that of young Black female dropouts declined by 11% (from $240 to $213), and that of young White female dropouts by 10% (from $250 to $226). Thus, among young male dropouts, Latinos were on a par with Blacks in 1996, having closed a 4% wage gap since 1990, and the Latino-White gap narrowed from 20% to 17% between 1990 and 1996. Among young female dropouts, Latinas earned more than Blacks or Whites in 1996. They earned 8% more than Blacks, having been on a par with them in 1990, and 2% more than Whites, having earned 4% less in 1990.

## Mature dropouts (aged 35-64)

The wages of mature Hispanic dropouts declined more between 1990 and 1996 than those of mature White and Black non-Hispanics without a high school diploma. Among mature male dropouts, the median real weekly wage of Hispanics declined by 13% (from $367 to $320), while that of Whites declined by 12% (from $509 to $450), and that of Blacks declined by 9% (from $384 to $350). Among mature female dropouts, wages of Hispanics declined by 8% (from $264 to $244), and the median wages of Whites and Blacks declined by 3%, from $300 to $290 and $288 to $280, respectively. Therefore, among mature men without a high school diploma, the Latino-Black gap grew from 4% in 1990 to 9% in 1996, and the Latino-White gap grew slightly (from 28% to 29%). Among mature women who did not finish high school, the Latina-Black and Latina-White gaps both grew (from 8% to 13% and 12% to 16%, respectively).

## Young high school graduates (without a BA)

Between 1990 and 1996, the median real weekly wage of young men and women with 12-15 years of education declined by the same percentage for Hispanics as for Whites, and more than for Blacks. The decline was 9% for Hispanic and White men (from $384 to $350 and $480 to $438, respectively), 6% for Black men (from $360 to $340), 6% for Hispanic and White women (from $331 to $310 and $360 to $340, respectively), and 4% for Black women (from $312 to $300). Among young men and women who finished high school but not college, Hispanics had higher wages than Blacks, but the gap narrowed from 6-7% in 1990 to 3% in 1996; while the Hispanic-White gap remained the same – 20% for men and 8-9% for women.

## Mature high school graduates (without a BA)

The median real weekly wage of mature Hispanics with 12-15 years of education declined more for Hispanics than for Blacks or Whites from 1990 to 1996. Among men, Latinos' wages fell by 10% (from $553 to $500) and Whites' fell by 3% (from $660 to $640), while Blacks' wages remained at $480. Among women, Latinas' wages declined by 7% (from $406 to $376) and Blacks' declined by 5% (from $396 to $375), while Whites' remained virtually the same, rising from $420 to $423. Thus, among mature men who finished high school but not college, Latinos had higher wages than Blacks, but their advantage narrowed from 15% in 1990 to 4% in 1996; and the Latino-White gap grew from 16% to 22%. Among mature women with a high school diploma but not a BA, Latinas had 3% higher wages than Blacks in 1990, but this small difference disappeared by 1996; and the Latina-White gap grew from 3% to 11%.

## Young college graduates

The median real weekly wage of young Hispanics with a BA or higher degree rose between 1990 and 1996, while those of young Black and White college graduates declined. Among men, Latinos' wages grew by 6% (from $600 to $634), while Blacks' and Whites' declined by 8% (from $600 to $550 for Blacks and $720 to $663 for Whites). Among women, Latinas' wages rose by 5% (from $540 to $565), while Blacks' declined by 7% (from $495 to $461) and Whites' declined by 5% (from $576 to $548). Thus, among young male college graduates, Latinos' wages were 15% higher than Blacks' in 1996, after having been the same in 1990; and the Latino-White gap narrowed from 17% to 4%. Among young female college graduates, Latinas earned more than either Blacks or Whites in 1996. They earned 23% more than Blacks and 3% more than Whites, after having earned 9% more than Blacks and 6% less than Whites in 1990.

## Mature college graduates

The median real weekly wage of mature Hispanic men with a BA or higher degree declined between 1990 and 1996, while that of White and Black male college graduates rose. Latinos fell by 3% (from $810 to $782), Whites rose by just 1% (from $989 to $1,000), and Blacks rose by 7% (from $720 to $769). Thus, among mature male college graduates, Latinos had higher wages than Blacks, but their advantage narrowed from 13% in 1990 to 2% in 1996; and the Latino-White gap widened from 18% to 22% between 1990 and 1996.

The median real weekly wages of mature women with a BA or higher degree rose more for Latinas than for Whites or Blacks between 1990 and 1996. The increase for Latinas was 13% (from $612 to $692), for Whites 5% (from $693 to $730), and for Blacks just 1% (from $630 to $638). Thus, among mature female college graduates, Latinas earned 8% more than Blacks in 1996, having earned 3% less in 1990; and the Latina-White gap narrowed from 12% to 5%.

In sum, we find that Latinos continue to lag behind Whites with similar education and age; the Latino-White gaps have generally grown since 1990 for mature men, but narrowed or remained the same for younger men. Among young men with at least a BA degree, Latinos who work full-time earn 15% more than Blacks and only 4% less than Whites. Hispanic men who finished high school or college generally have higher wages than Blacks in the same age group; but among those over age 35, the Latinos' advantage narrowed during the 1990s. Among mature dropouts as well, Latinos' wages declined relative to those of Blacks; whereas young Latino dropouts have caught up with Black dropouts.

The wages of Hispanic female college graduates have increased since 1990, so that now they earn more than Black female BAs in the same age group; and young Latinas also earn more than young White female BAs. Among young women with at least a BA degree, Latinas who work full-time earn 23% more than Blacks and 3% more than Whites. Mature Latinas with at least a BA earn 8% more than Blacks and only 5% less than Whites. With the exception of young high school dropouts, Hispanic women without a college degree suffered larger wage declines since 1990 than Black or White non-Hispanic women of the same age and education level. Young Latinas still earned higher wages in 1996 than young Black women with the same level of education, but mature Latinas fell further behind Whites and Blacks among women who had not finished college.  Among young high school dropouts, Latinas' wages fell less than the wages of young Black and White non-Hispanic women, so that by 1996 Latinas were earning more than either Whites or Blacks.

## D.  By National Origin, for Hispanics (see Tables 4 & 5)

Mexicans and Central and South Americans continue to have lower median wages than the other Latino groups, including Puerto Ricans and Cubans.  In 1996, there was a 25-30% difference between the median wages of Puerto Ricans and Cubans, on the one hand, and Central and South Americans and Mexicans of the same gender, on the other.  The "Other Hispanic" group slipped from first to third place between 1990 and 1996, because their wages dropped the most – by 15% (from $498 to $421) for men and by 6% (from $384 to $360) for women.  Meanwhile, men's wages dropped within all the other Latino groups as well: for Mexicans by 6% (from $360 to $340); for Puerto Ricans by 7% (from $480 to $445); for Cubans by 8% (from $480 to $441); and for Central and South Americans by 9% (from $384 to $350).  However, women's wages rose among Puerto Ricans, Central and South Americans, and especially Cubans – by 1% for both Puerto Ricans (from $370 to $375) and Central and South Americans (from $300 to $304), and by 6% (from $378 to $400) for Cubans.  However, the median wage of Mexican women dropped by 4%, from $312 to $300.  Thus, the gender wage gap narrowed within each group, as men's wages declined while women's wages rose, or fell less.

**Table 4**

**Median Real Full-time Weekly Earnings of Hispanic Males
by Hispanic Origin (1996 $)**

| | | | Hispanic Origin | | |
| --- | --- | --- | --- | --- | --- |
| Year | Mexican | Puerto Rican | Cuban | C & S American | Other Hispanic | Total |
| 1990 | 360 | 480 | 480 | 384 | 498 | 384 |
| 1996 | 340 | 445 | 441 | 350 | 421 | 360 |

Source: Author's tabulations of weighted data on current weekly earnings of full-time workers in Current Population Survey Merged Outgoing Rotation Groups microdata files.

**Table 5**

**Median Real Full-time Weekly Earnings of Hispanic Females
by Hispanic Origin (1996 $)**

| | | | Hispanic Origin | | |
| --- | --- | --- | --- | --- | --- |
| Year | Mexican | Puerto Rican | Cuban | C & S American | Other Hispanic | Total |
| 1990 | 312 | 370 | 378 | 300 | 384 | 330 |
| 1996 | 300 | 375 | 400 | 304 | 360 | 320 |

Source: Author's tabulations of weighted data on current weekly earnings of full-time workers in Current Population Survey Merged Outgoing Rotation Groups microdata files.

## E. By National Origin, Age, and Education (see Tables 6 & 7)

Some of the wage differences among the Hispanic national origin groups are no doubt due to differences in their educational levels and average age.*

### Dropouts
Among mature Latino dropouts, Puerto Ricans earned considerably more than Mexican and Central and South American men their age, perhaps because Puerto Ricans are concentrated in the Northeast, a higher wage region than the Southwest, where the majority of Mexicans live. Within national origin groups, the wages of mature Hispanic dropouts tended to drop more than those of young dropouts from 1990 to 1996. The median real weekly wage of young male Mexican and Central and South American high school dropouts declined by 10% between 1990 and 1996, the Mexicans' from $288 to $260 and the Central and South Americans' from $300 to $270. The wages of mature Mexican male dropouts declined by 9% (from $353 to $320), while those of mature Puerto Rican male dropouts declined by 13% (from $432 to $376) and those of mature Central and South American male dropouts declined by 17% (from $360 to $300). For all ages combined, Other Hispanic male dropouts' median wage dropped 31%, from $432 in 1990 to $300 in 1996. Meanwhile, the median real weekly wage of Central and South American female dropouts remained at $240, the median real weekly wage of young female Mexican dropouts declined by 4% (from $240 to $230), and that of mature Mexican female dropouts declined by 11% (from $270 to $240).

### Young high school graduates (without a BA)
The median real weekly wages of all groups of young Hispanic high school graduates who did not finish college declined between 1990 and 1996. Wages of Mexican men declined 6% (from $372 to $350), of Central and South American males 11% (from $360 to $320), and of Puerto Ricans and Other Hispanic men 19% (from $480 to $390 for Puerto Ricans and $432 to $350 for Other Hispanic). Wages of Puerto Rican females declined 3% (from $360 to $350), of Central and South American females 4% (from $300 to $288), of Mexican females 5% (from $318 to $302), and of Other Hispanic females by 11% (from $336 to $300).

---

\* Cubans are omitted from this discussion because the numbers in specific age-education cells are so small that estimates of median wages are unreliable. Only those Hispanic-origin age-education groups with at least 100 in the sample are discussed here.

## Mature high school graduates (without a BA)

The median real weekly wage of mature Central and South American men and women and Other Hispanic men who had completed high school but not college rose, while wages of all other Hispanic-origin groups at this education level declined between 1990 and 1996. Wages of Central and South American men rose slightly (from $480 to $486) and those of Other Hispanic men rose by 8% (from $553 to $600), while wages of Puerto Rican men declined by 7% (from $547 to $507), and those of Mexican men declined by 13% (from $576 to $500). Among mature women with 12-15 years of schooling, the median real weekly wage of Central and South American women rose by 13% (from $339 to $384), while that of Puerto Ricans fell by 8% (from $415 to $380), that of Mexicans fell by 11% (from $420 to $375), and that of Other Hispanics fell by 13% (from $432 to $376).

## College graduates

The median real weekly wage of Mexican women and young Mexican men with college degrees rose between 1990 and 1996, but mature Mexican men and Central and South Americans did not fare so well. The wages of young Mexican men with a BA or higher degree grew by 20% (from $529 to $634), and those of Mexican women with at least a BA (all ages combined) increased by 10% (from $576 to $634); while wages of mature Mexican men with college degrees fell by 8% (from $840 to $769). Among Central and South Americans, the median real weekly wage of men with college degrees (all ages combined) fell by 8%, from $696 to $640, while those of women college graduates remained the same ($540).

## Table 6

## Median Real Full-time Weekly Earnings of Hispanic Males
## by Hispanic Origin, Education, & Age (1996 $)

| Year, Education, and Age | Hispanic Origin | | | | | |
| | Mexican | Puerto Rican | Cuban | C & S American | Other Hispanic | Total |
|---|---|---|---|---|---|---|
| **1990** | | | | | | |
| *No Diploma* | | | | | | |
| 16-34 | 288 | 336 | 360 | 300 | 312 | 288 |
| 35-64 | 353 | 432 | 384 | 360 | 480 | 367 |
| Total | 300 | 399 | 376 | 336 | 432 | 312 |
| *12-15* | | | | | | |
| 16-34 | 372 | 480 | 473 | 360 | 432 | 384 |
| 35-64 | 576 | 547 | 487 | 480 | 553 | 553 |
| Total | 450 | 492 | 480 | 408 | 480 | 456 |
| *>= BA* | | | | | | |
| 16-34 | 529 | 706 | 613 | 660 | 600 | 600 |
| 35-64 | 840 | 960 | 840 | 720 | 819 | 810 |
| Total | 693 | 720 | 721 | 696 | 660 | 720 |
| **1996** | | | | | | |
| *No Diploma* | | | | | | |
| 16-34 | 260 | 320 | 260 | 270 | 283 | 260 |
| 35-64 | 320 | 376 | 340 | 300 | 320 | 320 |
| Total | 284 | 352 | 300 | 280 | 300 | 288 |
| *12-15* | | | | | | |
| 16-34 | 350 | 390 | 425 | 320 | 350 | 350 |
| 35-64 | 500 | 507 | 505 | 486 | 600 | 500 |
| Total | 400 | 450 | 450 | 400 | 450 | 400 |
| *>= BA* | | | | | | |
| 16-34 | 634 | 647 | 576 | 600 | 680 | 634 |
| 35-64 | 769 | 950 | 800 | 660 | 800 | 782 |
| Total | 692 | 865 | 738 | 640 | 800 | 692 |

Source: Author's tabulations of weighted data on current weekly earnings of full-time workers in Current Population Survey Merged Outgoing Rotation Groups microdata files.

## Table 7

### Median Real Full-time Weekly Earnings of Hispanic Females by Hispanic Origin, Education, & Age (1996 $)

| Year, Education, and Age | Hispanic Origin | | | | | |
|---|---|---|---|---|---|---|
| | Mexican | Puerto Rican | Cuban | C & S American | Other Hispanic | Total |
| **1990** | | | | | | |
| *No Diploma* | | | | | | |
| 16-34 | 240 | 300 | 240 | 216 | 216 | 240 |
| 35-64 | 270 | 300 | 240 | 259 | 288 | 264 |
| Total | 240 | 300 | 240 | 240 | 247 | 240 |
| *12-15* | | | | | | |
| 16-34 | 318 | 360 | 390 | 300 | 336 | 331 |
| 35-64 | 420 | 415 | 360 | 339 | 432 | 406 |
| Total | 360 | 388 | 384 | 312 | 384 | 360 |
| *>= BA* | | | | | | |
| 16-34 | 538 | 623 | 480 | 600 | 624 | 540 |
| 35-64 | 660 | 720 | 660 | 485 | 618 | 612 |
| Total | 576 | 646 | 540 | 540 | 624 | 582 |
| **1996** | | | | | | |
| *No Diploma* | | | | | | |
| 16-34 | 230 | 279 | 400 | 230 | 310 | 230 |
| 35-64 | 240 | 285 | 234 | 250 | 280 | 244 |
| Total | 230 | 280 | 234 | 240 | 280 | 240 |
| *12-15* | | | | | | |
| 16-34 | 302 | 350 | 360 | 288 | 300 | 310 |
| 35-64 | 375 | 380 | 360 | 384 | 376 | 376 |
| Total | 326 | 365 | 360 | 324 | 340 | 340 |
| *>= BA* | | | | | | |
| 16-34 | 576 | 550 | 550 | 538 | 576 | 565 |
| 35-64 | 730 | 800 | 660 | 576 | 800 | 692 |
| Total | 634 | 673 | 576 | 538 | 604 | 600 |

Source: Author's tabulations of weighted data on current weekly earnings of full-time workers in Current Population Survey Merged Outgoing Rotation Groups microdata files.

## F. By Birthplace, for Hispanics (see Tables 8 & 9)

Hispanics born outside the mainland U.S. (foreign-born) have lower wages than those born in the mainland U.S., due to their lower education levels, language problems, and lack of experience in the U.S. labor market, and because of discrimination against the foreign-born. (For example, the average Mexican immigrant in California and Texas in 1990 had completed fewer than seven years of school, while the average U.S.-born Mexican American in those states had finished high school.) Therefore, some of the differences discussed above between Latinos and Black and White non-Hispanics, and among the Latino national origin groups, may be due to the different proportions of immigrants in their populations. In 1994, the CPS began including data on place of birth, enabling one to determine the median wages of Latinos born on the mainland U.S. and abroad.* In 1996, the median wage of Hispanic men who were born on the U.S. mainland was $442, 38% more than the wage of men born abroad ($320). The median wage of U.S.-born Hispanic women was $360, 29% more than the wage of for-eign-born Hispanic women ($280). The median wages of both Latinos and Latinas who were born in the U.S. declined 3% in the two years between 1994 and 1996, while the wages of those born abroad remained stable.

### Table 8

### Median Real Full-time Weekly Earnings of Hispanic Males by Nativity (1996 $)

| | Where Born | | |
|---|---|---|---|
| Year | U.S. Mainland | Abroad | Total |
| 1994 | 455 | 318 | 366 |
| 1996 | 442 | 320 | 360 |

Source: Author's tabulations of weighted data on current weekly earnings of full-time workers in Current Population Survey Merged Outgoing Rotation Groups microdata files. Nativity before 1994 is not available.

* When referring to place of birth, "U.S." means the mainland United States, and "abroad" includes Puerto Rico and other U.S. territories, as well as foreign countries.

## Table 9

### Median Real Full-time Weekly Earnings of Hispanic Females by Nativity (1996 $)

| | Where Born | | |
| --- | --- | --- | --- |
| Year | U.S. Mainland | Abroad | Total |
| 1994 | 371 | 285 | 318 |
| 1996 | 360 | 280 | 320 |

Source: Author's tabulations of weighted data on current weekly earnings of full-time workers in Current Population Survey Merged Outgoing Rotation Groups microdata files. Nativity before 1994 is not available.

### G. By Birthplace, Age, and Education (see Tables 10 & 11)

Latina college graduates and young Latina high school dropouts had rising wages between 1994 and 1996 regardless of where they were born, as did U.S.-born male college graduates.

### U.S.-born

Among U.S. mainland-born Hispanics, the only age-education groups whose median real weekly wages rose from 1994 to 1996 were men and women with BA or higher degrees and young female high school dropouts. Among mainland-born Hispanic college graduates, young females' wages increased by 10% (from $508 to $561), those of mature females increased by 8% (from $673 to $730), and those of males increased by 6% (from $635 to $673 for young men and $814 to $865 for mature men). The wages of young mainland-born Hispanic female dropouts rose by 8% (from $258 to $279).

At the same time, most other age-education groups experienced declines of 5-6% (from $296 to $280 for young male dropouts, $371 to $352 for mature male dropouts, $400 to $380 for young males with 12-15 years of school, $339 to $320 for young females with 12-15 years of school, and $423 to $400 for mature females with 12-15 years of school). The wages of mature mainland-born Latino males who had 12-15 years of education declined by 1% (from $582 to $575). That of mature Hispanic female dropouts remained constant at $262.

## Foreign-born

Women with BA or higher degrees and young females who did not finish high school were the only age-education groups among Hispanic immigrants whose wages rose between 1994 and 1996. Among foreign-born Latina college graduates (including island-born Puerto Ricans), the median real weekly wage of young women increased by 18% (from $489 to $576) and of mature women by 13% (from $561 to $634). The wages of young foreign-born Latinas with less than 12 years of schooling rose by 4% (from $212 to $220). The wages of foreign-born Hispanic males who did not complete high school remained virtually the same during 1994-96, $260 for young men and $320 for mature men.

Meanwhile, the wages of Hispanic immigrants in other age-education-gender groups declined. Wages of males with a BA or higher degree fell the most, by 9% (from $508 to $462) for young men and by 12% (from $753 to $660) for mature men. Among those with 12-15 years of education, wages declined by 6% for young males (from $339 to $320), 5% for mature females (from $366 to $346), 4% for mature males (from $482 to $462), and 2% for young females (from $296 to $290). Wages of mature females without a high school diploma declined by 6% (from $254 to $240).

## Table 10

### Median Real Full-time Weekly Earnings of Males
### by Nativity, Race/Ethnicity, Age, & Education (1996 $)

|  | Where Born and Race U.S. Mainland | | | |
|---|---|---|---|---|
| Year, Age, and Education | Hispanic | Black NH | White NH | Total |
| **1994** | | | | |
| *16-34* | | | | |
| No diploma | 296 | 265 | 318 | 318 |
| 12-15 | 400 | 339 | 427 | 423 |
| >= BA | 635 | 529 | 662 | 651 |
| Total | 389 | 343 | 468 | 448 |
| *35-64* | | | | |
| No diploma | 371 | 371 | 455 | 423 |
| *12-15* | 582 | 508 | 635 | 633 |
| >= BA | 814 | 762 | 997 | 977 |
| Total | 570 | 508 | 716 | 688 |
| **1996** | | | | |
| *16-34* | | | | |
| No diploma | 280 | 255 | 312 | 300 |
| 12-15 | 380 | 340 | 438 | 412 |
| >= BA | 673 | 553 | 654 | 653 |
| Total | 385 | 346 | 470 | 450 |
| *35-64* | | | | |
| No diploma | 352 | 360 | 451 | 420 |
| 12-15 | 575 | 480 | 640 | 604 |
| >= BA | 865 | 761 | 1000 | 972 |
| Total | 550 | 480 | 702 | 680 |

*Continued on next page*

## Table 10 (Cont.)

## Median Real Full-time Weekly Earnings of Males
## by Nativity, Race/Ethnicity, Age, & Education (1996 $)

| Year, Age, and Education | Where Born and Race Abroad | | | |
|---|---|---|---|---|
| | Hispanic | Black NH | White NH | Total |
| **1994** | | | | |
| *16-34* | | | | |
| No diploma | 262 | 265 | 318 | 265 |
| 12-15 | 339 | 318 | 423 | 347 |
| >= BA | 508 | 488 | 733 | 635 |
| Total | 296 | 339 | 508 | 318 |
| *35-64* | | | | |
| No diploma | 318 | 296 | 508 | 318 |
| 12-15 | 482 | 476 | 635 | 529 |
| >= BA | 753 | 705 | 1017 | 916 |
| Total | 381 | 476 | 733 | 488 |
| **1996** | | | | |
| *16-34* | | | | |
| No diploma | 260 | 314 | 320 | 262 |
| 12-15 | 320 | 362 | 422 | 350 |
| >= BA | 462 | 538 | 690 | 630 |
| Total | 290 | 375 | 500 | 320 |
| *35-64* | | | | |
| No diploma | 320 | 320 | 404 | 320 |
| 12-15 | 462 | 450 | 650 | 519 |
| >= BA | 660 | 769 | 1000 | 898 |
| Total | 375 | 480 | 722 | 478 |

Source: Author's tabulations of weighted data on current weekly earnings of full-time workers in Current Population Survey Merged Outgoing Rotation Groups microdata files. Nativity before 1994 is not available.

## Table 11

### Median Real Full-time Weekly Earnings of Females by Nativity, Race/Ethnicity, Age, & Education (1996 $)

| Year, Age, and Education | Where Born and Race U.S. Mainland | | | |
| --- | --- | --- | --- | --- |
| | Hispanic | Black NH | White NH | Total |
| **1994** | | | | |
| *16-34* | | | | |
| No diploma | 258 | 218 | 238 | 233 |
| 12-15 | 339 | 296 | 339 | 337 |
| >= BA | 508 | 476 | 551 | 549 |
| Total | 339 | 318 | 385 | 371 |
| *35-64* | | | | |
| No diploma | 263 | 275 | 296 | 290 |
| 12-15 | 423 | 385 | 427 | 423 |
| >= BA | 673 | 671 | 733 | 733 |
| Total | 423 | 410 | 488 | 472 |
| **1996** | | | | |
| *16-34* | | | | |
| No diploma | 279 | 210 | 226 | 228 |
| 12-15 | 320 | 300 | 340 | 326 |
| >= BA | 561 | 461 | 543 | 538 |
| Total | 332 | 315 | 384 | 365 |
| *35-64* | | | | |
| No diploma | 262 | 280 | 294 | 280 |
| 12-15 | 400 | 376 | 423 | 415 |
| >= BA | 730 | 638 | 730 | 717 |
| Total | 400 | 400 | 480 | 465 |

*Continued on next page*

## Table 11 (Cont.)

## Median Real Full-time Weekly Earnings of Females
## by Nativity, Race/Ethnicity, Age, & Education (1996 $)

| Year, Age, and Education | Where Born and Race Abroad | | | |
|---|---|---|---|---|
| | Hispanic | Black NH | White NH | Total |
| **1994** | | | | |
| *16-34* | | | | |
| No diploma | 212 | 212 | 240 | 212 |
| 12-15 | 296 | 318 | 320 | 318 |
| >= BA | 489 | 508 | 549 | 529 |
| Total | 265 | 345 | 391 | 305 |
| *35-64* | | | | |
| No diploma | 254 | 238 | 349 | 254 |
| 12-15 | 366 | 371 | 427 | 397 |
| >= BA | 561 | 651 | 713 | 678 |
| Total | 296 | 375 | 468 | 371 |
| **1996** | | | | |
| *16-34* | | | | |
| No diploma | 220 | 245 | 240 | 225 |
| 12-15 | 290 | 300 | 341 | 305 |
| >= BA | 576 | 480 | 570 | 565 |
| Total | 260 | 340 | 400 | 300 |
| *35-64* | | | | |
| No diploma | 240 | 276 | 280 | 245 |
| 12-15 | 346 | 360 | 415 | 375 |
| >= BA | 634 | 600 | 730 | 692 |
| Total | 295 | 375 | 474 | 360 |

Source: Author's tabulations of weighted data on current weekly earnings of full-time workers in Current Population Survey Merged Outgoing Rotation Groups microdata files. Nativity before 1994 is not available.

## H. By Occupation (see Tables 12 – 17*)

Regardless of group or year, even low-level "white collar" workers (e.g., technical, sales, and clerical workers) have higher wages than "blue collar" workers (e.g., crafts, machine operators, and laborers), who in turn have higher wages than service workers.

### Men

Among male white-collar workers, Latinos earn the same as or more than Blacks, but less than White non-Hispanics. Among the Hispanic national origin groups, Cuban male white-collar workers had the highest median weekly wage ($576 in 1996), followed by Other Hispanic, then Puerto Ricans, then Central and South Americans. Mexican men had the lowest median weekly wage ($480). All had dropped since 1990, by 7-16%.

**Table 12**

**Median Real Full-time Weekly Earnings of Males
by Race/Ethnicity & Occupation (1996 $)**

| Year and Race | High White Collar | Low White Collar | Service | Blue Collar | Total |
|---|---|---|---|---|---|
| **1990** | | | | | |
| Hispanic | 720 | 480 | 300 | 372 | 384 |
| Black NH | 660 | 466 | 336 | 415 | 432 |
| White NH | 900 | 600 | 420 | 528 | 600 |
| Total | 875 | 600 | 384 | 480 | 576 |
| **1996** | | | | | |
| Hispanic | 680 | 426 | 288 | 332 | 360 |
| Black NH | 673 | 430 | 307 | 400 | 403 |
| White NH | 880 | 577 | 404 | 507 | 600 |
| Total | 865 | 560 | 352 | 475 | 553 |

Source: Author's tabulations of weighted data on current weekly earnings of full-time workers in Current Population Survey Merged Outgoing Rotation Groups microdata files.

---

* The samples of certain Hispanic-origin groups of workers were too small to estimate median wages reliably.

But among male blue-collar and service workers, Latinos earn less than Blacks. Puerto Ricans and Other Hispanics had the highest median wages of Hispanic male blue-collar workers ($400 in 1996), while Mexicans and Central and South Americans had the lowest ($320). Cubans were in between ($360). All blue-collar workers had declined since 1990, by 11-17%. Among male service workers, Puerto Ricans' median wage was $375 and Mexicans' and Central and South Americans' was $280 in 1996. All service workers except Cubans and Other Hispanics had declined since 1990, by 3-11%.

**Table 13**

**Median Real Full-time Weekly Earnings of Hispanic Males by Hispanic Origin & Occupation (1996 $)**

| Year and Occupation | | Hispanic Origin | | | | |
| --- | --- | --- | --- | --- | --- | --- |
| | Mexican | Puerto Rican | Cuban | C & S American | Other Hispanic | Total |
| **1990** | | | | | | |
| White Collar | 540 | 600 | 660 | 600 | 600 | 570 |
| Service | 288 | 420 | 347 | 312 | 346 | 300 |
| Blue Collar | 360 | 480 | 432 | 378 | 480 | 372 |
| Total | 360 | 480 | 480 | 384 | 498 | 384 |
| **1996** | | | | | | |
| White Collar | 480 | 538 | 576 | 505 | 560 | 505 |
| Service | 280 | 375 | 415 | 280 | 350 | 288 |
| Blue Collar | 320 | 403 | 360 | 325 | 400 | 332 |
| Total | 340 | 445 | 441 | 350 | 421 | 360 |

Source: Author's tabulations of weighted data on current weekly earnings of full-time workers in Current Population Survey Merged Outgoing Rotation Groups microdata files.

Within broad occupational categories, U.S. mainland-born Latino men earned more than men born elsewhere. The difference was smallest (14%) for service workers, and largest (28%) for blue-collar workers. The median wages of both U.S. and foreign-born Hispanic male white- and blue-collar workers declined between 1994 and 1996, as did those of U.S.-born Hispanic male service workers. However, the median real wage of Hispanic male service workers who were born abroad rose.

---

### Table 14

### Median Real Full-time Weekly Earnings of Hispanic Males by Nativity & Occupation (1996 $)

| Year and Occupation | Where Born | | |
| --- | --- | --- | --- |
| | U.S. Mainland | Abroad | Total |
| **1994** | | | |
| White Collar | 561 | 508 | 529 |
| Service | 342 | 265 | 285 |
| Blue Collar | 423 | 318 | 339 |
| Total | 455 | 318 | 366 |
| **1996** | | | |
| White Collar | 550 | 468 | 505 |
| Service | 320 | 280 | 288 |
| Blue Collar | 400 | 312 | 332 |
| Total | 442 | 320 | 360 |

Source: Author's tabulations of weighted data on current weekly earnings of full-time workers in Current Population Survey Merged Outgoing Rotation Groups microdata files. Nativity before 1994 is not available.

---

Within most occupational categories, male Hispanics' wages declined more between 1990 and 1996 than Blacks' or Whites'. The exception was service workers, where Latinos' wages declined the same as Whites' and less than Blacks'. The median wage of Latino managers and professionals dropped 6% (from $720 to $680), while among

White males it dropped 2% (from $900 to $880) and among Blacks it increased 2% (from $660 to $673). The wages of Latino low-level white-collar and blue-collar workers declined 11% from 1990 to 1996 (from $480 to $426 for white collar and $372 to $332 for blue collar), while the wages of White men in these occupations declined 4% (from $600 to $577 for white collar and $528 to $507 for blue collar). The wages of Black male blue-collar workers also declined 4% (from $415 to $400), while that of Black male low-level white-collar workers declined 8% (from $466 to $430). Among male service workers, on the other hand, the median real wage of Hispanics and Whites declined 4% (from $300 to $288 for Latinos and from $420 to $404 for Whites) while the wages of Blacks declined 9% (from $336 to $307).

Thus, the White-Hispanic gaps among men within broad occupational groups generally grew from 1990 to 1996, and Latino white-collar workers lost their advantage over Black men. Latino blue-collar and service workers earned less than Black men in those occupations in both years, but the gap narrowed from 11% to 6% for service workers and widened from 10% to 17% for blue-collar workers. (Latino blue-collar workers are much more likely to be farm laborers, a lower-paid occupation than crafts, where Black men are more likely to be found.) In 1996, Latino managers and professionals earned only 1% more than Black men, whereas they had earned 9% more in 1990; and Latino low-level white-collar workers earned 1% less than Blacks, whereas they had earned 3% more in 1990. The White-Latino gap remained 29% among service workers, but grew from 20% to 23% among male managers and professionals, from 20% to 26% among low-level white-collar workers, and from 30% to 35% among blue-collar workers.

### Women

Hispanic women earn less than Blacks and Whites in all occupational categories. Among Latina white-collar workers, in 1996, Cubans had the highest median wage ($480), followed by Puerto Ricans ($425), Central and South Americans ($415), Other Hispanics ($400), and Mexicans ($375). The Other Hispanic women's wage had dropped 11% since 1990, when they were in first place. Wages of Mexican and Central and South American female blue-collar and service workers were about $250 in 1996. For the blue-collar workers, this represented a 3-7% decline since 1990; while the service workers' wage had risen 0-4%.

## Table 15

## Median Real Full-time Weekly Earnings of Females
## by Race/Ethnicity & Occupation (1996 $)

| Year and Race | Occupation | | | | |
|---|---|---|---|---|---|
| | High White Collar | Low White Collar | Service | Blue Collar | Total |
| **1990** | | | | | |
| Hispanic | 570 | 360 | 240 | 264 | 330 |
| Black NH | 600 | 384 | 277 | 300 | 360 |
| White NH | 600 | 393 | 270 | 336 | 421 |
| Total | 600 | 390 | 270 | 319 | 414 |
| **1996** | | | | | |
| Hispanic | 538 | 347 | 247 | 250 | 320 |
| Black NH | 550 | 370 | 260 | 300 | 360 |
| White NH | 623 | 400 | 276 | 340 | 442 |
| Total | 611 | 392 | 266 | 320 | 415 |

Source: Author's tabulations of weighted data on current weekly earnings of full-time workers in Current Population Survey Merged Outgoing Rotation Groups microdata files.

## Table 16

### Median Real Full-time Weekly Earnings of Hispanic Females by Hispanic Origin & Occupation (1996 $)

| Year and Occupation | Hispanic Origin | | | | | |
|---|---|---|---|---|---|---|
| | Mexican | Puerto Rican | Cuban | C & S American | Other Hispanic | Total |
| **1990** | | | | | | |
| White Collar | 396 | 420 | 432 | 406 | 450 | 415 |
| Service | 240 | 252 | 288 | 240 | 276 | 240 |
| Blue Collar | 270 | 300 | 240 | 258 | 254 | 264 |
| Total | 312 | 370 | 378 | 300 | 384 | 330 |
| **1996** | | | | | | |
| White Collar | 375 | 425 | 480 | 415 | 400 | 400 |
| Service | 240 | 280 | 300 | 250 | 265 | 247 |
| Blue Collar | 250 | 280 | 234 | 250 | 300 | 250 |
| Total | 300 | 375 | 400 | 304 | 360 | 320 |

Source: Author's tabulations of weighted data on current weekly earnings of full-time workers in Current Population Survey Merged Outgoing Rotation Groups microdata files.

Among Hispanic female white-collar workers, the median weekly wage did not vary by nativity in 1996. The wages of U.S.-born women had declined since 1994, while those of the foreign-born remained virtually constant. But mainland-born Hispanic female blue-collar and service workers' median weekly wages were higher in 1996 than the wages of those born abroad. The former had increased since 1994, while the latter had declined or remained constant.

**Table 17**

**Median Real Full-time Weekly Earnings of Hispanic Females
by Nativity & Occupation (1996 $)**

| Year and Occupation | Where Born | | |
| --- | --- | --- | --- |
| | U.S. Mainland | Abroad | Total |
| **1994** | | | |
| White Collar | 420 | 397 | 410 |
| Service | 249 | 238 | 241 |
| Blue Collar | 309 | 254 | 256 |
| Total | 371 | 285 | 318 |
| **1996** | | | |
| White Collar | 392 | 400 | 400 |
| Service | 260 | 240 | 247 |
| Blue Collar | 323 | 240 | 250 |
| Total | 360 | 280 | 320 |

Source: Author's tabulations of weighted data on current weekly earnings of full-time workers in Current Population Survey Merged Outgoing Rotation Groups microdata files. Nativity before 1994 is not available.

Hispanic female white-collar workers' wages dropped the same or less than those of Blacks from 1990 to 1996, while those of Whites rose. Latina blue-collar workers' wages also dropped, while those of Blacks and Whites stayed the same. On the other hand, Latina service workers gained even more than Whites, while Blacks' wages fell. Among women managers and professionals, Latinas' median real wage dropped 6% (from $570 to $538), while Blacks' declined 8% (from $600 to $550) and Whites' rose 4% (from $600 to $623). Among female low-level white-collar workers, Hispanics' and Blacks' wages both declined by 4% (from $360 to $347 for Latinas and from $384 to $370 for Blacks), while the wages of Whites rose 2% (from $393 to $400). The wages of Hispanic female blue-collar workers dropped by 5% (from $264 to $250), while the wages of Blacks stayed at $300 and those of Whites increased just 1% (from $336 to $340). Hispanic female service workers gained 3% (from $240 to $247), while Whites gained 2% (from $270 to $276) and Blacks declined 6% (from $277 to $260).

Thus, Latinas earned less than Black or White women in the same occupational category, and the White-Latina gaps mostly widened between 1990 and 1996. Although the White-Latina gap among service workers remained 11%, it increased from 5% to 14% among managers and professionals, from 8% to 13% among low-level white-collar workers, and from 21% to 26% among blue-collar workers. The Black-Latina gap among managers and professionals narrowed from 5% to 2%, and that among service workers narrowed from 13% to 5%; but in both 1990 and 1996, Latina low-level white-collar workers earned 6% less than Blacks, and the Black-Latina gap among blue-collar workers widened from 12% to 17%.

## IV. Explanations of Wage Gaps and Trends

**The wage differences between Hispanics and Black and White non-Hispanics may be due to differences in composition of these ethnic groups within the broad categories used in this chapter.** When we compare within broad age-education levels, for example, Latinos are likely to have dropped out of school earlier, on average, and to be younger than the average Black or White within the "young high school dropout" grouping. The overwhelming majority of Blacks and Whites were born in the U.S., where school attendance is compulsory until at least age 16. This means they have at least ten years of schooling, while a substantial fraction of Hispanics are immigrants with less than an eighth-grade education. Indeed, the average Mexican immigrant in California and Texas in 1990 had less than a seventh-grade education. At the other end of the spectrum, among college graduates, Latinos are less likely than Whites to have advanced professional degrees. Age and education differences may also help explain why the wages of Cubans and Puerto Ricans are so much higher than those of Mexicans and Central and South Americans. The proportion of foreign-born also helps to explain wage gaps. The continuing influx of immigrants with little education, by changing the composition and therefore the overall averages for the Mexican American and overall Hispanic populations, obscures what is happening to the education and earnings levels of U.S.-born Latinos. Quite apart from the compositional effect of immigration, the educational attainment and wages of Latinos are affected by school quality, school financing, financial aid policies, and other factors that encourage (or discourage) completing high school, continuing to college, and thus increasing earning power.

Training programs and anti-discrimination policies also provide opportunities for both U.S.-born and immigrant Latinos to move into higher-paying occupations.

Immigrants suffer from other handicaps in the U.S. labor market besides low education levels, among them lack of fluency in English and lack of access to the networks and contacts that U.S. natives have (see Meléndez and Falcón, Chapter 7, for a discussion of social networks). In addition, limited access to English-language programs, as well as employment discrimination against those perceived to be "foreign," are also factors in their labor market experiences (see Grenier and Cattan, Chapter 4, and Morales, Chapter 2, for explanations of these points). With the exception of employment discrimination, these problems diminish with time in the U.S., so that groups with relatively little recent immigration – Puerto Ricans, for example – would tend to have rising wages over time, relative to groups with large continuing inflows.

Furthermore, studies suggest that discrimination against Hispanics increased after the Immigration Reform and Control Act was enacted in 1986, since some employers' fear of sanctions for hiring undocumented immigrants has caused them to avoid hiring Latinos in general.[2]

Differences in educational experiences also help to explain the wage gaps between Hispanics, Blacks, and Whites within broad occupational groupings. Other factors that may account for some of the wage differences between Latinos and other groups are the quality of education, the particular subjects studied, and the amount and type of training received on the job. Overall, Latinos and Blacks, who tend to live in large cities and be poor, have less access to good schools than do Whites in the suburbs. They then are less likely to get jobs in industries that offer good training programs and promotion opportunities. Insofar as Latino and Black male college graduates disproportionately prepare for the lower-paid human service professions, such as teaching and social work, their average earnings will be lower than those of Whites.[3]

Another reason why wages may differ between Latinos and other ethnic groups, and among the Latino national origin groups, and why the wage gaps may change over time, is that the Latino groups are concentrated in particular regions of the U.S. For the most part, Puerto Ricans continue to reside primarily in the Northeast, Cubans in Florida, and Mexicans in the Southwest. Blacks are more likely than Latinos to be in the rest of the South and the Midwest, and less likely to be in the West. Wage levels are generally higher in the Northeast than in the Southeast and Southwest, which would help explain Puerto Ricans' higher wages. Moreover, these regions do not all undergo economic expansions and downturns at the same time. Therefore, one group may be experiencing a tight labor market that lifts its wages at the same time that another group is experiencing a regional recession.

Changes in the industrial structure and the decline of unionized jobs also affect Hispanics, Blacks, and Whites differently, insofar as they are concentrated in different occupations and industries. Furthermore, because changes that affect fewer than half of a group will not change the median, a minimum wage increase would not affect the median wage of a group directly unless 50% of the group were earning less than the new minimum wage (which was not the case for any group examined in this chapter). But it could have a "ripple" effect on wages not far above the minimum.

Beyond these factors that differ across ethnic groups, Hispanics have been caught in the same changes in the U.S. wage structure since 1990 as other groups. For reasons that are probably related to the pace and type of technological change, the continuing decline of unionization, and the deterioration of the purchasing power of the minimum wage, wages have become more unequal in the U.S. since the late 1970s. This growing inequality has taken the form of increasing returns to education and work experience, as well as of increasing inequality among workers of the same age, education, occupation, industry, etc. The wages of workers with less than a college education have fallen dramatically, carrying groups with below-average education levels, such as Hispanics, downward on average, too. At the same time, persons with college and advanced professional degrees have experienced rapidly-rising wages, and highly-educated Hispanics have benefited from this trend.

## V. Conclusions and Policy Implications

We have seen that wages of Hispanics were lower in 1996 than in 1990, except for those of the college-educated and of females in service occupations. In a continuation of the trend that began in the late 1970s and that has affected all ethnic groups in the U.S., wages of Latinos without college degrees deteriorated until at least 1994. There is some evidence of an upturn since 1994 as the labor market has tightened, but wages of high school graduates and dropouts have not yet regained their 1990 level, and it is too soon to tell whether the apparent improvement is more than a sampling variation. The bright spot in this picture is that Hispanic college graduates' wages have improved since 1990, even more than Blacks' and White non-Hispanics'. As a long-run strategy for raising Latinos' wages, higher college attendance and completion rates are essential. This highlights the importance of access to college and financial aid for young low-income Hispanics.

It is not clear how the median wages of less-educated Latinos can be raised. Making it easier to organize unions would help those who retain or obtain higher-paid unionized jobs, but employers might employ fewer workers and raise hiring qualifications in response to wage increases. Thus, unionization could mean that some less-skilled Latinos would find that their job opportunities had deteriorated. Increasing the minimum wage also may result in fewer jobs for low-skilled workers, while improving the wages of those who retain jobs at the new minimum. Moreover, the federal minimum wage in 1990 was only $3.80 ($4.56 in 1996 dollars); for most of 1996 it was $4.25. (It was raised to $4.75 on October 1, 1996 and to $5.15 on October 1, 1997.) At 40 hours per week, a minimum wage job, therefore, paid only $182 per week (in 1996 dollars) in 1990 and $175 per week on average during 1996. This is about 85% of the median wage of the lowest-earning Latino subgroup examined in this chapter – young foreign-born female high school dropouts – half of whom earned more than $212 per week in 1994. Thus, at best, a minimum wage increase would benefit a minority of low-skilled Latinos, without raising their median wage.

Barring a dramatic unforeseen improvement in the demand for workers with a high school education or less, we cannot look to the labor market to solve the problem of low and deteriorating wages for this large group of Latinos. Redistribution of income via tax relief and transfer payments is perhaps the only way to improve the living standards of workers with a high school education or less. This calls for increasing the refundable Earned Income Tax Credit (EITC), together with greater efforts to make sure that all eligible workers receive the amount due them. In addition, credits to offset low-wage workers' Social Security (FICA) and other payroll taxes would give them greater take-home pay without their having to rely on wage increases.

# NOTES

1. U.S. Bureau of the Census, *Money Income in the United States: 1996*. Current Population Reports Series P-60, No. 197. Washington, DC: U.S. Government Printing Office, September 1997.

2. For a discussion of increased employment discrimination due to IRCA, see U.S. General Accounting Office, *Immigration Reform: Employer Sanctions and the Question of Discrimination*, Washington, DC: March 1990; and *Unfinished Business: The Immigration Reform and Control Act of 1986*, Washington, DC: National Council of La Raza, December 1990.

3. Author's tabulations of the 1994-96 CPS files show that 11% of White non-Hispanic, 13% of Hispanic, and 17% of Black males with a BA or higher degrees were in the lower-paid human service professions (teachers, counselors, social workers, recreation workers, religious workers, nurses, physicians' assistants, dieticians, and therapists). For male college graduates, the average full-time weekly salary in these professions was 15% lower than the average across all other occupations. Among female college graduates, these human service professions paid 1.5% more than all other occupations, on average; and 32% of Latinas, 35% of White non-Hispanics, and 36% of Blacks were in these human service professions.

# 6

# Benefit Coverage for Latino and Latina Workers

**Richard Santos, Ph.D.**
*Department of Economics*
*University of New Mexico*

**Patricia Seitz, Ph.D.**
*Department of Arts and Sciences*
*Albuquerque Technical-Vocational Institute*

## Abstract

*Hispanics are less likely than other workers to obtain fringe benefits at the work-place. The extent of benefit coverage also varies by Hispanic group and gender; Mexican American men represented the lowest proportion (49%) and Cuban women the highest proportion (77%) of workers with private health insurance in 1995. Although about 60% of employed White men and women had access to a pension plan at work, fewer than 40% of Hispanic men and only 45% of Hispanic women had access to an employer-sponsored pension plan. Results from a 1993 national survey of young adults ages 28-36 show that among full-time employed Hispanics, women had greater access than men to employment benefits such as dental insurance, life insurance, profit-sharing, training and education, flex-time, maternity/paternity leave, and child care. With some exceptions, Whites were more likely to have access to these types of benefits than Hispanics. Other characteristics of workers associated with greater benefit coverage include unionization, higher levels of educational attainment, and larger establishment size. The disparity in benefit coverage by worker group suggests that the economic situation of Hispanic workers relative to that of other workers extends beyond differences in earnings.*

# I. Introduction

Nearly 13 million Hispanics were employed in 1997, representing about 10% of workers in the nation.[1] For most of these workers, jobs are the major source of income and provide access to a wide array of economic and social benefits. But jobs are not comparable in remuneration and benefits; among full-time workers ages 16 and older, Hispanic men earned 62% and Hispanic women earned 53% of the median weekly earnings earned by White men in 1997.[2] As such, the unfavorable earnings situation of Hispanic workers has received considerable attention; significantly less is known about other aspects of compensation, i.e., "fringe" benefits. Of note, wages and salaries accounted for 72% of private employer compensation costs; paid leave (6.4%), supplemental pay (2.8%), life, disability, and health insurance (6.5%), retirement/savings (3.1%), legally-required benefits (9.1%), and other benefits (0.2%) accounted for 28% of compensation costs in 1997.[3] With the exception of private health insurance coverage, the extent and type of benefits available to employed Hispanics have not been studied.

In this chapter, we provide an overview of the employment benefits for Hispanic workers and compare their benefit coverage with the status of White and African American workers.

Prior to assessing the level of fringe benefit coverage among working Hispanics, it is important to provide some general observations about the nature of employment benefits.

First, unlike those in other industrialized nations, workers in the United States rely more on the labor market than on government mandates to provide numerous social and health benefits. Benefits, therefore, are not universal in the U.S. – hence, the adjective "fringe." Access to benefits is largely dependent on employment and may cease upon job termination. Although employers are legally required by government to provide some benefits, including Social Security and unemployment compensation, benefits legislation is a maze of state and federal regulations. More than 700 state laws collectively govern health insurance provisions alone.[4] This disparity in legally-mandated coverage presents dilemmas for researchers. More important, because employers often do not offer benefits without encouragement from the government, the regulations translate to differential access based on state of residence.

Second, access to health care insurance, pension savings vehicles, life insurance, vacations, sick leave, education and training opportunities, and other benefits are primarily determined by one's employment situation. Persons in well-paying primary-sector jobs are more apt to enjoy benefit coverage than workers in low-wage secondary-sector jobs. Primary-sector jobs are often in industries that are large and fairly stable; and by virtue of size, these sectors are able to offer numerous benefits that small employers cannot afford. To illustrate, the cost of benefits ranges from two dollars per hour for service workers to more than nine dollars per hour for managers.[5] As Chapters 1 and 2 in this book demonstrate, Latino workers are not typically located in primary-sector positions, and therefore are not likely to receive or have access to the range of fringe benefits that have become critical for financial security.

Third, fringe benefits are family benefits. Although we focus on benefit coverage for workers, it is important to remember that receipt of benefits – or, more critically, non-receipt of benefits – has far-reaching implications for the socioeconomic status and quality of life of Latino families. For example, financial access to medical services to treat diabetes and other ailments, which affect many Hispanic families, tends to depend on the worker's insurance coverage. In addition, workers' families who receive subsidized tuition for higher education, or subsidized child care through their jobs, have an advantage over other families. The well-being of Hispanic families is thus tied to the benefits available to their wage earners; access to health care, educational opportunities, and child care are essential resources for improving the economic situation of Hispanic families.

## II. Methodology

Two methodological considerations merit attention. First, systematic data collection on benefits available to workers is lacking. When data are gathered from employers (such as the Bureau of Labor Statistics establishment surveys), it is not possible to ascertain the extent of benefit coverage by race, ethnicity, or gender among workers. Of particular note, the Bureau of Labor Statistics survey excludes the federal government and agricultural sector.

Second, we must differentiate between access to benefits and utilization of benefits. The issue of access addresses whether employers make benefits available to Hispanic workers and their families. Low-wage workers, part-time workers, workers employed by companies with few employees, and those without union representation are the least likely to have access to benefits. Employers' or insurance carriers' eligibility definitions of family units, marital status, and dependents likewise affect access to benefits. Workers can also elect not to utilize certain benefits because of costs; selection of benefits thus becomes an obstacle for workers if choosing the benefit translates to lower take-home pay. Additional reasons for not selecting benefits might include: benefits are available through another family member's employment plan, the benefit is not considered important to the worker, or coverage can be obtained through a credit union or other private entities, such as insurance companies or mutual aid (community-based, self-help) organizations.

For this study, we use two major government surveys to provide a benchmark of fringe benefits among Hispanics: the 1995 March Current Population Survey (CPS) and the 1993 National Longitudinal Surveys of Youth Labor Market Experience (NLSY). Unfortunately, neither a comprehensive survey nor a uniform time period is available to examine the access to and utilization of benefits among Hispanic workers in detail. By using both the 1995 March CPS and 1993 NLSY, we can obtain estimates of benefit coverage by race, ethnicity, and gender. Problems such as identifying which family members are eligible for benefits and whether workers make use of employer benefits are not completely eliminated. To differentiate better between access and use of benefits, results from other studies are used, where applicable, to explain levels of benefits among Hispanic workers.

The chapter begins with data from the 1995 March CPS in order to determine the level of health insurance and pension coverage among workers ages 18-64. Data from the NLSY are then used to offer a comprehensive look at benefit coverage, including health insurance and pensions, and life insurance, training/education, profit-sharing, and other benefit options. The NLSY focuses on workers ages 28-36. The next section of the chapter discusses job safety risks and benefits available to workers who are injured or become unemployed. In the last section, we provide a summary and assessment of the employment benefits among Hispanic workers.

# III. Health Insurance

Among employed adults ages 18-64, Table 1 shows that 85.1% of White women and 84.0% of White men had private health insurance in March 1995, compared to 63.5% of Hispanic women and 52.7% of Hispanic men. The rate of insurance coverage for Blacks was less than that of Whites and more than that of Hispanics.

## Table 1
### Health Insurance Coverage: Employed Persons Ages 18-64, 1995
### (in percentages)

| | Private Insurance | Medicaid | Medicare | CHAMPUS* | No Health Care Insurance |
|---|---|---|---|---|---|
| **Women** | | | | | |
| Hispanic | 63.5% | 6.9% | 0.1% | 2.2% | 30.4% |
| Mexican American | 61.8 | 6.9 | 0.1 | 1.9 | 32.0 |
| Cuban | 76.7 | 5.5 | 0.6 | 3.7 | 16.9 |
| Puerto Rican | 74.0 | 10.1 | 0.4 | 3.8 | 17.9 |
| Other | 60.3 | 6.1 | — | 1.9 | 34.6 |
| Black | 72.7 | 8.7 | 0.6 | 3.9 | 19.7 |
| White | 85.1 | 3.3 | 0.3 | 3.2 | 11.8 |
| **Men** | | | | | |
| Hispanic | 52.7 | 3.8 | 0.2 | 1.7 | 43.7 |
| Mexican American | 49.1 | 4.2 | 0.1 | 1.7 | 47.0 |
| Cuban | 74.2 | 2.3 | 1.9 | 1.2 | 23.9 |
| Puerto Rican | 70.0 | 4.5 | — | 4.0 | 25.3 |
| Other | 53.8 | 2.7 | — | 1.2 | 43.5 |
| Black | 71.2 | 3.2 | 0.7 | 4.1 | 25.3 |
| White | 84.0 | 1.8 | 0.2 | 3.1 | 14.2 |

* CHAMPUS is the Civilian Health and Medical Program of the Uniformed Services, the health coverage offered for military dependents.

Note: Persons can be classified in more than one category.

Source: Current Population Survey; data are weighted.

For Hispanics, private health insurance coverage is lowest among Mexican Americans and persons of "other" Hispanic origin.[6] Cubans, irrespective of gender, were the most likely to have health insurance among Hispanics, although their incidence of coverage (76.7% for women and 74.2% for men) was lower than that for Whites. Private insurance coverage for employed Puerto Rican men and women is comparable to that of Cubans. The observation is significant because the conventional economic yardstick generally shows that Puerto Ricans exhibit a disadvantaged economic status which tends to be more similar to that of Mexican Americans than to the more favorable situation of Cubans.

Most adults obtain private health insurance at the workplace because group coverage allows cost-sharing by employers; more than 90% of employed workers who had health coverage listed in their name obtained the insurance through their employer.

Table 1 also indicates that public insurance plays a minimal role in providing health insurance to employed workers; fewer than 5% of employed men, irrespective of race or ethnicity, were covered by Medicaid in 1995. For employed women, Medicaid coverage ranges from 3.3% for Whites to 10.1% for Puerto Ricans. In essence, Medicaid is not an option for most able adults, and the higher public insurance coverage among employed women is probably due, in part, to poverty and the presence of children. Furthermore, Medicare is designed for persons age 65 and older or those with special medical needs (e.g., renal dialysis) and, in fact, fewer than 2% of adults ages 18-64 were covered by Medicare. CHAMPUS is another type of government insurance available to dependents of military service personnel or those retired from the military; 4% or fewer of employed adults were covered by CHAMPUS. For employed Hispanic workers, Medicare, Medicaid, and CHAMPUS are not significant sources of health insurance, although 10.1% of Puerto Rican women, 8.7% of Black women, and 6.9% of Mexican American women secured Medicaid coverage.

Table 1 indicates that 43.7% of employed Hispanic men and 30.4% of employed Hispanic women did not have either private or public health insurance, i.e., were uninsured in 1995. For Whites, the uninsured rates were 11.8% for women and 14.2% for men; the rates for Blacks were 19.7% for women and 25.3% for men.

Among Hispanics, Cuban women and Puerto Rican women were the most likely to have some type of health insurance coverage, reflected in uninsured rates of 16.9% and 17.9%, respectively, in 1995. The effective combination of private and public insurance coverage most likely contributes to the low proportion of uninsured Puerto Rican women.

Close to one-half (47.0%) of Mexican American men and nearly one-fourth (23.9% and 25.3%, respectively) of Cuban and Puerto Rican men were uninsured.

The weak link for Hispanic workers between private health insurance and the workplace, especially for Mexican American men, is troubling. Research suggests that low family income constrains the purchase of health insurance for Hispanics.[7] A link between income and insurance is also implied by Fronstin et al. (1997); wage differences accounted for about 23% of the insurance disparity between Mexican American and Cuban men for 1988-1993.[8] Nevertheless, it is estimated that 60% of coverage differences between Hispanics and other workers cannot be explained by conventional variables (e.g., education, income, state of residence, firm size, industry, or occupation).[9] Furthermore, few studies have addressed the effects of changes in the economy, such as the increase in part-time work, fewer fringe benefits given by firms, and the growth of low-wage jobs, on the insurance situation of Hispanics. However, some scholars suggest that the lack of insurance has been compounded by these economic conditions.[10]

## IV. Retirement Benefits

Table 2 shows the extent of pension coverage among adults ages 18-64 in the 1995 March CPS. About 60% of Whites and Blacks had employer- or union-sponsored pension plans that year.

For Hispanics, the availability of pension plans was dramatically less than for Whites or Blacks; only 37.1% of Hispanic men and 45.0% of Hispanic women had retirement programs available. Among Hispanics, the lowest rates were for Cuban men and women and Mexican American men; Puerto Rican men and women had the greatest access to pension coverage from an employer.

Gender is not associated with differential access to retirement programs; that is, the relative percentage of men and women with employer- or union-sponsored pensions is fairly uniform within the racial/ethnic groups shown in Table 2. Mexican Americans are the exception; 34.8% of men versus 46.3% of women had access to pensions through work.

**Table 2**

**Pension Coverage:  Employed Persons ages 18-64, 1995**

| | Pct. with Pension Plan offered by Employer or Union | Pct. with Coverage of Those with Employer-/ Union-Pension Plan |
|---|---|---|
| **Women** | | |
| Hispanic | 45.0% | 70.5% |
| Mexican American | 46.3 | 70.9 |
| Cuban | 36.7 | 77.8 |
| Puerto Rican | 52.8 | 73.3 |
| Other | 40.7 | 66.7 |
| Black | 61.4 | 74.4 |
| White | 58.8 | 76.8 |
| **Men** | | |
| Hispanic | 37.1 | 74.8 |
| Mexican American | 34.8 | 74.1 |
| Cuban | 36.2 | 85.4 |
| Puerto Rican | 52.3 | 76.5 |
| Other | 39.3 | 74.1 |
| Black | 58.8 | 80.2 |
| White | 59.9 | 84.2 |

Source: Current Population Survey; data are weighted.

The vast majority of workers, irrespective of race or gender, elected to enroll in pension plans when offered, although women opt slightly less frequently for pension coverage than men.  Cuban men (85.4%) and White men (84.2%) were foremost in pension participation and the lowest participation rates were for Mexican American women (70.9%) and "other" Hispanic women (66.7%).  More research is necessary to assess why workers elect not to join pension programs.

Analysts often liken retirement income to a three-legged stool, with income shares derived from (1) private pensions and Social Security, (2) earnings, and (3) assets, such as savings and dividends. For workers who retire with limited resources, public assistance (e.g., welfare, food stamps, and Medicaid) constitutes a fourth potential source of income. Research on these income sources paints a less-than-encouraging retirement picture for Hispanics.

Because retirement income is largely dependent on labor market attachment and the type of job held when one was active in the labor force, it is not surprising that "Hispanic retirees have a less stable retirement seat on average, with two legs – pensions and assets – shorter than [those of] their White counterparts."[11] Only 12% of Hispanic women, and 25% of Hispanic men, age 65 and older have pension benefits other than Social Security.[12]

Due to the shortfall in pensions and assets, it is not uncommon for Hispanics age 65 and older to hold jobs. Of those employed in their retirement years, 13% garnered 100% of their income by continuing to work; the corresponding percentages for Blacks and Whites were 6% and 2%, respectively.[13]

Income from assets cannot compensate for the shortfall left from inadequate pension coverage and low earnings. The mean financial assets of Hispanics age 70 and over were $8,355 during 1993 and 1994, compared to $65,116 for Whites. Moreover, the gap is wider among those in their pre-retirement years[14] and, according to the 1998 Employee Benefit Research Institute (EBRI) Retirement Confidence Survey (RCS), far fewer Hispanics (37%) are currently able to set aside savings specifically targeted for retirement than Whites (66%).[15]

The difficulties of retirement planning have not escaped the Latino community. Data from the 1998 RCS show that more than one-third of Hispanics (37%), versus 13% of Whites and 26% of Blacks, are not confident that their retirement income will cover basic expenses. Retirement planning is further complicated by the lack of easy-to-understand investment information and Hispanics' lack of comfort with banks and financial institutions. Hispanics more frequently express these sentiments than either Whites or African Americans.[16]

## V. Range of Benefits Offered

Although employer benefits extend beyond health insurance and pension coverage, there is little information on the availability of alternative benefits to Hispanic workers. To explore the question, we used the 1993 NLSY, which includes information on whether the current or last employer offered nine different types of benefits: health insurance, dental insurance, life insurance, a pension plan, profit-sharing, training and education, flex-time, maternity/paternity leave, and child care.[17] The age of workers included in the survey is limited to those 28-36 years old, but the NLSY is the only source, to our knowledge, that asks individuals about a range of benefits. No data were collected on whether workers opted to acquire coverage or whether the employer paid for the benefit. Although health insurance and pensions were discussed earlier, we include statistics on these benefits for comparative purposes.

### A. Benefits by Race, Ethnicity, and Gender

Table 3 offers a snapshot of nine selected fringe benefits among full-time workers (those working 35 or more hours per week) and part-time workers (those working less than 35 hours per week) by race, ethnicity, and gender. As one would expect, the data readily show that the availability of benefits favors full-time workers. With the exception of flexible scheduling, part-time workers are less likely to have access to fringe benefits. Indeed, about two-thirds of Hispanic women (69.6%) and men (62.9%) who work part-time have access to flex-time. We do not know the extent to which flex-time is a worker benefit to accommodate family obligations, school enrollment, or second jobs, or simply an employer program to control hours of employment and payroll costs at the employer's discretion. Because most persons ages 28-36 are employed full-time, we direct our attention to these workers.

Without question, health insurance is the most common benefit offered to workers by employers. For women, maternity leave provisions are the next most frequent benefit offered, followed by life insurance and pension coverage. For men, life insurance options are ranked after health insurance, followed by dental insurance and pension plans.

Training and education are the next-most-offered benefit after pension plans; 44.4% of Hispanic men employed full-time and 56.2% of Hispanic women who worked full-time had access to training and education benefits through their employer. Flex-time, profit-sharing, and child care round out the fringe benefits extended to full-time workers.

## Table 3

## Fringe Benefits Offered by Employer:  Persons ages 28-36 in 1993
## (in percentages)

|  | Hispanic Women | Black Women | White Women | Hispanic Men | Black Men | White Men |
|---|---|---|---|---|---|---|
| **Pct. of Persons Employed** | 64.7% | 63.3% | 72.7% | 79.2% | 70.1% | 77.6% |
| Part-time | 18.9 | 18.2 | 29.4 | 7.1 | 9.3 | 6.0 |
| Full-time | 81.1 | 81.8 | 70.6 | 92.9 | 90.7 | 94.0 |
| **Health Insurance** | | | | | | |
| Part-time | 40.1 | 48.2 | 43.0 | 40.5 | 22.7 | 27.6 |
| Full-time | 81.6 | 82.4 | 86.4 | 74.0 | 74.1 | 82.2 |
| **Dental Insurance** | | | | | | |
| Part-time | 34.3 | 38.2 | 31.8 | 28.0 | 14.1 | 16.4 |
| Full-time | 67.8 | 71.5 | 65.9 | 56.9 | 58.6 | 58.8 |
| **Life Insurance** | | | | | | |
| Part-time | 22.6 | 41.5 | 34.7 | 30.7 | 16.4 | 21.1 |
| Full-time | 72.3 | 73.3 | 77.4 | 61.4 | 62.8 | 68.9 |
| **Pension Plan** | | | | | | |
| Part-time | 26.9 | 41.5 | 38.0 | 32.2 | 16.0 | 25.8 |
| Full-time | 68.8 | 69.3 | 71.3 | 54.8 | 57.6 | 63.7 |
| **Profit-Sharing** | | | | | | |
| Part-time | 13.4 | 19.0 | 17.3 | 29.2 | 13.5 | 8.9 |
| Full-time | 33.1 | 26.4 | 34.0 | 29.3 | 27.5 | 33.1 |
| **Training & Education** | | | | | | |
| Part-time | 30.1 | 30.5 | 37.1 | 24.6 | 21.9 | 16.0 |
| Full-time | 56.2 | 59.0 | 61.9 | 44.4 | 42.7 | 52.8 |
| **Flex-Time** | | | | | | |
| Part-time | 69.6 | 60.8 | 75.5 | 62.9 | 36.6 | 66.3 |
| Full-time | 49.8 | 51.7 | 52.2 | 41.4 | 42.0 | 48.6 |
| **Maternity/Paternity leave** | | | | | | |
| Part-time | 48.0 | 56.4 | 58.9 | 34.6 | 13.4 | 19.7 |
| Full-time | 79.5 | 80.2 | 84.4 | 51.9 | 53.3 | 51.9 |
| **Child Care** | | | | | | |
| Part-time | 4.6 | 5.7 | 11.5 | N/A | 2.0 | 5.5 |
| Full-time | 8.3 | 13.5 | 9.0 | 5.8 | 9.5 | 4.7 |
| N (unweighted) | 579 | 923 | 1521 | 687 | 1003 | 1871 |

Note: Full-time workers are those reporting 35 or more hours per week

Source: National Longitudinal Survey of Youth Labor Market Experience; data are weighted.

Few Hispanic men (5.8%) or women (8.3%) had access to company-provided, or reimbursement for, child care. The relative ranking of these four benefits is fairly consistent by race, ethnicity, and gender.

Although the ranking of benefits does not vary significantly by race and ethnicity, we observe marked disparities in benefit availability for Latinos, African Americans, and Whites. With few exceptions, Whites have greater access to these nine benefits than Hispanic (or Black) workers. Among full-time women workers, the differences between Whites and Hispanics are minimal, with the exception of training/education options and maternity leave. The estimates for the two populations are about five percentage points apart for each of these benefits, with White women exhibiting greater access.

Significantly larger racial/ethnic differences in benefit access are noted for men working full-time. Although the discrepancies between Hispanic and Black men are negligible, the differences between Hispanic and White men are upwards of seven to nine percentage points for some benefits (i.e., training/education, life insurance, and flextime, in addition to health care and pension coverage).

One last observation highlights the striking gender differences in benefit availability between Latino men and women. Hispanic women consistently have more access than Hispanic men to the nine benefits included in the survey. The most plausible explanation is differences in job placement, given that Hispanic women are more likely than Hispanic men to work in low-paying, but primary-sector jobs (e.g., clerical work and semi-skilled professions) that offer such benefits.

## B. Benefits by Hispanic Subgroup

Table 4 offers a closer examination of the benefit data elicited in the NLSY survey for the four Hispanic subgroups, i.e., Mexicans, Cubans, Puerto Ricans, and "other" Hispanics. All else being equal, we expect the variations in benefits by origin status to reflect the labor market status of the respective group.

In conjunction with conventional labor market indicators, such as earnings, Cubans consistently outrank Mexican, Puerto Rican, and other Hispanic workers in access to the nine selected benefits.

Traditional labor market measures would suggest further that Hispanic women enjoy

## Table 4
## Benefits Offered by Employer by Hispanic Origin Status:
## Persons ages 28-36 in 1993
## (in percentages)

| | Men | | | | Women | | | |
|---|---|---|---|---|---|---|---|---|
| | Mexican American | Cuban* | Puerto Rican | Other | Mexican American | Cuban* | Puerto Rican | Other |
| Health insurance | 70.2% | 78.2% | 75.6% | 74.4% | 80.1% | 72.4% | 64.0% | 78.9% |
| Dental insurance | 50.5 | 68.0 | 60.2 | 61.4 | 66.1 | 66.2 | 57.4 | 63.0 |
| Life insurance | 57.0 | 79.2 | 59.7 | 61.3 | 69.4 | 65.9 | 58.3 | 65.7 |
| Pension plan | 51.9 | 60.1 | 52.9 | 57.0 | 68.5 | 57.7 | 52.1 | 63.0 |
| Profit-sharing | 26.9 | 56.9 | 22.9 | 30.7 | 33.6 | 30.6 | 26.8 | 26.8 |
| Training | 39.6 | 47.6 | 47.1 | 49.7 | 55.2 | 59.4 | 39.1 | 56.1 |
| Flex-time | 46.0 | 49.6 | 28.9 | 40.1 | 54.0 | 53.3 | 43.6 | 52.5 |
| Maternity/ Paternity leave | 50.4 | 58.8 | 48.9 | 52.4 | 82.6 | 72.4 | 61.0 | 70.6 |
| Child care | 4.7 | 7.4 | 6.8 | 6.0 | 8.7 | 2.5 | 5.4 | 9.3 |
| Mean # benefits | 3.9 | 5.0 | 4.0 | 4.3 | 5.2 | 4.7 | 4.0 | 4.9 |
| Median # benefits | 4.0 | 5.0 | 5.0 | 5.0 | 6.0 | 6.0 | 4.0 | 5.0 |
| % with 0 benefits | 15.4 | 5.3 | 20.0 | 18.6 | 6.6 | 13.6 | 17.4 | 10.8 |
| Unweighted N | 411.0 | 47.0 | 95.0 | 132.0 | 339.0 | 34.0 | 90.0 | 115.0 |

* Given the small sample sizes, caution should be exercised in the interpretation of the estimates for Cuban workers.

Source: National Longitudinal Survey of Youth Labor Market Experience; data are weighted.

less-favorable benefit coverage than men, due to gender disparity in employment. This argument, though, is not supported in the descriptive data in Table 4.

Mexican American women outrank Mexican American men for the entire range of nine benefits. Although speculative, gender differences in occupational location potentially account for the higher benefit coverage of Mexican American women. The low employment/population ratios of Mexican American women also suggest that those in the labor market are more employable; in 1997, fewer than 55% of Mexican American women age 16 and older were in the civilian labor force.[18]

Women of "other" Hispanic origin outrank their male counterparts for eight of the nine benefits; profit-sharing is the exception. Gender differences in benefit coverage for Cuban and Puerto Rican men and women are mixed.

Table 4 also presents the mean and median number of benefits among the Hispanic sub-groups. Four of the eight groups had a mean of five benefits – Cuban men and women, Mexican American women, and women of "other" Hispanic origin; a mean of four benefits is observed for Puerto Rican men and women, Mexican American men, and men of "other" Hispanic origin. Of note, about one-fifth of Puerto Rican men (20.0%), a slightly lower proportion of Puerto Rican women (17.4%), and 15.4% of Mexican American men, had no benefits available to them at work. Cuban men (5.3%) and Mexican American women (6.6%) are the least likely to work for an employer who offers no benefits.

## C. Benefits by Selected Characteristics

Table 5 examines the extent of benefit access among Hispanics by selected characteristics, i.e., place of birth, education, unionization, and employer size.

The data show that foreign-born Latinos generally have less access to benefits than U.S.-born Latinos, although the disparity is modest. Differences of two to six percentage points are observed between foreign- and native-born Latino workers. Differences in benefit coverage by educational attainment are more dramatic. Simply put, persons with more years of schooling have greater access to benefits. To illustrate, from Table 5:

- Hispanics who complete high school or attend college are 1.2 and 3.3 times, respectively, more likely than those with less than 12 years of schooling to have access to these nine job benefits.

- Of particular interest, fewer than one-fourth (23%) of Latinos who did not complete high school – those who theoretically could profit the most from training – have access to company-sponsored training or subsidized education, compared to

44% of high school graduates, 58% of those with some post-secondary schooling, and 77% of Latinos who completed college.

- Only profit-sharing exhibits minimal variation by educational level, ranging from 23% for high school dropouts to 29%-37% for those who have completed high school or attended college.

Data on unionization show important positive effects on benefit coverage for Hispanics.

## Table 5

### Benefits Offered by Employer by Selected Job and Worker Characteristics: Persons ages 28-36 in 1993, Hispanics only (in percentages)

| | Nativity | | Educational attainment | | | | Covered by Collective Bargaining | | Employer size | | | |
|---|---|---|---|---|---|---|---|---|---|---|---|---|
| | U.S.-born | Foreign-born | <12 years | 12 years | 13-15 years | 16+ years | No | Yes | 1-20 | 21-100 | 101-500 | 501+ |
| Health insurance | 75 | 72 | 57 | 74 | 83 | 87 | 71 | 90 | 55 | 81 | 90 | 92 |
| Dental insurance | 60 | 57 | 40 | 58 | 67 | 76 | 54 | 81 | 35 | 65 | 78 | 85 |
| Life insurance | 64 | 58 | 47 | 59 | 74 | 79 | 60 | 75 | 39 | 69 | 82 | 88 |
| Pension plan | 59 | 55 | 38 | 56 | 68 | 76 | 53 | 80 | 34 | 66 | 78 | 78 |
| Profit-sharing | 30 | 30 | 22 | 29 | 37 | 29 | 32 | 23 | 19 | 29 | 43 | 47 |
| Training | 49 | 44 | 23 | 44 | 58 | 77 | 45 | 58 | 32 | 47 | 61 | 74 |
| Flex-time | 47 | 46 | 34 | 43 | 57 | 57 | 48 | 41 | 45 | 48 | 48 | 53 |
| Maternity/Paternity leave | 62 | 60 | 47 | 61 | 71 | 70 | 59 | 75 | 38 | 71 | 80 | 82 |
| Child care | 6 | 8 | 4 | 7 | 6 | 9 | 7 | 6 | 3 | 5 | 8 | 18 |
| N (unweighted) | 957 | 309 | 250 | 555 | 308 | 151 | 975 | 259 | 577 | 384 | 244 | 158 |
| % within category | 76 | 24 | 20 | 44 | 24 | 12 | 79 | 21 | 42 | 28 | 18 | 12 |

Source: National Longitudinal Survey of Youth Labor Market Experience; data are weighted.

Persons covered by collective bargaining agreements (i.e., union contracts) are 1.2 to 1.5 times more likely to secure benefits than workers without collective bargaining coverage. Ninety percent of union workers, for example, have health insurance, compared to 71% of non-union workers. Profit-sharing and flexible scheduling are exceptions to the higher coverage among union workers. One-third of non-union workers (32%) can tap into profit-sharing, compared to slightly fewer than one-fourth of union workers (23%); and almost one-half of those without union contracts (48%) have flex-time options versus two-fifths of union workers (41%). One explanation for these exceptions is that unions have historically been more eager to rely on negotiated or specified benefits within a contract rather than on management's ability to make profits or to maintain flexibility in arranging work time.

As for the size of an employer, Hispanics in smaller firms are especially disadvantaged in terms of benefit coverage. Consider dental, retirement, and training/education benefits in Table 5; about one-third of Hispanics in establishments with 20 or fewer employees have access to these options, compared to more than three-fourths of those in establishments with more than 500 or more employees. Of note, about 18 of 100 Hispanics in the largest firms have access to employer-sponsored child care, compared to three to five of 100 Hispanics in smaller firms.

To conclude, it is significant that the majority of Hispanics in the age range represented in Table 5 have minimal education (i.e., 12 or fewer years), are not unionized workers, and are working in smaller companies. Hence, the benefits' advantages associated with education, collective bargaining, and employer size do not have a sizable impact on the Hispanic community.

## VI. Risks and Job Loss Benefits

The disparity in benefit coverage among Hispanic workers reflects only part of the job-outcomes picture. Hispanic workers also bear a disproportionate share of hazardous working conditions and disability risks. Hispanic workers lost a median of six days of work in 1995 due to non-fatal occupational injuries and illnesses; the median for Black and White workers was five days.[19]

Table 6, derived from the CPS, offers illustrative data on the distribution of Hispanics in jobs with higher-than-average fatality rates. The most apparent conclusion is that Hispanic workers, both men and women, are more often employed in occupations with high fatal-

**Table 6**

**Percentage of Persons in Most Hazardous Occupational Categories
by Race/Ethnicity and Gender, 1995**

| | Fatality Rate* | Hispanic Men | Black Men | White Men | Hispanic Women | Black Women | White Women |
|---|---|---|---|---|---|---|---|
| **Protective service** | 14 | 2.0% | 4.6% | 2.7% | 0.6% | 1.8% | 0.4% |
| **Farming, forestry, & fishing** | 23 | 7.8 | 2.0 | 3.5 | 1.7 | 0.1 | 1.1 |
| Farmworkers, including supervisors | 30 | 3.3 | 0.8 | 0.5 | 0.7 | 0.0 | 0.1 |
| Forestry & logging | 90 | 0.1 | 0.1 | 0.2 | — | — | 0.0 |
| **Precision production, craft, & repair** | 8 | 20.3 | 14.0 | 19.6 | 3.6 | 2.4 | 1.9 |
| Construction trades | 12 | 9.1 | 5.3 | 7.6 | 0.2 | 0.1 | 0.2 |
| **Operators, fabricators, & laborers** | 11 | 19.1 | 22.8 | 13.4 | 11.3 | 9.2 | 5.2 |
| Transportation & material moving occupations** | 22 | 7.0 | 11.0 | 6.5 | 0.6 | 1.2 | 1.0 |
| **Handlers, equipment operators, helpers & laborers** | 13 | 10.5 | 10.1 | 3.9 | 2.6 | 1.7 | 1.3 |
| Construction laborers | 39 | 3.0 | 1.8 | 0.8 | 0.1 | 0.1 | 0.0 |
| Laborers, except construction | 16 | 2.3 | 2.5 | 1.5 | 0.9 | 0.5 | 0.4 |
| **Total** | 5 | 59.2 | 53.1 | 43.6 | 19.7 | 15.3 | 9.9 |

* Fatalities per 100,000 employed workers; taken from Table 2 in Guy Toscano and Janice Windau, 1997, "National Census of Fatal Occupational Injuries, 1995," pp. 1-12 in U.S. Department of Labor, Bureau of Labor Statistics, *Fatal Workplace Injuries in 1995: A Collection of Data and Analysis*. Washington, DC: USGPO. The fatality rate across all occupations is five per 100,000.
**Includes truck drivers, taxicab drivers, and so forth.
Note: Universe includes any person reporting an occupation.

Source: Current Population Survey; data are weighted.

ity rates. Fully three-fifths of Latinos (59.2%) and one-fifth of Latinas (19.7%) work in the five occupational categories that feature exceptionally dangerous working conditions. Notably, the percentages for both Latinos and Latinas are markedly larger than those for White and Black workers, as shown in Table 6. Specific occupations with high fatality rates include construction trades, in which 9.1% of Hispanic men are employed, transportation and material moving jobs (7.0%), and construction labor (3.0%).

The results for farmworkers, especially for men, are noteworthy. More Hispanics work in farming, fishing, and forestry than Black or White workers – 7.8% of Hispanic men and 1.7% of Hispanic women – and these occupations have a fatality rate more than 400% higher than the average across all occupations. The dangers of agricultural work are reinforced when one considers that almost 40% of the injury and illness cases among agricultural workers that prompted time off from the job involved Hispanic workers.[20] Moreover, data on fatalities and injuries represent a serious understatement of the extent of job risks, as almost 300,000 farmworkers suffer pesticide poisoning annually.[21]

What is the recourse for Hispanics injured on the job, or the recourse for their families if they are killed on the job? We do not have enough information to address the question, and suggest that occupational injuries is an area that merits further research. Worker compensation and disability insurance are, for the most part, governed by state laws, and hence uniform data collection is not yet established. Of particular interest, Texas is one of only three states that lack legal requirements for workers' compensation, although most large employers carry some type of liability; one-fifth (20.5%) of the U.S. Hispanic workforce resides in Texas.[22]

Again, the issues of access and utilization are relevant. We can speak with some confidence that workers in unionized settings, especially those in blue-collar jobs, are more apt to secure workers' compensation benefits than workers without collective bargaining coverage.[23] Union workers most likely accrue these benefits because there is greater dissemination of information about, and assistance with, workers' compensation claims.

Unemployment compensation is covered by state law as well, and these regulations and their associated administrative practices vary considerably, thus resulting in disparate unemployment insurance (UI) coverage for Latino workers. Of the nine states with the largest Latino populations, six had UI recipiency rates of less than 30% in

## Legal Exclusion of Farmworkers*

Agricultural workers are typically exempt from federal labor standards. The following points illuminate the lack of legal coverage for farmworkers:

- Only one-half of farmworkers are covered by minimum wage laws.
- Farmworkers are excluded in worker compensation laws in almost one-half of states, and hence workers injured on the job cannot recoup lost wages or medical expenses.
- The Occupational Safety and Health Administration (OSHA) does not regulate farmworkers' exposure to toxic materials – the only occupation exempt from coverage. In addition, OSHA does not monitor working conditions on farms with fewer than 11 employees.
- Farmworkers are not covered under the National Labor Relations Act, which governs unionization and collective bargaining for the majority of the labor force.

The legal exclusion of farmworkers from basic human rights protection in the workplace underscores their economic vulnerability. Other private-sector workers are legally covered by minimum wage protection, safety regulations, and the right to engage in collective bargaining.

* Valerie A. Wilk, "The Occupational Health of Migrant and Seasonal Farmworkers in the United States," Farmworker Justice Fund, 1986.

1989, which indicates that the majority of unemployed (and Hispanic) workers did not collect unemployment insurance. These states include Illinois (where 28.6% of unemployed persons secured benefits), New Mexico (24.9%), Colorado (23.9%), Arizona (21.1%), Texas (19.5%), and Florida (17.0%). UI receipt was highest in New Jersey (50.1%), California (44.9%), and New York (40.1%).[24]

Specific data on unemployment insurance coverage and receipt of benefits for Latinos is practically nonexistent. One study reports that unemployed Latinos and non-Latinos in California have an equal probability of procuring benefits. In contrast, in Texas, one of six unemployed minority workers was awarded UI compared to one of four non-minority workers.[25] Like workers' compensation, receipt of UI benefits is substantially greater in unionized organizations, especially for blue-collar workers.[26]

## VII.  Policy and Research Implications

In the United States, jobs provide access to health insurance, retirement programs, life insurance, and other benefits for most workers.  For the nearly 13 million Hispanic workers, the level of access and utilization of job benefits are not commensurate with those of other workers.

**Although Hispanic men have the highest labor force participation rate of any group in the economy,[27] Hispanic men are significantly less likely than Black or White men to receive benefits.** Among Hispanics, benefit coverage is more likely for women than men, but the benefit situation is moderated by the lower earnings of women relative to those of men.  **Although Hispanic women are less likely than White or Black women to enter the labor force,[28] Latinas who work may be better-educated, work full-time, and have jobs in the primary sectors, characteristics associated with greater benefit coverage.**  The contributions of women earners to the economic well-being of Hispanic families underscores the importance of having specific benefits available through employers, including family/maternity leave and child care.

**In addition to gender, differences in benefit coverage were evident between Hispanic subgroups; the level of overall coverage was more favorable for Cubans and least favorable for Mexican Americans and others of Hispanic origin.**  Among the Hispanic subgroups, Cuban men and women were among those least likely to work for an employer who offered a pension plan; yet if a plan was offered, Cubans were the most likely to participate.  Puerto Ricans, especially women, fared as well as Cubans in health insurance coverage and were more likely than other Hispanics to work in establishments that offered a pension plan.  More extensive benefit coverage offered by employers and industries in the Northeast, where a significant proportion of Puerto Ricans is concentrated, could account for the benefit differential.  Of note, the disparity of benefit coverage between Hispanics and other workers is not explained by the presence of immigrant workers; the findings indicate only modest differences in access to benefits between U.S.- and foreign-born Latinos.

**Characteristics of workers found to be associated with greater benefits include: union-ization, more educational attainment, and employment in large establishments.** Unionization represents a significant avenue to strengthen and extend benefits for Hispanic workers and their families. Unionized employees not only enjoy a wider range of benefits, but research suggests that health and safety issues attract greater attention in union settings.[29] Likewise, the level of benefit coverage favors more educated workers, and the educational gap between Hispanic and other workers must be eliminated. Hispanics would also benefit from more consumer education about the value of accessing and using the benefits earned in the workplace. The benefit advantage associated with employment in large firms, especially with a unionized workforce, indicates that opportunities in the primary sectors of the economy are beneficial to Hispanics. Employment access to the primary sectors could be increased by more job search information and additional education and training, and by combating discrimination in the workplace (see Chapters 2 and 7 for additional discussion of these issues).

**As an employment policy issue, the large proportion of uninsured Hispanics illustrates the weakness of using the labor market to provide health insurance and other types of basic benefits for workers and their families.** Government should address these deficiencies and promote equality of opportunity to obtain basic employment benefits for all workers. Access to benefits has improved for Hispanics and other workers when the government has legally required employers to participate in Social Security, workers' compensation, and unemployment insurance. To illustrate, let us suppose that access to education for children were determined by the parents' employment, rather than by a universal right. Would it be acceptable to society to have one-fifth of the population without financial access to an education? Although the U.S. does not link education to employment, an equally critical benefit – health insurance – is often dependent, for many Hispanics, on their placement in the labor market.

To improve access to and utilization of fringe benefits, we believe that government efforts, including those at the state level, to provide universal health insurance coverage for workers are especially promising for Hispanics and other low-income workers. We also believe that government policy-makers should explore strategies to assist small employers and certain industries in which fringe benefit coverage is low because of regulations or lack of competitive insurance premiums. Use of insurance cooperatives, i.e., where small employers can band together to obtain lower insurance premiums, may enhance the ability of these companies to offer benefits. Of note, the national debate to reform the Social Security program, including privatization of retirement accounts or increasing the retirement age, should receive careful scrutiny for its effects on Hispanic workers. These reform efforts must recognize that the fringe benefit experiences of Hispanics in the private market have not been encouraging, and that low family income minimizes savings and participation in pension programs. Other areas where government can assume leadership are workplace safety, workers' compensation, and unemployment compensation, given that the findings of this chapter indicate that Hispanics are over-represented in dangerous occupations and industries. Farmworkers deserve special attention in this regard. Evidence also shows that Hispanics have been especially vulnerable to recent recessions and other structural changes in the economy.[30] For Hispanic workers, job safety and full-time, stable employment opportunities are thus critical concerns.

Last, we recommend that more research resources be devoted to monitoring the level of benefit coverage by race, ethnicity, and gender. The Bureau of Labor Statistics and other organizations involved in data collection efforts should explore this option. Further research is required to understand better the reasons why some workers decline benefit coverage, as well as the effects of mandated benefit coverage on employment opportunities and job mobility. Regional differences in benefit coverage also warrant an inquiry into how state employment laws and administrative practices, especially in states where Hispanics are geographically concentrated, affect coverage.

# NOTES

1. U.S. Department of Labor, Bureau of Labor Statistics, *Employment and Earnings*, January 1998, Table 12.

2. *Employment and Earnings*, Table 37.

3. U.S. Department of Labor, Bureau of Labor Statistics, "Employer Costs for Employee Compensation – March 1996," News Release #96-424, October 10, 1996, Chart A.

4. Ford, Jason, "State-Mandated Employee Benefits: Conflict with Federal Law?" *Employee Benefits Survey: A BLS Reader*, Washington, DC: U.S. Government Printing Office, 1995.

5. Levine, Chester, "Employee Benefits: Growing in Diversity and Cost," *Occupational Outlook Quarterly*, V. 37, No. 4, 1994, pp. 38-42.

6. Persons of "other" Hispanic origin are principally those of Central and South American origin.

7. Andersen, Ronald, Sandra Zelman Lewis, Aida L. Giachello, Lu Ann Aday, and Grace Chiu, "Access to Medical Care among the Hispanic Population of the Southwestern United States, " *Journal of Health and Social Behavior*, V. 22, March 1981, pp. 78-89; and Valdez, R. Burciaga, Hal Morganstern, E. Richard Brown, Roberta Wyn, Chao Wang, and William Cumberland, "Insuring Latinos Against the Cost of Illness," *Journal of the American Medical Association*, V.269, 1993, No. 17, February 17, 1992, pp. 889-894.

8. Fronstin, Paul, Lawrence G. Goldberg, and Philip K. Robins, "Differences in Private Health Insurance Coverage for Working Male Hispanics," *Inquiry*, V. 34, Summer 1997, pp. 171-180.

9. Valdez et al., *op.cit.*

10. *Ibid.*

11. Snyder, Donald C., "The Economic Well-Being of Retired Workers by Race and Hispanic Origin," in R.V. Burkhauser and D.L. Salisbury, editors, *Pensions in a Changing Economy*, Washington, DC: Employee Benefit Research Institute, 1993, pp. 67-78.

12. Social Security Administration, "Income sources by age, sex, race, and Hispanic origin: Percent of persons aged 55 or older with money income from specified sources, 1994," Table I.9 (PDF file), 1995, http://www.ssa.gov.

13. Social Security Administration, "Relative importance of income sources by sex, marital status, race, and Hispanic origin: Percentage distribution of aged units 65 or older receiving particular sources of income, 1994," Table VI.B.4 (PDF file), 1995, http://www.ssa.gov. Note that the percentages reported in the text do not include persons with veterans' benefits.

14. Smith, James P., *Unequal Wealth and Incentives to Save*, Santa Monica, CA: Rand Corporation, 1995.

15. Employee Benefit Research Institute, "Boom Times a Bust for Retirement Assurances: Results of the 1998 Retirement Confidence Survey," News Release, Washington, DC, June 2, 1998.

16. *Ibid.*

17. The training/education question in the NLSY asks about company-provided training or reimbursement; the child care question asks about company-provided or subsidized child care.

18. *Employment and Earnings*, Table 6.

19. U.S. Department of Labor, Bureau of Labor Statistics, "Lost-Worktime Injuries: Characteristics and Resulting Time Away From Work," News Release #97-188, June 12, 1997, Table 7.

20. *Ibid,* Table 2.

21. Goldstein, Bruce, "An Overview of Migrant and Seasonal Farmworkers in the 1990s," Washington, DC: Farmworker Justice Fund, Fall 1995.

22. Nichols, Marion E., Isaac Shapiro, and Robert Greenstein, *Unemployment Insurance in States with Large Hispanic Populations,* Washington, DC: Center on Budget and Policy Priorities, 1991.

23. Hirsch, Barry T., David A. MacPherson, and J. Michael Dumond, "Workers' Compensation Recipiency in Union and Nonunion Workplaces," *Industrial and Labor Relation Review,* V. 50, No. 2, 1997, pp. 213-236.

24. Nichols, Shapiro, and Greenstein, *op.cit.*

25. *Ibid.*

26. Budd, John W., and Brian P. McCall, "The Effect of Unions on the Receipt of Unemployment Insurance Benefits," *Industrial and Labor Relations Review*, V. 50, No. 3, 1997, 478-492.

27. Fullerton, Howard N., Jr., "Labor Force 2006: Slowing Down and Changing Composition," *Monthly Labor Review,* V. 120, No. 11, 1997, pp. 23-38.

28. *Ibid.*

29. Sloane, Arthur A., and Fred Witney, *Labor Relations,* Saddle River, NJ: Prentice Hall, 1997.

30. Morales, Rebecca, and Frank Bonilla (eds.), *Latinos in a Changing U.S. Economy: Comparative Perspectives on Growing Inequality,* Newbury Park, CA: Sage Publications, 1993.

# Closing the Social Mismatch: Lessons from the Latino Experience

**Edwin Meléndez, Ph.D.**
*Robert J. Milano Graduate School of Management and Urban Policy*
*New School for Social Research*

**Luis M. Falcón, Ph.D.**
*Sociology Department*
*Northeastern University*

## Abstract

*In this chapter, we compare the job search experience of Latinos to that of Blacks and Whites in Boston and Los Angeles. Compared to Blacks and Whites, Latinos are more likely to use relatives as job contacts and to use open-market search strategies like want ads and walk-ins. These search strategies are associated with less desirable labor market outcomes. In contrast, Latinos use job intermediaries less often than other groups – a search strategy that, in our analysis, leads to better job outcomes. We examine intervention programs that assist Latino workers to enter the job market. The Center for Employment Training and Project QUEST are examples of best-practice training programs that have succeeded in connecting Latino social networks to regional employers and better job opportunities – that is, to close the social mismatch between the skills and contacts that Latinos bring to the labor market and the mechanisms needed to access good jobs in the regions where they live.*

# I. Introduction

It is generally accepted in the literature that social networks play a critical role in connecting job seekers to jobs. Latinos are a clear example of a population whose connections to the labor market are rooted in contacts provided by friends and relatives – what often is referred to in the literature as "social networks." While social networks seem to be instrumental in the attainment of jobs by Latino workers, our recent work suggests that social networks may contribute to continued social inequality by steering job seekers to jobs with limited opportunities for wage gains and occupational advancement (Falcón, 1995; Falcón and Meléndez, 1996; Meléndez and Falcón, 1997).

Social networks are just one of various search strategies available to job seekers. The choice of social networks as a strategy to find a job is, in part, determined by the availability of alternative search strategies, and the potential outcomes associated with the use of other methods. Job-matching institutions, such as employment agencies (both private and state-owned), training programs, and school-based placement centers, have a key role to play. If social networks are potentially limiting better employment opportunities for Latinos, it is possible that other strategies could compensate for the lack of labor-market connections and facilitate better access to good jobs. In particular, job-market intermediaries, which will be discussed in detail below, may be critical to providing the contacts and facilitating the connections to employers that might not be available to Latino job seekers otherwise.

The objectives of this chapter are twofold. The first is to examine the evidence regarding Latinos' utilization of social networks and labor-market intermediaries, and the effect of these strategies on their labor-market standing. We use data from the Multi-City Study on Urban Inequality (MCSUI) for Los Angeles and Boston. This survey provides a unique data set regarding social-network utilization for Latinos and other workers in urban labor markets. The evidence presented here indicates that Latinos have search patterns different from those of other workers in these cities and that these differences are associated with poorer labor-market outcomes. In short, Latinos rely more on social networks and open-market search strategies, and use intermediary organizations such as schools and private agencies less frequently, and less successfully, than other workers. This disconnection of Latino workers from intermediaries that may link them to employers' recruiting networks, and that may result in better employment opportunities, indeed represents a "social mismatch."

The second objective is to present examples and discuss the characteristics of programs that are well-known intermediaries serving primarily Latino populations. The Center for Employment Training (CET) in San Jose, California and Project QUEST (Quality Employment Through Skills Training) in San Antonio, Texas are programs that have proven to be very effective in establishing long-lasting connections to employers. We propose that these programs are successful because they simultaneously deal with improving the skills and job-readiness of participants while establishing close links to industry. In short, effective intermediaries are those able to close the social gap between the search strategies employed by Latinos, largely through social networks, and the recruiting networks established, used, and trusted by employers.

## II. Social Networks and How Latinos Search for Jobs

The use of social networks is the most commonly used method of searching for employment, not only for Latinos, but also for other groups. Finding jobs through family, friends, or neighborhood acquaintances is relatively inexpensive and accessible to all job seekers, regardless of employment or socioeconomic status. However, while most individuals do have a web of contacts around them, not all networks are equal. The quality of social networks, in terms of providing information and facilitating employment and access to better jobs, is, in part, determined by the social position of the job seeker and the heterogeneity of the social network to which they belong. Because individuals usually belong to networks consisting of other individuals who share many of the same traits, social networks tend to be rather homogeneous. The closer (or stronger) the social connection of a job seeker is to a network contact, the more likely it is that the information provided by the contact will lead to jobs similar to the socioeconomic status of the job seeker. Thus, it is assumed within the literature that weaker ties, rather than stronger ties, may be more likely to provide better information, because weaker ties may have connections to other networks and therefore increase the pool of potential job contacts and available information. In other words, weaker ties increase the range of an individual's network, which increases the chance of reaching out to sources of information of a different social status.

Job seekers can also find employment information through newspapers, want ads, and other publications, and get referrals from schools, state agencies, and many other job-market intermediaries. To the extent that these sources provide better information and access than informal, network-based connections, job seekers may benefit from diversifying search methods and contacts. For Latinos, as we will explain in more detail below, access to good jobs depends strongly on the use of strategies other than social networks. Reliance exclusively on social networks has a very strong negative effect on Latinos' access to good jobs and better employment opportunities.

Employers' hiring patterns and established recruitment networks also play a significant role in determining the effectiveness of job seekers' search strategies. Employers often recruit for entry-level jobs from referrals provided by their own employees. Employee-based referrals reduce the cost of recruitment for employers. Current employees are able to provide more accurate information about the workplace and to select those who could potentially fit the requirements of the job. Employers also go to more specialized recruiting sources for skilled workers and professionals, such as unions, college fairs, head-hunters, and private agencies. Alternative, more formal recruitment methods are costly, but might be necessary if labor markets are tight or the desired level of skills and experience are hard to identify among job applicants.

In this context, it is evident that the success of a particular search method is, in part, determined by the segments of the job market targeted by the job seeker and the likelihood of connecting to the employers' recruitment methods within those segments. Employers' direct recruitment, based on referrals by current employees or the use of intermediaries for referrals and screening of candidates, may have adverse consequences for Latinos and other inner-city residents. Disadvantaged workers may be affected simply by the lack of connections to the employers' recruitment networks or because they are screened out by existing intermediaries. These circumstances are particularly problematic when inner-city workers seek jobs in suburban areas – they may lack the connection to those already employed there, or may be screened out because of racial, ethnic, or language differences, or commuting distances and lack of transportation.

To examine some key aspects of the job search process, we use data from the Boston and Los Angeles samples of the MCSUI. The data set includes samples of non-Hispanic Whites, Blacks, Latinos, and Asians in the two cities. Data were collected based on a cluster-stratified random sample design and are presented here using the appropriate sampling weights. The analysis focuses on respondents who searched for a job during the five years prior to the survey interview. Table 1 shows data on the various search methods used by the respondents during their last job search. As suggested in our discussion earlier, the use of friends and relatives as a job-search method is very common among all groups. The vast majority of respondents within all groups did contact a friend in the process of looking for their last job. The use of relatives, on the other hand, while fairly common, is not as widespread. Latinos are the exception to this pattern. In both cities, they present the highest use of relatives as a search method. Latinos also present

## Table 1

### Methods Used During Last Search by Race/Ethnicity of Respondent and City

|  | Boston | | | Los Angeles | | |
|---|---|---|---|---|---|---|
|  | NHW* | Black | Latino | NHW* | Black | Latino |
| **Social Network:** |  |  |  |  |  |  |
| Friends | 71% | 64% | 70% | 77% | 74% | 82% |
| Relatives | 49% | 51% | 54% | 46% | 46% | 59% |
| Average | 60% | 61% | 59% | 61% | 60% | 70% |
| **Market:** |  |  |  |  |  |  |
| Newspaper | 76% | 82% | 58% | 69% | 68% | 61% |
| Want Ads | 22% | 46% | 44% | 25% | 32% | 38% |
| Walk-Ins | 45% | 68% | 61% | 48% | 53% | 59% |
| Sent Résumé | 69% | 69% | 35% | 70% | 60% | 33% |
| Average | 53% | 66% | 50% | 53% | 53% | 48% |
| **Intermediary:** |  |  |  |  |  |  |
| Union | 4% | 10% | 3% | 5% | 5% | 6% |
| State Agency | 21% | 29% | 22% | 18% | 21% | 14% |
| Private Service | 21% | 16% | 14% | 25% | 22% | 6% |
| Temp Agency | 11% | 25% | 13% | 21% | 30% | 17% |
| School Placement | 14% | 17% | 5% | 12% | 12% | 7% |
| Average | 13% | 17% | 11% | 15% | 17% | 9% |
| N | 292 | 283 | 390 | 366 | 499 | 555 |

* Non-Hispanic White.

Source: Authors' estimates based on data from the Multi-City Study on Urban Inequality, 1995.

a higher use of want ads and walk-ins than other groups, while they under-utilize sending résumés, or using private agencies, school referrals, and even newspapers. The pattern of search methods displayed by Latinos is clearly in contrast to the one used by Blacks and non-Hispanic Whites. These latter groups rely more on newspapers, sending résumés, and the use of private agencies than do Latinos.

Search methods can be grouped or categorized based on the implicit relationship that they represent. Friends and relatives are part of a job seeker's social networks and represent informal access to employers and information about jobs. Organizations that facilitate information and connections to employers are often referred to as "intermediaries." In our data set, these are represented by private, temporary, and state agencies, unions, and schools. We will refer to methods based primarily on exchange of information as part of "open-market" job search strategy. This category includes the use of want ads, newspapers, and contacting employers directly by sending résumés or visiting their offices (walk-ins). Once search methods are grouped this way, it is evident from Table 1 that social networks are the strategy used most often by all groups, followed by open-market, and, a distant third, intermediaries. For Latinos, the sharpest contrast to other groups regards their under-utilization of sending résumés as a search method and using intermediaries as a search strategy. These differences can be attributed to an overall lower educational level in the case of using schools and sending résumés, and to a lack of institutional connections in the case of intermediaries. From the public policy and community strategy points of view, these might represent areas for targeted intervention.

Job seekers can choose from a variety of search methods with different levels of investment of resources and time. A social-network-based search requires the presence of individuals within a network with information or access to jobs. Using intermediaries such as state agencies and private services may require language skills that some Latino immigrants may lack. This raises the question, are the search strategies of Latinos different from those commonly used within the labor markets in which they find themselves? And, is the pattern of search in any way associated with differential payoffs and job opportunities?

To answer the first question, we used a factor-analysis model in which methods were grouped according to the pattern of relationships established by job seekers' searches. The factor analysis organizes the various dimensions of the job-search methods exhibited by groups into a pattern. The emerging patterns, then, could provide a better picture as to how the various groups package a search strategy – in other words, based on the job-search methods individuals choose, we can determine which methods go together.

In this exercise, the number of factors and the combination of search methods for Latinos and for all groups together responded completely to the convergence of methods into factors representing search strategies. For example, the grouping of friends and relatives would suggest that these two methods are typically used together and constitute a distinct search strategy, which we have referred to as "social networks." A simplified ver-

## Table 2

### Grouping of Search Methods into Strategies Using Factor Analysis

| Factor | Boston | | Los Angeles | |
| :---: | :---: | :---: | :---: | :---: |
| | **All Groups** | **Latinos** | **All Groups** | **Latinos** |
| 1 | Walk-Ins | State Agencies<br>Send Résumé<br>Want Ads<br>Walk-Ins<br>Newspapers | Private Agencies<br>Temp Agencies<br>State Agencies | State Agencies<br>Private Agencies<br>Temp Agencies<br>School Referral |
| 2 | Private Agencies<br>Unions<br>Temp Agencies<br>State Agencies | Friends<br>Relatives | Want Ads<br>Newspapers<br>Walk-Ins<br>Unions | Friends<br>Relatives |
| 3 | Send Résumé<br>School Referral<br>Newspapers | Unions<br>Private Agencies<br>Temp Agencies | Friends<br>Relatives | Send Résumé<br>Want Ads<br>Walk-Ins<br>Newspapers |
| 4 | Friends<br>Relatives | School Referral | School Referral<br>Send Résumé | Unions |

Source: Authors' estimates based on data from the Multi-City Study on Urban Inequality, 1995.

sion of the results from the factor analysis is presented in Table 2. The groupings of search methods for Latinos and for all groups are presented by city.

In order to ascertain differences in the ways Latinos search for jobs, it is important to establish a general structure of job searches for both cities. The grouping of methods in the general markets of Boston and Los Angeles suggest four separate search strategies that differ according to the type of connection to the job market (e.g., weak or strong ties) and the type of intermediary linking the job seeker to the employer. The job-search methods fall into four distinct search packages that we have labeled *Social Network, Open-Market, Credential-Based*, and *Job Placement Services*. The last two strategies rely on the use of intermediaries to establish the link to employers.

The social network strategy (friends, relatives) and the open-market strategy (walk-ins, want ads) are at opposite extremes of the job-search spectrum. If social networks represent the establishment of strong ties, where job seekers use close contacts to intercede for them, open-market strategies represent no ties at all, where the seeker contacts the employer directly. Between these two extremes, there are two strategies based on qualitatively different types of intermediaries. Obviously, the methods of sending résumés and using school referrals are associated with credential-based occupations, while the use of private, state, and temporary agencies, as well as unions, is associated with job-placement services (information, referral, and limited screening).

With a few exceptions, the bundling of job-search methods is fairly similar across the two cities. We can conclude that there are recognizable search strategies that job seekers follow when searching for jobs. While there are some differences in the bundling of strategies across cities – for example, the use of school-based referrals does not emerge as a search strategy in Los Angeles – the social networks, the job placement services, and the open-market strategies do fully emerge in both cities.

The results of the factor analysis suggest some differences in the way Latinos search for work compared with the patterns established by all groups in the regional labor market. In Boston, open-market search strategies (want ads and walk-ins) also include the use of state and temporary agencies, and newspapers. This bundling of search strategies suggests that, in this case, the agencies are used primarily as sources of information and not as referral intermediaries. Latinos in Boston also differ in terms of their bundling of the credential-based methods – school referral and sending résumés – with the private placement services method. This suggests a skill level that allows them to make use of such credential-based resources. As for the general market, the use of social networks emerges as a separate strategy. Finally, unions stand out as a single-method search pattern.

The Latino job-search experience in Los Angeles is somewhat different from that in Boston. It is apparent from the ranking of factors that Latino job seekers use job-placement intermediaries more often in Los Angeles than they do in Boston. All three job intermediaries stand out as a unique search pattern for Latinos in Los Angeles. The open-market approach of directly contacting employers through responding to ads is also well defined. The use of social networks as a single strategy is consistent with what is found in Boston and in the general labor market. The last strategy, the use of union intermediaries, is bundled together with school referrals, suggesting that skills training programs (e.g., vocational skills) may be an important part of the school-based referrals. The analysis of search-method utilization indicates that Latinos follow job-search strategies that are similar to those of other workers in their regional labor markets. The descriptions presented in Table 1, however, suggest that Latinos are more likely to use open-market and social-network-based strategies than intermediaries.

These findings have important implications. The reliance by Latinos on social networks connected to familiar occupations and industries, as well as on open market search strategies that are disconnected from employers' recruitment networks, may contribute to the perpetuation of job segmentation in low-wage labor markets. A corollary of this proposition is that the use of labor-market intermediaries in the job search could be associated with better labor-market outcomes. Thus, as we will discuss in more detail in the next section, movement away from traditional search methods and the adoption of more effective strategies may result in better labor-market outcomes for Latinos.

## III. Latinos and the Role of Intermediaries in Job Search

Private, state, and temporary agencies, unions, and colleges often play the role of intermediary in the labor market. They identify the personnel needs of employers and facilitate recruitment. In general, intermediaries provide information to job seekers, prepare them for interviews and tests, assist them in preparing references and other documentation, and refer job candidates to targeted employers. Such intermediaries as technical schools and community colleges provide extensive skills training and basic education, and provide job placement as a service to students. Regardless of whether the emphasis of the intermediary is on education or making connections to employers, intermediaries negotiate the employment transaction by matching workers to job openings. In short, intermediaries are an alternative to other job-search strategies – social networks and open-market strategies – in the matching of workers to employment opportunities.

Intermediaries facilitate hiring for employers by screening applicants and, through a better match, reducing turnover and recruitment costs. Particularly for entry-level jobs, employers seek job-specific skills and job readiness. More than a high school diploma, as such, employers prefer direct certification that the candidate has basic skills (such as reading and writing, arithmetic, and computer literacy) that can be applied to a specific work context. Employers also seek soft skills, such as punctuality, ability to follow directions, ability to deal appropriately with customers, and commitment to the job. The importance of screening for these skills could be the leading force explaining the increasing use of intermediaries by employers for recruitment. In order to reduce the cost of worker recruitment, employers need some reassurance of the skills possessed by the worker. This can occur formally as it does through intermediaries, or informally through referral and direct recruitment by trusted employees.

At first glance, there are no reasons to believe that the increased use of intermediaries in labor markets is detrimental to the employment opportunities, access to good jobs, and long-term economic position of Latinos. As proposed by Moss and Tilly (1996) and Kirschenman, Moss, and Tilly (1995), given the stereotypical views of Blacks and Latinos, and the prevalence of discriminatory recruiting practices, better screening of job seekers can actually benefit qualified Latinos and other racial minorities.[1] Conversely, exclusion from employers' recruiting networks, whether based on direct referrals by other employees or on connections made by intermediaries, may result in the systematic exclusion of Latinos from better job opportunities. The essence of the problem is, to what extent are Latino workers affected by using ineffective social networks and not having access to intermediaries?

Understanding the institutional context of how labor markets operate is critical to improving the labor-market standing of Latinos. The above discussion suggests that the payoff associated with a particular job-search strategy, as well as the ability to utilize a particular strategy, could be different for Latinos when compared with other groups. For example, the benefits generally associated with social networks for White or Black job seekers could be negative for Latinos, given the group's overall position in the labor market and their lack of the appropriate connections in the more desirable industries and occupations. We propose that Latino job seekers use different strategies, depending on the information available to them (through formal or informal contacts) and their assessment of the potential for success of a particular search strategy.

In the end, every worker aspires to a job, although the quality of the job attained may vary according to the search mechanism employed. Given the differences in access to social resources, we expect that among Latinos, the association between particular search methods, and such labor-market outcomes as wages, occupational status, and employment, will differ from that of other groups. These differences should be seen in two ways: in the significance and in the direction of the association. By "significance" we refer to the method statistically showing an effect that could not happen in these data just by chance. We expect that methods found to be important to Latinos may not necessarily be so for other groups. The direction of the association has to do with the effect the particular method has on the outcome (e.g., wages, occupational status, and employment). Some methods may have a negative effect on wages or occupational status – that is, they lower the wages obtained or lead to a lower-quality job. Other methods may have the totally opposite effect – they increase wages or occupational status – and some may have no effect at all. In sum, Latinos may be adversely impacted by exclusion from better recruitment channels or the use of search methods associated with less desirable labor-market outcomes.

The central questions to be explored in the experiments that follow are: how are the choice of strategies in general, and the use of intermediaries in particular, related to the efficiency (i.e., getting a job), effectiveness (i.e., getting a good job), and long-term potential (i.e., connection to a good employer) of a job search? We tested these hypotheses regarding the impact of the choice in search strategy on labor market outcomes using regression analysis and the MCSUI data for Boston and Los Angeles.[2] For analytical purposes, labor market outcomes can be divided into the three groups suggested above. We used whether the person is employed or not to ascertain whether the search strategy was effective or not in getting a job for the job seeker. Employability is coded as "1" if the respondent was employed at the time of the survey, and "0" otherwise.

To test for the quality of job obtained, we used the Socioeconomic Index (SEI), the natural logarithm of hourly wage, and the number of benefits of the last job. The SEI is a standard measure of the relative status of the job, a commonly-used variable in sociological analysis. The log of hourly wages is calculated directly from reported hourly wages or indirectly from calculating hourly wages based on annual or monthly earnings and the number of weekly hours per worker. To ascertain the potential of a particular job, we used three indicators: firm size, whether the workplace is primarily employing minority workers, and whether the workplace is primarily employing co-ethnic workers (workers of the same race/ethnicity as the respondent). The presumption here is that job mobility is better in a large establishment and that minority workplaces are associated with a segmented workforce and a lower likelihood of advancement.

The analysis focuses on the effect of the use of social networks, intermediaries, and open-market strategies on the already-described set of labor market outcomes. Search methods are grouped into the three aforementioned strategies and operationalized as variables by adding the frequency of use of each method into a particular strategy. Thus, the social network strategy has a value from 0 to 2, depending on whether a job seeker used friends, relatives, both friends and relatives, or none in their last search. The intermediaries' variable ranges from 0 to 5 and the open-market variable from 0 to 4.

An important methodological problem to consider is that the method chosen by the job seekers depends to a large extent on the characteristics of the job that the job seeker would like to get. In other words, a carpenter knows that the only way to get access to a certain employer is through the union, or a clerical worker knows that a targeted bank only accepts résumés through the mail. This implies that the choice of using a specific method, relative to others, may be influenced by the type of job being searched for and the searcher's knowledge of which methods are conducive to such a job. To correct for this problem, we estimated the model in two steps. First, we created an estimate of the predicted frequency of use of the three search strategies – social networks, intermediaries, and open-market. We did so by estimating the use of each of the strategy variables in an equation that included, as independent variables, indicators for a series of characteristics of the job and industry in which the worker is employed. We consider these to be matching variables – elements that employers consider when making a decision about hiring a worker. They include the level of job-specific experience, the number of tests given to a job applicant, the frequency of use of academic and communication skills on the job, and the number of work-related and non-work-related references used by the job applicants. In addition, we included indicators for the industry location of the job and control variables for the personal characteristics of the workers.

The predicted values for frequency of use of social networks, intermediaries, and open-market strategies were then used in estimating the effects of job strategies on labor-market outcomes. In this formulation of the independent variables, a job seeker can use none,

### Table 3

### Population Characteristics

|  | Boston | | | Los Angeles | | |
|---|---|---|---|---|---|---|
|  | NHW* | Blacks | Latinos | NHW* | Blacks | Latinos |
| **Ethnicity:** | | | | | | |
| Mexican | | | 1% | | | 70% |
| Puerto Rican | | | 45% | | | 1% |
| Dominican | | | 10% | | | 0% |
| Other Latino | | | 43% | | | 20% |
| **Sex:** | | | | | | |
| Male | 46% | 49% | 57% | 51% | 50% | 54% |
| Female | 54% | 51% | 43% | 49% | 50% | 46% |
| **Age:** | | | | | | |
| Average | 38.6 | 36.8 | 34.8 | 40.97 | 37.25 | 35.5 |
| 21-25 | 14% | 19% | 18% | 10% | 16% | 21% |
| 26-34 | 27% | 32% | 37% | 23% | 33% | 32% |
| 35-44 | 31% | 28% | 29% | 25% | 24% | 27% |
| 45-64 | 28% | 17% | 17% | 38% | 27% | 20% |
| **Education:** | | | | | | |
| Average | 14.27 | 12.36 | 10.99 | 14.36 | 13.49 | 10.3 |
| No High School | 4% | 22% | 44% | 4% | 7% | 47% |
| High School or GED | 41% | 54% | 41% | 36% | 54% | 32% |
| Some College | 9% | 15% | 8% | 22% | 21% | 10% |
| College | 48.6 | 13.2 | 2.3 | 41.8 | 16.2 | 9.3 |
| **Immigrant Characteristics:** | | | | | | |
| US-Born | 95% | 63% | 15% | 84% | 90% | 27% |
| Speaks English Poorly | 0% | 3% | 20% | 0% | 0% | 35% |
| **Occupation:** | | | | | | |
| Prof. & Managers | 46% | 29% | 25% | 53% | 30% | 25% |
| Clerical | 30% | 30% | 14% | 26% | 38% | 20% |
| Crafts | 6% | 6% | 1% | 7% | 3% | 12% |
| Services | 10% | 29% | 19% | 9% | 25% | 19% |
| Laborers | 9% | 12% | 36% | 6% | 4% | 25% |

\* Non-Hispanic Whites.

Source: Authors' estimates based on data from the Multi-City Study on Urban Inequality.

one, or several strategies in combination and at different degrees of intensity. We measured the net effect of a particular search strategy on labor market outcomes, controlling for job and industry-related effects on the determination of the method chosen for the average use of the other strategies.

Before presenting the regression results, it is important to note the distribution of some of the other variables used to control for the effects of search strategies in the analysis. Table 3 presents descriptive statistics for non-Hispanic Whites, Blacks, and Latinos in Boston and in Los Angeles. In general, the characteristics of this sample are similar to those of other studies of Latinos. As a whole, Latinos are younger than Blacks and non-Hispanic Whites. Compared to Blacks and Whites, they have lower educational attainment, on average, and are more likely to be foreign-born. As such, Latinos tend to have less-developed communication skills in English and are more likely to be employed in low-skill occupations than non-Hispanics. The outcome variables are distributed in an expected pattern. Latinos have lower employability, a lower log of hourly wages, and a lower SEI than either Blacks or non-Hispanic Whites.

Table 4 summarizes the results of the association between search strategies and labor-market outcomes. As suggested before, these effects are net of other individual characteristics and of the frequency of use of search strategies given by industry sectors and employers' hiring practices. The presentation in the table has been simplified; no regression coefficients are shown. Instead, a plus or a minus sign is displayed indicating the direction of the association for each search-method coefficient that was significantly different from zero at P>.05, P>.10, or P>.20.[3] Search methods with negative signs reduce the magnitude of the labor market outcome, while methods with a positive sign have an increasing effect. Methods with no sign displayed show no effect in this analysis. The more signs shown, the stronger the effect of that particular method.

Search strategies show distinct patterns of impact on the labor market outcomes of White, Black, and Latino job seekers. In both Boston and Los Angeles, a greater use of intermediary-based methods in the search has a clearly positive impact on the quality of jobs obtained by job seekers and steers them away from more segmented workplaces, although the impact on employability varies by ethnic group. In contrast, increased use of social networks-based methods has an overall negative impact on the quality of jobs. The results for open-market strategies are more ambiguous.

What can be said about specific impacts for each ethnic group? Blacks in Los Angeles seem to benefit the most from intermediaries, improving both employability and their

# Table 4

## Search Strategies' Effects on Labor Market Outcomes

| | Boston | | | | Los Angeles | | | |
|---|---|---|---|---|---|---|---|---|
| | Networks | Intermed. | Market | N | Networks | Intermed. | Market | N |
| **Whites** | | | | | | | | |
| Employment | | | | 265 | | | | 337 |
| Socioeconomic Index | - - - | + + | | 274 | | + + + | | 349 |
| Wages | | + | | 228 | + + + | | - - | 266 |
| Benefits | - - - | + + + | + + | 280 | - - - | | + + | 350 |
| Firm Size | | + + + | - - - | 266 | | + | | 346 |
| Minority Workplace | + + + | - - - | | 251 | - - - | | | 345 |
| Co-ethnic Workplace | - - - | + + + | | 251 | + + | | | 345 |
| **Blacks** | | | | | | | | |
| Employment | - - | | | 235 | + + + | | - - | 420 |
| Socioeconomic Index | - - - | + + + | | 244 | + + + | | - - | 443 |
| Wages | | | | 212 | | + + | | 372 |
| Benefits | - - - | + + + | + + | 256 | - - - | + + + | | 445 |
| Firm Size | - - - | + + + | + + | 231 | | | | 437 |
| Minority Workplace | | - - - | + + + | 229 | | | | 440 |
| Co-ethnic Workplace | | - - | + + + | 236 | | | | 440 |
| **Latinos** | | | | | | | | |
| Employment | - - - | + + | | 341 | -- - | - - - | +++ | 533 |
| Socioeconomic Index | - - - | | + + + | 323 | - - - | | + | 525 |
| Wages | - - - | | + + + | 314 | | + + + | | 504 |
| Benefits | - - - | + + + | | 356 | - - - | + + | + | 539 |
| Firm Size | + | | | 314 | | | | 518 |
| Minority Workplace | + + + | - - - | + + + | 306 | | _ _ | | 528 |
| Co-ethnic Workplace | | | | 306 | + | | | 528 |

Notes: a) Or + indicate significance at the 20% level.
       - - Or + + indicate significance at the 10% level.
       - - Or + + + indicate significance at the 5% level.
     b) Models include controls for age, age square, sex, high school, college, if married, has children, and poor English.

Source: Authors' estimates based on data from the Multi-City Study on Urban Inequality, 1995.

access to good jobs. For Whites in both cities and Blacks in Boston, intermediaries improve access to occupations with a higher SEI, and to jobs that pay better hourly wages and have more benefits. For these two groups in Boston, intermediaries also steer job seekers to larger employers and away from minority workplaces. Open-market strategies have the opposite effect, steering Black and White job seekers to smaller firms and to minority workplaces.

The impact of intermediaries on Latinos' labor market outcomes is more limited. In Boston, intermediaries improve employability, improve job benefits, and steer applicants away from minority-dominated workplaces. However, intermediaries have no effect on other labor market variables that impact job quality, such as wages or occupational status. In Los Angeles, Latinos face a somewhat similar situation. Intermediaries improve wages and benefits, but have a negative effect on employability. Latinos seem to benefit the most from open-market search strategies. In Boston, open-market strategies improve occupational position and wages, while in Los Angeles they also improve employability. One plausible explanation for these effects, which are in sharp contrast to those of Whites and Blacks in both cities, is that given the low socioeconomic status, and the high segmentation, experienced by Latinos in low-wage jobs, any strategy which diversifies contacts that are made primarily through social networks will have a positive impact on the labor market standing of Latinos. This is a reasonable explanation in the context of intermediaries' not providing a more rewarding strategy to Latino job seekers.

These results are consistent with two previously-argued propositions about the role of intermediaries in labor markets; first, that some intermediaries may better serve employers' needs by screening candidates and facilitating a better match, and, second, that the benefit ethnic groups derive from matchmakers depends on their own community resources and contacts. The importance of community resources is also evident when comparing the role of institutional intermediaries with that of open-market or social-network search strategies. Evidently, social-networks-based strategies are the least advantageous for all groups. The use of friends and relatives is generally associated with negative labor-market outcomes for all groups in both cities. Of all groups, Latinos in Boston seem to be the most adversely affected by making employment contacts through social networks. By contrast, the negative outcomes associated with social-network use are less pronounced for Latinos in Los Angeles.

What are the implications of these results for improving the employment and labor-market standing of Latinos? Most research in the area of job searches has paid attention to the role of social networks in facilitating employment and access to better jobs. As a group with a large number of immigrants, Latinos share a propensity toward using social networks, as we have previously demonstrated. However, it is apparent from the above discussion that intermediaries are associated with better labor-market outcomes and may offer an alternative to the use of social networks, which may have fewer connections to better jobs, or to less effective open-market search strategies. The relative benefit of a job search assisted by labor-market intermediaries may be related to how closely they are linked to employers' networks and preferences and how effectively they can connect job-ready applicants through such channels.

Not all search strategies have the same impact on labor-market outcomes, and not all job seekers are affected in the same manner by these strategies. The questions that follow from this discussion are: if the institutional context of the matching of workers and employers matters, and we know that some intermediaries seem to impact the various groups positively, while social-network or open-market strategies seem to affect them negatively, do we find examples of mechanisms used to narrow this social mismatch? If the preferred search strategies of Latinos are those associated with negative outcomes, and the strategies preferred by employers are associated with positive ones, how do we bridge the gap? Are there examples of intermediaries that have proven to be effective in servicing Latinos? If so, what makes these programs work?

## IV. Making the Links: Lessons from the Latino Experience

Intermediaries can be divided into categories according to the core functions they per-form within the labor market. These core functions include providing information and referrals (job placement), job-readiness preparation, and skills training. Some intermedi-aries specialize in one of these functions, while others integrate two or more services into a comprehensive program. For example, one-stop centers, a federal government-funded employment service, focus exclusively on job placement, providing information to job seekers and employers, and arranging for referrals and interviews. In most states, these functions are complemented with referrals to social and training services. Similarly, community colleges provide academic degrees and technical certification, but offer min-imal job-placement or job-readiness services. Temporary employment agencies focus on job placement, but often, particularly with the recent advent of "work-first" programs and support for home-to-work transitions, also offer job-readiness courses. Depending on the program, job-readiness programs typically last from one week to five or six weeks, and include such topics as orientation to the world of work, training options and career exploration, planning and goal setting, job-search and retention skills, life-management skills, internship placement for direct work experience, and, occasionally, short-term English-as-a-Second-Language or basic academic-skills remedial work. Community-based training programs servicing economically or socially disadvantaged populations typically integrate all core functions. In general, training programs serve as a second choice system for those who are unable to succeed in more traditional school or community college systems.

To understand why some programs are successful, it is necessary to have a general understanding of why many programs seeking to match disadvantaged job seekers to employment opportunities fail to achieve their objectives. For Grubb (1996), the shortcomings of employment training programs are related to several factors. In general, many programs offer little or no training at all and have no significant impact on the basic and vocational skills of program participants. Often, classroom training or job placement is disconnected from other complementary services that are necessary to serve disadvantaged populations. Furthermore, when skills training is offered, it is often disconnected from the needs of employers and the industry. These programs do not adopt best instructional practices when servicing populations with significant deficiencies in their education. Given the above context, placing job seekers in marginal jobs increases the odds that they will be looking for another job in the near future. And, lacking connections to the educational system, participants rarely enroll in adult education programs or community colleges on their own.

A growing body of literature (Harrison and Weiss, 1998; Joyner, 1996; Siegel and Kwass, 1995; Stokes, 1996) is documenting, from case-study research, the institutional features of second-chance training and placement programs that make them successful when compared with other programs. A recent report by the General Accounting Office (GAO) identifies four key features shared by effective employment and training programs:

1. Ensuring that clients are committed to training and getting jobs.
2. Removing barriers, such as lack of child care and transportation, that might limit the clients' ability to finish training and get and keep a job.
3. Improving clients' employability skills, such as getting to a job regularly and on time, working well with others while there, and dressing and behaving appropriately.
4. Linking occupational skills training with the local labor market (Joyner, 1996).

These findings are based on programs that range from intense case management with no direct skills provided by the program, to short-term employability and placement programs, to more comprehensive skills training with integrated support and placement services. Because of the targeted population, these programs are either community-based or operated in conjunction with a community-based organization. The above context is important to understanding the contribution to the employment training field of the San Jose-based (mostly Chicano) Center for Employment and Training (CET). A recent survey of the literature from the U.S. Department of Labor found that CET was the only program where rigorous studies based on random assignment of participants demonstrated a (statistically) significant impact on participants' earnings and employability (U.S. Department of Labor, 1995). This finding has been supported by a number of independent studies that have established CET training as best practice in the field (Cave, Bos, Doolittle, Toussaint, 1993; Hollister, 1990; Kerachsky, 1994; Zabrowski and Gordon, 1993). However, these studies have paid little attention to program design or the role of social networks, and how they affect program success. In particular, it is important to link our understanding of how Latinos search for jobs and the degree to which they rely on social networks and not on intermediaries to the design of effective programs matching disadvantaged workers to employment opportunities.

Previous work by Meléndez (1996) and Meléndez and Harrison (1997) offers valuable insight into the key elements for the success of CET and how it relates to our previous discussion on social networks, and, more specifically, on how Latinos search for jobs. From the findings of the CET case study, they propose that there is asymmetry between network structures that facilitates the employment process on the supply and demand sides of the labor market (Meléndez and Harrison, 1997: 4). On the workers' side, CET established a strong connection to the existing networks of Chicano farm workers. It was precisely this identification with the Chicano farm workers' movement that allowed them to expand through California and the Southwest, creating and operating more than 35 centers by the mid-1990s. CET provides access to entry-level positions with major regional employers by inserting itself directly into their recruiting networks. The secret of CET's success is precisely its ability to channel Latino networks to the right type of connections with employers while at the same time preparing workers, in terms of job-specific and employability skills, to meet employers' expectations of a reliable labor force. CET institutionalizes relations with employers and transfers these contacts to Latino and other job seekers who otherwise would not have had access to such job-market connections. One of the obvious disadvantages of short-term (up to about six months) training programs like CET, though, is their limited potential to enhance skills significantly.

Project QUEST in San Antonio targets disadvantaged workers, most of whom are Chicanos, attending community colleges in the area. Although QUEST has not been evaluated to the extent that CET has, it received the Innovation in American Government Award in 1995, as well as wide acknowledgment by local authorities, such as the Alamo Workforce Development Council, for placing welfare recipients in work, and has been the subject of two recent studies (Osterman and Lantsch, 1996; Morales, 1996). In short, QUEST is a community-based organization that provides case management, support services, counseling, financial aid, job readiness, and job placement to community college students attending regular two-year programs. Like CET, QUEST establishes close connections to employers in the area and steers students to enrollment in programs that target occupations and industry sectors for which there is a strong forecasted demand. One of the most important findings from recent studies is that QUEST has induced systemic reforms in participating community colleges. Thus, QUEST links students to employers and supports their education. But how is this related to Latino social networks, and what difference does it make?

Like CET, QUEST is part of the region's Latino social movement, particularly that of the activist Catholic Church. QUEST relies on community-outreach teams to recruit neighborhood residents and to support them during the duration of the program. QUEST was created by COPS (Communities Organized for Public Service) and the Metro Alliance, characterized by a largely African American membership. Both of these organizations are affiliated with the community-activist Industrial Area Foundation. These community links and origins are important for understanding how QUEST has received critical political support to leverage resources for the program. These links also provide the legitimacy to engage employers in supporting the program and hiring participants, as well as to community colleges and social service agencies that provide critical services to participants. Until 1995, about 70% of program participants were Latino and about one-half were economically disadvantaged.

CET and QUEST are examples of what Harrison and Weiss (1998) have labeled "community-based workforce development networks." In this type of network, the community-based organization itself serves as the labor-market intermediary and articulates participants' relations with employers and other support services. Other types of networks were characterized by structured relations among CBOs, or anchored by public agencies or community colleges. The single element these community-based networks have in common, and one that distinguishes them from other more traditional labor-market intermediaries, is their capacity to connect to existing community (in our case, Latino) social networks and the propensity to use them. Friends and family contacts are directed to programs that simultaneously can improve basic, vocational, and employability skills and have established institutional relations with employers and other support service agencies. As these two examples illustrate, Latino organizations are at the forefront of the best practices in the field of employment training and community-based job-market intermediaries.

# V. Conclusions and Policy Implications

The lessons from ongoing research on how job seekers are matched to employment opportunities and how programs can assist in maximizing the potential gain from job searches have to be understood in the appropriate social context. To begin with, the two cities used from the MCSUI data set are not necessarily representative of the conditions and social environment of Latinos in the United States. Boston and Los Angeles offer interesting cases from a research point of view: Los Angeles has the largest influx of immigrants in the nation, and even though the native-born Latino population is under-represented, Latinos constitute a significant proportion of the overall population and the largest racial or ethnic minority group in the city. In contrast to the community in Los Angeles, Latinos in the greater Boston metropolitan area make up a smaller proportion of the population. The Latino population in Massachusetts, as a whole, is of more recent origin, with about half of the over 300,000 Latinos in the state having arrived during the 1980s. With Puerto Ricans as the largest group, and Dominicans as the rapidly-growing, second-largest Latino group, this is a population overwhelmingly composed of the immigrant generation, with all the characteristics of a community in the settlement stage. While Blacks in Los Angeles are a smaller population than Latinos, Blacks in Boston constitute the largest and most influential racial minority group.

Research on the institutional context that mediates the connections between disadvantaged populations and employment opportunities is in its infancy. Very few empirical studies exist on this subject, whether one is referring to survey-based quantitative studies or detailed case studies based on qualitative analysis. In other words, the lessons from this study are limited by the small number of cities that provide a social context for labor market dynamics and by the limited number of studies on what explains employment training program effectiveness. In particular, there is insufficient research on Latino experiences in employment training programs nationally and by region, and on what constitutes effective workforce development strategies or areas to pursue for this significant segment of American workers.

We began this chapter by stating that, when compared with other groups, there are differences in the ways Latinos search for employment. Those differences are not in the type of search strategies that Latinos pursue, but on the propensity to favor some search methods over others. The differences between the job-search patterns of Latinos and those of other groups are partly a function of the immigrant character of Latinos and differentials in the level of resources Latino communities have. We have presented evidence that Latinos are able to bundle together search packages that are not that different from those of other groups. However, their emphasis on social contacts, particularly those of kin, sets them apart from other groups. We have further presented evidence that not all search strategies have an equal impact on labor market strategies. Net of individual characteristics, we have shown that the different strategies are associated with qualitatively different rewards. What we have called the social-network strategy is associated with negative labor market outcomes in most cases, and the open-market strategy is largely inconsequential to job seekers, except for Latinos. The most consistent pattern of positive association is for the intermediaries – the private temporary and government employment agencies, or the school- or union-based referrals. These are the search methods least likely to be used by Latinos. Hence, the social mismatch.

How do we orient the social networks of Latinos toward building structures of support and reaching out to institutions that can provide access to employers' recruitment networks? More than that, how do we create resources that allow for Latino workers to vouch for their skills and credentials? What have we learned from best-practice programs servicing Latinos? Within the context of the above-stated limitations, what can we recommend to policy makers, community organizations, educational institutions, and training programs? We have two key recommendations.

First, Latinos should be encouraged to use intermediaries more often in their job searches, and intermediaries should be encouraged to provide services to Latinos more often. Our data and analysis show that intermediaries do have a positive impact on improving access to good jobs and to better employment opportunities. However, Latinos are not taking full advantage of existing match-makers. We have presented examples of programs that have been able to bridge the gap between Latino workers and employers in their regional labor markets. They have been able to do so by building on and strengthening already-existing structures of social support within Latino communities to remove barriers, facilitate the completion of training programs, and, most importantly, improve employability skills which include the range of behavior expected within a workplace.

Second, given the socioeconomic characteristics of Latinos, intermediaries must be more responsive to the multiple needs of this population. Latino workers face some fairly large barriers in improving access to good jobs. These barriers range from the lack of "support services," like child care for the many young mothers in the community, and transportation, to the lack of solid work references for those who have never been in the labor force, or those whose last employment was in another country. These barriers are further complicated by inadequate language skills and limited knowledge of what is expected in the workplace. In addition, employment discrimination and a host of both human capital and structural economic factors affect Latino labor market experiences and outcomes. (For a discussion of these issues, see Chapters 1 and 2 of this volume.) Any successful intermediary must deal with all of these issues simultaneously. Resolving the social mismatch problem becomes, then, an institutional problem. Service providers must approach Latino clients in a way that addresses the host of problems we have just highlighted.

Employers want workers who will be productive; they also want to minimize the costs of continued turnover and recruitment that contribute to the increasing cost of labor. But to deal with the issue of a social mismatch, it is not enough to provide access to employers. It requires some qualitative changes in the characteristics of the Latino labor supply. Closing the social mismatch does not mean starting from scratch, however, since many of the resources already exist within Latino communities.

# NOTES

1.  A classic example of a discriminatory practice is when employers lack the resources to evaluate the qualifications of each applicant and rely on a group perception to make hiring decisions. For example, an employer may be less inclined to interview a Latino for an office receptionist position because, in general, "Latinos speak poor English." Another example is when employers are less likely to interview a resident in a particular neighborhood because that area is known as a "high crime area." In both cases, the individual is not given the opportunity to be employed because he or she is associated with a (perceived) group attribute (lack of communication skills, more likely to be in contact with criminals) that the employer wants to avoid. The argument here is that an intermediary may screen applicants for desirable attributes and increase the probability that some individuals will be considered for jobs who would not have been considered by employers otherwise.

2.  We estimated ordinary least square regressions for the natural logarithm of hourly wages and the socioeconomic index, benefits, firm size, and a logistic regression for current employment, minority workplace, and co-ethnic workplace. The estimated models are as follows:

    $$Pi(E) = f1 \ (Si, \ Xi) + U1$$
    $$SEIi = f3 \ (Si, \ Xi) + U3$$
    $$\log \ (Wi) = f2 \ (Si, \ Xi) + U2$$
    $$Bi = f4 \ (Si, \ Xi) + U4$$
    $$FSi = f5 \ (Si, \ Xi) + U5$$
    $$MWi = f6 \ (Si, \ Xi) + U6$$
    $$CEWi = f7 \ (Si, \ Xi) + U7$$

    where $Pi(E)$ is the probability of employment for the ith individual, $\log \ (Wi)$, the log of the hourly wages, and $SEIi$ is the socioeconomic index; $Si$ and $Xi$ are the vectors of search strategies used by job seekers and personal characteristics control variables (age, experience, education, marital status, presence of children, and hours worked), respectively; $Bi$ are the number of benefits received by a worker; $FSi$ represents the number of employees in a firm; $MWi$ is whether most of the workers in the respondents' workplace are minority; and $CEWi$ is whether most of the workers in the respondents' workplace are of the same ethnicity as the respondent.

3.  Tables including coefficients and standard errors for the models are available from the authors upon request.

# The Impact of Latino Workers on the U.S. Economy: Implications for Effective Employment Policy

**Sonia M. Pérez**
**Charles K. Kamasaki**
*National Council of La Raza*

## Abstract

*This discussion summarizes major issues and key findings from the previous chapters and analyzes the relevance of this research to public policy, specifically at the federal level. It also points to national developments that suggest that a focus on national employment policy – particularly involving Latino workers – is timely, relevant, and important. It emphasizes that, given the growth of the Latino population and the share of all U.S. workers they represent, it is imperative that the nation turn its attention to enhancing their employment characteristics, status, and outcomes. The authors suggest that investments in current and future Latino workers are necessary to ensure their productivity in the economy in the new century, and conclude by identifying policy interventions that can effectively improve the status of such workers.*

## Introduction

The U.S. Hispanic population is poised to be the economic fuel that drives the nation's continued prosperity in the 21st century. Latinos are now at least 11% of the nation's residents and are almost as likely to live in Omaha, Nebraska or Wilmington, North Caroli-

The authors appreciate the research assistance of Sandra Gallardo, NCLR Policy Fellow, in completing this article.

na as they are to live in Los Angeles, California or Brooklyn, New York. Almost half of Latinos are under 25 years old and, as such, represent a significant pool of workers entering their prime years in the labor force. Recent studies have pointed to a rise in the Latino middle class, a Hispanic annual purchasing power of more than $350 billion, and Hispanic entrepreneurs as a significant factor in the overall increase of America's small businesses.[1] At the time of this writing, there were further positive signs. Hispanic household income had experienced increases since the mid-'90s, and there was the beginning of a downward trend in the too-high Latino poverty rate – attributed largely to a continued strong economy and a consistently high level of workforce activity on the part of Hispanics.

In fact, one of the most positive employment characteristics of Latino workers – men, in particular – is their high labor force participation rate and workforce activity. But these high levels of workforce participation alone are insufficient for Latinos to reach parity with other American workers in terms of employment status and economic well-being. In the current economy, consistent and even full-time, year-round work does not guarantee that workers will have earnings that lift them above the poverty level. Rather, the key mechanisms that will improve these workers' status and propel the nation's continued economic expansion lie in increased worker education levels and productivity. In this regard, there are some areas both of concern and of opportunities for improving the lot of Latino workers.

As this volume illustrates, the employment status of a significant segment of Latinos is characterized by low-skilled jobs at inadequate wages with few benefits. Moreover, these jobs are often vulnerable to displacement resulting from changes in the economy. The heavy concentration of Latino workers in such employment has relegated a sizeable share of Hispanics to the bottom of the economic ladder. The consequences for these Hispanic workers and their families have been unstable employment, limited economic mobility, low wages, and stubbornly high poverty, especially among working families with children. While these consequences have an immediate impact on the Latino population, there are also potential effects on the cities and states where Latinos live – and on the nation as a whole.

Demographic data show that changes in the composition of the U.S. population mean that Latinos now represent an increasing share of students, workers, and taxpayers. In specific industries that have experienced labor shortages, Hispanics entering their prime working years represent a valuable a pool of talent and energy. Already, Latino workers and their high productivity have sustained and expanded meat and poultry plants, agricultural businesses, and a host of industrial sectors. Moreover, the aging of the U.S. population has meant that the nation is becoming increasingly dependent on young Latino workers. For example, once there were 17 workers for every Social Security recipient; today that ratio is 3:1 and in 10 years it will be 2:1. The future solvency of the nation's social insurance systems is thus dependent, at least in part, on the productivity of Hispanic workers. Given the growth of the Hispanic population, its relative youth, and its strong attachment to the labor market, improvements in Latinos' employment status and prospects are critical to all Americans. Similarly, the continued segmentation of Hispanics in low-wage work translates into major losses for the nation as a whole.

Consequently, efforts to raise the economic status of Latinos – especially through improvements in educational attainment and employment status – would have significant benefits for all Americans. To maximize their potential to drive the U.S. economy, however, more attention is needed to address the gaps in earnings and employment opportunities between Latinos and other Americans. Specifically, employment policy must become a national priority to both manage the challenges of the changing workforce and sustain the country's economic growth and prosperity.

This chapter highlights the key themes that emerge from research on the employment status of Latino workers in an effort to illuminate areas for further study and public policy action. It also underscores the value of Latino economic well-being to the larger U.S. economy, and argues that, with concerted effort and investments, the employment status of Hispanics – and overall economic benefits to the nation – can be improved substantially.

## Themes from the Research

Several issues have defined traditional research on Hispanics in the workforce. These include extensive documentation of the status of Latino workers, with an emphasis on low skills, low wages, and occupational segmentation. Additionally, there has been a focus on either human capital characteristics or structural economic changes as the principal factors in explaining Latino labor force outcomes. A new, emerging subset of the literature focuses on the contributions of Latino workers and underscores the assets of Hispanic communities, including their strong attachment to the labor force and their tendency to form and live in two-parent, working families. Many of these families are also reaping benefits from the current vibrant economy. In reward for their hard work, unemployment is declining, and earnings and income are rising. In turn, their economic contributions have meant that many cities and neighborhoods have been regenerated.[2] Not enough research exists on this "successful" segment of Latinos, the reasons for their successes, and their specific paths to economic mobility, and much more information is needed on these aspects of Hispanic economic status to understand how these benefits can be spread and shared more broadly.

Their strong attachment to the workforce, the gains made in business ownership, and other indicators of upward economic mobility notwithstanding, Latinos, as a group, are likely to be employed in low-paying jobs without important benefits like health insurance and pension coverage. In large measure, particularly in light of the changing economy and emphasis on knowledge and skills, this status can be attributable to inadequate educational preparation. Hispanics are significantly less likely than African Americans or Whites to have a high school diploma; similarly, fewer than one in 10 Latinos has a college degree. In this increasingly computerized, technological, and knowledge-based economy, such a lack of educational attainment is a serious problem. From a structural standpoint, the shift from manufacturing to services and from factories to office work has bypassed many Latino workers. They neither have the skills these new employers demand, nor tend to live in some of the areas where these jobs are available. Moreover, the widening educational gap between Latinos and other Americans that has occurred over the past several decades has put Hispanic workers and their families at a serious disadvantage both in the labor market and economically.

By comparison, the majority of White workers have moved in sync with the changes of the economy; when high school degrees were not required for work at decent wages, White workers with low education levels were able to maintain their families. As employers changed and demanded more skill, the educational attainment levels of Whites increased. For a host of historical and other reasons, both Black and Latino workers have had to make significant leaps to catch up to their White peers in terms of education and skill levels. One promising sign is that African Americans have begun to narrow that divide, as demonstrated by major gains in high school educational attainment levels that have put them close to parity with Whites. By contrast, the relative increase in Latino high school graduation rates since the 1970s has been negligible. As a result, only a small segment of Hispanic workers has been able to move into well-paying jobs that demand high levels of education and skill. For many other Latinos, these discrepancies cannot be closed overnight in response to what this current labor market requires.

While significant disparities remain between Whites and African Americans in a variety of other educational indicators, the near convergence of White and Black high school graduation rates over the past 25 years is noteworthy. If nothing else, it demonstrates that education gaps of the same order of magnitude as those currently faced by Hispanics can be closed, albeit over an extended period of time.

Two other issues have stood out in recent labor market research on Latinos. First, the extent to which the presence of Latino immigrants has affected the overall employment profile of Hispanic and other workers has been given substantial attention by researchers, policy makers, and the press. Second, while largely ignored by the press and policy makers, research has confirmed the importance of employment discrimination on Latino labor market opportunities.

## The Immigrant Factor

There has been a growing tendency by both researchers and policy-makers to attribute the stagnant economic status of Hispanic workers to Latino immigrants, particularly as the proportion of the Hispanic population that is foreign-born has increased over the past two decades. About two-thirds of Hispanics (56.5% of them native-born and 6.9% naturalized citizens) were U.S. citizens in 1996, and four in five Latino children were native-born (84.3%).

As a group, Hispanic immigrants indeed tend to have very low levels of educational attainment and limited skill levels. For example, while only slightly more than half of native-born Hispanics 25 years and older (55.9%) have completed high school, the same is true for only one-third of comparable foreign-born Hispanics. Higher education data show that fewer than one in 14 (7.4%) foreign-born Hispanics 25 or older, compared to little more than one in nine native-born Hispanics (11.5%), have college diplomas.[3] Poverty rates are also higher for immigrant communities, in general. For example, national-level data show that, in 1990, the most recent year for which strictly comparable native-born and foreign-born data are available, the poverty rate of U.S.-born Mexican Americans was 24.0%, while that of immigrant Mexicans was 28.6%.

However, even when immigration data concerns are held constant, there continue to be gaps in both education and poverty levels between native-born Mexicans (the largest Latino subgroup and the largest single immigrant group) and Whites. Specifically:

- While education does tend to be higher among U.S.-born Latinos, third-generation Mexican Americans have not attained educational levels comparable to those of non-Hispanic White natives. Moreover, when the Mexican population is disaggregated by birth cohort, data show that both male and female third-generation Mexican Americans have lower education levels than those in the second generation; in other words, educational attainment is actually declining in those generations.[4] In addition, although U.S.-born Latinos complete more education than their foreign-born counterparts, they still do not reach the education levels of African Americans and Whites.[5]

- A recent study on Latinos in California indicates that "being native-born does not necessarily guarantee a step up in the economic ladder."[6] One in five (21%) native-born Latinos in California does not have a high school diploma, compared to one in 14 (7%) non-Latinos. Furthermore, 17% of third-generation Latinos, compared to 7% of non-Latinos, have not completed high school; and, while only 10% of this segment of Latinos have a college degree, 30% of non-Latinos have a B.A. Therefore, in the case of California, low levels of educational attainment are not a problem solely of immigrants, and "relying on time alone" to address this serious concern "does not appear to be the best prescription."[7]

- With respect to poverty, the latest available data (from the 1990 Census) suggest that U.S-born Mexicans have only a slightly lower poverty rate than their foreign-born counterparts (24.0% and 28.6%, respectively), while both native-born and foreign-born Cubans have a remarkably similar rate (14.3% and 14.5%, respectively). Compared to native-born Whites, who in 1990 had a poverty rate of 8.0%, U.S.-born Mexicans are three times more likely to be poor. Therefore, even when foreign-born Mexicans are "removed" from the data to allow for native-born comparisons, a significant difference exists between U.S-born Mexican and White poverty rates.

Thus, it cannot fairly be said that the presence of large numbers of immigrants is the most important, or even a particularly significant, factor in Latinos' low levels of educational attainment or persistently high poverty rates. Another question that has surfaced in the literature with respect to the impact of Hispanic immigrants on the labor market is the extent to which "secondary effects" stemming from their presence in the labor force limit economic opportunities and status of U.S.-born low-wage workers, and of African Americans in particular. Although some job displacement and/or wage depression can be identified in certain economic sectors,[8] most such studies find few or no significant macro-level effects. For example, recent analysis of census data by Roger Waldinger and Nelson Lim indicates that between 1970 and 1990, there was a shift in employment among African Americans from industries where Latinos were present to those with few immigrants. In particular, the labor market niche of African Americans appears to exhibit a trend of movement into higher-skilled industries. Additionally, Blacks are well-represented in public-sector employment, an area of the economy where Latinos in general and immigrants in particular are significantly underrepresented. This suggests that, on the whole, Latino immigrants and African Americans are not competing for jobs.

In fact, some studies show, and common sense suggests, that Latino immigrants are more likely to be substitutes for previous immigrants and children of previous immigrants than for Black workers. To the extent that they frequently share labor market characteristics and live in the same communities, it is likely that some current Hispanic immigrants compete directly with native-born Latino workers, particularly in low-wage sectors of the economy. Even these common-sense notions, however, need to be interpreted with caution. For one thing, it is likely that the very presence of immigrants causes many of these low-wage jobs to persist in the country, in effect "creating" jobs, including higher-skilled supervisory positions, for native workers. Moreover, given the concentration of immigrants in many of these industries, the immigrants themselves are absorbing the brunt of any wage suppression that may be taking place, rather than causing economic hardship for other groups.

Furthermore, the presence of immigrants in the Latino community, with their strong work ethic, family unity, and espousal of core American values, arguably reinforces the strengths of Latino families overall. For example, a 1991 Children's Defense Fund report on child poverty noted that "male Latino immigrants are more likely to be working or seeking work than male Latinos born in the U.S."[9] Furthermore, data on homeownership – a key indicator of economic stability – show that more than half (57.1%) of foreign-born Hispanic U.S. citizens were homeowners in 1996, a proportion that approaches the national homeownership rate of 65.4%. By comparison, 48.1% of native-born Hispanics are homeowners.[10] In addition, one prominent researcher emphasizes the wide range of cultural benefits Latino immigrants provide, including strong family values and a healthy diet and lifestyle, which among other things translates into relatively high life expectancy and positive birth outcomes, despite limited access to medical care.[11] These factors almost certainly improve Latinos' socioeconomic status in areas that have experienced large-scale immigration. In any event, no reputable study has demonstrated that the marginal economic status of many U.S.-born Latino workers is primarily, or even largely, attributable to competition with immigrants.

These mixed data on the degree of influence that Latino immigrants have on the overall economic profile of Hispanics in the U.S. suggest that the conclusion that immigrants are "bad" for the Hispanic population's progress or for the U.S. is both simplistic and largely incorrect. The human capital characteristics of Hispanic immigrants are not valued by today's labor market, but that has not precluded them from actively seeking work or from getting hired. Their wages are lower than those of native-born Hispanics, but they are more likely than this group to be homeowners, so some of their "negative" economic effect on Latino wage and poverty data may be offset by positive effects of high labor force participation and homeownership rates, as well as other factors.

## Employment Discrimination

Recent studies indicate that employment discrimination against Latinos, in both the public and private sectors, is prevalent, and remains a significant factor in their employment and economic status – accounting for their significant interview rejection rate, wide earnings gap relative to Whites, and poor career advancement opportunities.

A variety of studies in the 1980s, using residual analyses of major data bases, found that a significant proportion of the White-Hispanic unemployment and wage gaps were attributable to employment discrimination.[12] Beginning in 1989, a new technique known as the "hiring audit" was introduced; it tests for differential treatment by having closely matched pairs of testers, one from the majority group and the other from a minority group, inquire about or apply for the same job. The experiences of the testers are matched to determine whether or not differential treatment occurred; since the methodology attempts to control for "objective" human capital characteristics (e.g., age, education, and work experience), significant differences in treatment are attributed to discrimination. An Urban Institute study based on 360 hiring audits in San Diego and Chicago in 1989 found that Anglo applicants received 33% more interviews and 50% more job offers than equally-qualified Hispanic applicants; overall, 31% of the Latino applicants encountered unfavorable treatment, compared to 11% of Anglo applicants.[13] A 1992 hiring audit in the Washington, D. C. metropolitan area by the Fair Employment Council of Greater Washington found that Hispanic testers encountered discrimination about 22.4% of the time.[14]

Taken together, and despite a number of methodological issues and questions which remain to be resolved, these studies demonstrate that Latinos experience substantial labor market discrimination, which has a direct impact on employment opportunities. Although a statistically precise estimate of the scope and degree of such discrimination remains elusive, suffice it to say that the discrimination experienced by Latino workers appears to be of the same order of magnitude as that experienced by African Americans in comparable studies and markets.[15]

Moreover, the effects of employment discrimination go beyond jobs, wages, and employment opportunities. For Latinos, such discrimination is also a factor in overall economic status, as measured by the poverty rate. In fact, while many in contemporary policy discussions dismiss its effects as negligible, a growing body of social science research strongly suggests that employment discrimination does help to explain the high and persistent Hispanic poverty rate, not to mention its effect on the income gap between Latinos and Whites. An analysis conducted by NCLR suggested that, in 1993, one-fourth of poor Hispanic families with a full-time, full-year worker (26.5%) would be lifted above the poverty level if employment discrimination were eliminated.[16]

## New Findings

In addition to providing human capital explanations, analyses of the impact of structural economic changes on workers, the influence of immigrant workers, and the impact of employment discrimination on Latino workplace opportunities, the discussions in this volume point to several new findings in the examination of the employment status of Latinos.

First, the analyses on occupational distribution in the previous chapters continue to underscore not only that certain industries must do more to increase their representation of Latinos, but also that *new strategies* are needed to connect Latino workers to different jobs and sectors outside of those in which they typically seek jobs. As Meléndez and Falcón noted, part of the obstacle to improving Latino employment status is that, like most workers, Latinos are likely to seek employment through family and friends who tend to work in precisely those industries that limit their opportunities for higher wages and employment mobility. By relying almost exclusively on these (ineffective) family networks, Hispanics limit the range of job possibilities available to them. An important and encouraging sign related to the issue of occupational distribution is that there is good news for Hispanic women. Latinas do not have as much variability as their male counterparts, who tend to be employed in a broader range of jobs. However, they are more likely than Hispanic men to be represented in jobs that offer higher salaries, benefits, and opportunities for mobility. For example, in 1997, data show that 18% of Hispanic women, compared to 12% of Hispanic men, worked in professional and managerial positions. In addition, as Reimers notes in Chapter 5, young women are earning more than they used to, a positive trend for this group. Of note, while Hispanic women earn less than Black or White women in all occupational categories, Latina college graduates and young high school drop-outs had rising wages between 1994 and 1996, regardless of place of birth.

Second, in addition to the ethnic and national origin diversity within the Latino population, there is also significant variation in the labor market experiences of Hispanic workers according to subgroup. Puerto Ricans, U.S. citizens by birth, have a mixed employment history, which suggests that citizenship alone is not a guarantee of economic opportunity or progress. Current data show that Puerto Ricans tend to have lower labor force participation rates and higher unemployment rates than their other Latino counterparts. This is related, in part, to their historical ties to the manufacturing sector (which has rapidly dwindled in the U.S.) and to the areas of the country in which they have traditionally been concentrated, which have not had the most robust or expansive economies. Despite this underemployed status, Puerto Ricans who are in the labor force are more likely than Mexicans and other Hispanics to work in stable and better-paying industries. Consequently, their wages are higher than those for other Latinos, and they tend to have access to important benefits, like health insurance.

In terms of job type, a similar situation exists for Cubans, who are among the most likely of all Latinos to have high education levels and to have a stable connection to the labor force, defined by their relatively low unemployment rate. This positive employment profile is aided by their age; Cubans have the oldest median age among all Latinos, which suggests that they have more employment experience than younger Latinos; and all workers, as a group, are likely to experience increases in earnings as they age. Moreover, the largest cohort of Cuban refugees to the U.S. in the 1960s was a self-selected group of educated professionals and businesspeople, on average, and this abundance of human capital enabled many to transfer skills to the U.S. labor force, make a transition to employment, and develop businesses. In addition, a Cuban-assistance program sponsored by the U.S. government provided employment training to many of these refugees, which facilitated their integration into the U.S labor market,[17] although the effects of this modest assistance should not be exaggerated.

Mexican- and Central-American-origin Latinos are especially likely to be in the workforce. In fact, Mexican and Central American men have the highest labor force participation rates of all male worker groups, including Whites. A combination of factors affects their placement in the labor market, earnings, and opportunities. These groups have the lowest levels of education of all Hispanics. Also, they continue to have lower median wages than the other Latino subgroups. As their occupational distribution shows, they are most likely to be concentrated in low-wage jobs vulnerable to economic shifts. Both groups also count the foreign-born as a high proportion of their populations, which implies limited English fluency and poor employment networks. It also suggests that they are especially likely to experience employment discrimination in terms of both opportunities and wages.

A third element important to the discussion of Latino labor market experiences and ways to improve employment status is benefits. Critical benefits like health insurance are not available to most low-wage workers, many of whom are Latino. In particular, Mexican Americans are the most likely not to have health insurance. This means that routine preventive health care, as well as serious medical attention for specific injuries or illnesses, must be paid out of pocket or foregone by Latinos whose employers do not provide health care coverage. This has two effects. Workers with already-low earnings may have to choose between paying for medical costs and paying for basic necessities, like food or housing. In other cases, workers who do not seek preventive or needed care may risk either the well-being of others, if they work while they are sick, or a loss of jobs or wages, if they cannot work because their medical condition disables them.

Health insurance is the most obvious of "fringe" benefits, but there are other important benefits outside of wages that a significant proportion of Latino workers does not receive. For example, the recent public policy debate related to the solvency of Social Security has brought to light the importance of private savings and retirement planning benefits provided by employers. Yet, according to the Department of Labor, one-third of Hispanic workers does not participate in private pension plans – the highest proportion of any worker group. Moreover, a recent survey by the Employee Benefits Research Institute confirmed that two-thirds (66%) of Hispanic workers reported that they had not received employer-provided retirement education materials in the past 12 months, and only 14% of Latino workers cited employer-funded plans as a source of income in retirement.[18] While shifts in occupational distribution and increases in wages are needed to enhance the employment status of Latino workers, more must be done to address the serious gaps in benefits that these workers experience. Necessary benefits, like pension coverage and health insurance, should no longer be seen as "extras" or optional elements of compensation. In this context, one important note to underscore is that of union representation. Latinos are the least likely of all workers to be members of unions, but stand to gain significantly, as several chapters in this volume note, from the increased wages and benefits that union membership offers.

A fourth finding suggested by the previous discussions is the growing economic bifurcation within the Latino population. Data suggest a trend in the employment mobility and economic status of Latino workers. On some key economic indicators, including income gains and poverty rates, Hispanics have not fared well recently, especially relative to Whites, and, in some cases, to Blacks. At the same time, a small but significant share of Latinos has enjoyed some measure of economic success. This paradox reflects a stagnation of wages and limited opportunities for economic mobility among low-income Hispanic workers, but a simultaneous growth in opportunity for upper-income Hispanic earners and business owners. Moreover, this bifurcation is occurring among *working* Latinos, which suggests a different set of policy responses from those geared toward the chronically unemployed, discouraged workers, long-term welfare recipients, or others with little or no experience in the labor market.

A final issue concerns the preparation of Latinos for better-paying jobs and their connection to employers. Given that "employment and training" and "workforce development" programs are not viewed in a positive light by many policy-makers, a finding from this research that may surprise some is that such programs can be extremely effective for Latinos. As Meléndez and Falcón discuss in Chapter 7, two programs in California and Texas have achieved significant gains for Latino workers in terms of skill enhancement, placement, and wages, and these programs have been rigorously reviewed by a number of outside evaluators. This issue and the concern regarding Latino social networks and job strategies discussed above suggest that community-based organizations can play important roles in both helping to provide Latino workers with job market skills and acting as intermediaries between them and employers.

## Research and Policy Implications

Taken together, the research discussed above and presented in this volume demonstrates that Latino employment and labor market issues, and the persistently wide economic gap that exists between them and their non-Hispanic counterparts, do not fit into the neat or traditional paradigms that most often tend to be discussed in the low-wage or ethnic literature. For example, the high poverty rate of Hispanic families is not explained by lack of work or labor force activity. Similarly, the progressive incorporation of generations of previous immigrants into the workplace and the larger society has not proven to be the typical model for much of that portion of the Hispanic community that is foreign-born. Furthermore, in the case of Puerto Ricans, their status as American citizens has not necessarily facilitated their entrée into the workforce, or their transition from declining industries to high-growth sectors of the economy.

Like the proverbial "square peg," the Latino experience in the workforce has resisted and confounded policy makers and others who wish to rely on the "round holes" of simplistic explanations. Those who prefer to do nothing, or who seek punitive strategies in response to their perceptions of the issues, can find precious little support in the research. This volume suggests that new research or policy responses designed to enhance the employability of Hispanics have to be multidisciplinary and integrated. Several areas deserve further attention.

First, a comprehensive assessment of the data and research shows that Latino workers possess important, positive characteristics that have value for the current labor force. Men are especially likely to work, despite a number of human capital characteristics and other challenges that would suggest that their workforce activity would be severely limited. Hispanic women are making some important strides, in terms of labor force participation rates, occupational distribution, and wages. A related point that this raises, however, is that new gender-oriented research is needed to understand both the gains made thus far by Hispanic women and why Latino men are mired in certain jobs and do not seem to be making as much earnings progress. Moreover, this bifurcation should be assessed for its potential impact on Hispanic family formation in the future.

Second, the data clearly show that some segment of the Latino immigrant population is not as economically mobile as previous immigrants before them. However, Latino immigrants are industrious and demonstrate a very strong attachment to the workforce. This suggests that policies should be adopted to increase their productivity, rather than to punish immigrants or all Latinos because of the perception that Hispanic economic progress is inhibited by the low skills of that segment of the population that is foreign-born. In response to the issues raised above of diversity within the Latino employment experience and potential economic bifurcation, research is needed within states and regions to understand the factors that affect employment status of specific Latino populations. For example, such research might examine ways to increase the education and skill levels of Central American workers in specific industries, so that the human capital of adult workers already in the labor market can be enhanced, facilitating mobility into other industries where Hispanics are underrepresented. Similarly, through the implementation of the Workforce Investment Act (WIA)* in areas where Puerto Ricans are concentrated, states should study ways effectively to integrate more Puerto Rican males into the labor market.

Third, wages and benefits continue to be key to the overall economic status of Latinos. In this sense, the nation's focus on job creation should be more comprehensive to include not only more jobs, but *better-quality jobs.* Adding more low-wage jobs without benefits will not help the overall economic progress of Latino or other less-skilled workers. In particular, two sets of benefits – health insurance and pension coverage – are critical to enhancing the employment status of Hispanics. In this connection, policy proposals that create incentives for employers to provide benefits, or that provide health and pension coverage directly through the government, show particular promise in addressing the interests of Latino workers, and should receive greater attention by researchers and policy-makers.

A fourth issue is related to the nation's system of training workers and assisting the existing pool of workers to meet the changing demands of employers and the U.S. labor market at a time of technological change and global competitiveness. The nation's most recent response to the need for "training" is the WIA, which gives priority to recipients of public assistance and other low-income individuals. Dislocated workers are also served. For Hispanics, WIA presents both some concerns and some opportunities. Much of WIA's funding and decision-making has been "devolved" to the states, where there is a noticeable absence of a Hispanic policy advocacy infrastructure. The extent to which the new system will respond to the distinct labor market needs of Latino workers is uncertain, and requires close scrutiny. In addition, a number of factors could lead to great unevenness and possible difficulties in various locales. These include: uncertainties in the implementation process, the law's shift away from previous near-exclusive targeting of low-income constituencies, the reliance on local workforce boards which may not have

* The WIA was signed into law on August 7, 1998, and replaces the Job Training Partnership Act. It revises law regarding governance, eligibility, and targeting of funds, establishes "one-stop centers" as the central vehicle for the delivery of employment training services, and provides funding streams for adults, dislocated workers, and youth. For a summary of the WIA, see *Workforce Investment Act of* 1998, Washington, DC: U.S. Department of Labor, Employment and Training Administration, September 1998.

connections to or representation from the Hispanic community, and the overall decentralizing thrust of the law. On the other hand, the potential for significantly improved performance of the entire workforce system offers possible opportunities for community-based service providers interested in and capable of seeking new partnerships in the workforce world, especially with private-sector employers. State-level implementation efforts, especially in areas like California, New York, Texas, and Illinois, should insure that Latinos are at the decision-making table, helping to shape the delivery of employment training services to the growing Hispanic workforce.

A fifth issue involves more information regarding Latino successes. This includes a better understanding of the growing Hispanic middle class and ways in which lessons learned from those achievements can be shared with low-income workers and families. In addition, not enough is known about Latino self-employment and the rise over the past decade in the number of Hispanic-owned businesses – especially those established by women. Given the importance of small businesses and entrepreneurship to American society, researchers should widen their lens to identify and document the reasons for the growth of Latino businesses. Similarly, the relatively higher immigrant homeownership rate is an intriguing, counter-intuitive finding that should be explored further.

**Investing In Latino Workers: Why Does This Matter and What Can We Do?**

The well-documented growth of the Latino population and their growing share of American workers underscore that concern for their employment status must extend beyond the Latino community to include the nation as a whole. Because of their youthfulness and population growth, Latino employment and economic outcomes will fuel – or impede – the nation's future prosperity.

The economic case is compelling. If Latinos had higher education and productivity levels, and were employed in high-growth, high-mobility occupations, the positive results would be measurable for Americans across the country. One recent analysis shows that increasing the education level of workers by a single year would result in productivity improvements of 8.5% in manufacturing industries and 12.7% in non-manufacturing industries.[19] For Hispanics specifically, a study by the Rand Corporation shows that every Hispanic who now has a high school education would earn between $400,000 and $500,000 more over his or her lifetime if he/she had a bachelor's degree. Beyond these individual economic gains, increasing the college completion rate of today's Hispanic 18-year-olds by as little as three percentage points (from 12% to 15%) alone would increase projected social insurance payments by $600 million. If this cohort's college completion rate were equal to that of White Americans (30%), social insurance payments would increase by about $6.6 billion. These estimates assume improvements only in a single cohort (18-year-old Hispanics). Were they applied to an entire generation, such as the birth cohort from zero to age 18, the increase in federal tax revenues from equalizing Hispanic college completion rates with those of Whites would be a staggering $10 billion each year.[20] A recent analysis of Latinos in California lends further support to these findings and demonstrates that increased education levels and economic status of Latinos would provide "indirect benefits to the state in the form of higher expenditures on goods and services, increases in tax revenues, and a reduction in the need of public programs for the poor."[21] Specifically, raising the educational attainment of Latinos in the labor force would result in an increase of $79 million in new state income tax revenues.[22]

The potential gains in societal equity and social cohesion are equally powerful. Despite "playing by the rules" and embodying "American" values, including hard work and two-parent families, the proportion of Hispanic families who are poor has grown over the past decade. The uneven economic progress that Hispanics have made since such data were collected in the 1970s is troubling. One basic American tenet holds that demonstrated work effort should be rewarded. If Hispanic Americans continue to struggle despite their initiative, what does that say about the integrity of "The American Dream"? Moreover, on a purely practical level, it is unhealthy for any society if its largest ethnic minority is denied equal economic opportunity. As the nation has learned in this century with respect to African Americans, the persistent denial of opportunity to any major ethnic group undermines the society as a whole – and has long-lasting and often unpredictable consequences. As the nation seeks ways to expand and prolong its current economic boom, it should ensure that all workers, at all levels, reap the benefits of labor force commitment and high productivity. When all Americans experience economic opportunity and mobility, the nation as a whole gains.

But this simply cannot happen unless Latinos become fully integrated into the nation's economic mainstream. Fortunately, many characteristics of the Latino workforce and the factors associated with their uneven employment status are amenable to well-designed policy prescriptions. Presented below are a series of such policy recommendations, grouped roughly into four categories – education, new workers, existing workers, and equal employment opportunity.

First, given the direct relationship between education and skill levels and employment and earnings prospects and status, **increasing Hispanic education levels** should be the top domestic priority for the current generation of policy makers. Policy makers would be foolish not to focus more resources and energy on narrowing the gaps in high school and college attainment levels between Latinos and other Americans, given chronic undereducation experienced by Hispanics and the demographic realities facing the nation.

While the development of comprehensive education policy proposals is far beyond the scope of this chapter, the research suggests that one seemingly simple step involves assuring equal opportunities for Latinos to participate in proven, effective federal education programs. It is ironic that Hispanics, who have low levels of educational attainment, are simultaneously severely underrepresented in federal education programs. As Chapter 1 notes, disparities in enrollment levels in early childhood programs can and should be addressed, in part through the admission of proportional levels of Hispanic children into Head Start. In addition, college preparation programs like Upward Bound have a proven track record of effectiveness in encouraging Latino youth to complete high school and prepare for higher education[23]; unfortunately, Hispanic participation in the program has fallen over the past two decades even as the population has risen rapidly.[24] Similarly, Latinos are underrepresented in programs such as Title I Compensatory Education for disadvantaged students, the Talent Search program serving at-risk high school students, and college loan and grant assistance.[25] Most observers recognize that the recent near convergence of African American and White high school graduation rates is attributable at least in part to the effective targeting of federal education programs to the Black community over the past three decades. Surely it is not unreasonable for policy-makers over the next several decades to assure Hispanics an equivalent opportunity to participate in these federal educational assistance efforts.

Second, **for non-college-bound youth, young adults, and others just entering the labor force**, several strategies are apparent. The research demonstrates that **workforce development programs** can have a positive impact on those who need to strengthen their skills. Such efforts should be expanded in several ways. The elements that are key to the effectiveness of the Texas and California programs, cited in Chapter 7, need to be replicated elsewhere. One aspect of this effort should include encouraging state and local officials who oversee implementation of the Workforce Investment Act to incorporate these key elements in their own programs. In addition, the pool of community-based and other organizations involved in job training with the technical and institutional expertise to implement such programs should be expanded significantly. Moreover, at a time of severe fiscal constraints, it is crucial that the public commitment to worker training be maintained. Thus, the total volume of federal and state resources allocated to workforce development should be expanded, and not diminished.

Furthermore, the need for alternative – and more effective – job recruitment networks suggests that several other promising workforce development strategies should be explored and tested. The current vogue in the field emphasizes a "work first" approach, which is predicated on the assumption that the principal policy objective is to get people into any job as quickly as possible. Given Latinos' high labor force participation rates and concentration in low-wage jobs without benefits, this approach is neither necessary nor useful. Instead, the research suggests, greater policy attention needs to be placed on **improving Hispanics' access to alternative job search and recruitment networks.** This implies more support for the development of so-called "soft skills" – resume writing, effective job application and interviewing techniques, etc. – among Latino jobseekers. In addition, both employers and community groups should have a common interest in improved job referral and placement systems, and more effort should be given to their development. Moreover, the existing school-to-work transition system clearly does not work for many Hispanics; as an example, Latinos are severely underrepresented in apprenticeship programs.[26] In this respect, expanding opportunities for school-based co-op and work experience programs, work-based internships, and cooperative apprenticeship efforts between employers and community groups would all seem to strengthen the exposure of prospective Latino workers to alternative recruitment and referral networks.

Third, for those Latinos already in the job market, proven **strategies for making work more rewarding** must be expanded. In particular for Latinos, the Earned Income Tax Credit (EITC) already is an effective tool for rewarding work; in 1998, the EITC reduced Hispanic after-tax poverty by 3.8 percentage points.[27] However, the policy goal of ensuring that no family with a full-time, year-round worker live in poverty is far from being realized, particularly for Latino workers. Some have proposed that tax reform proposals that seek to eliminate the "marriage penalty" also include commensurate benefits to EITC recipients, a proposal that would greatly benefit Latino workers. In addition, it would also make sense to expand EITC benefits in other ways, including deepening support to workers with larger families.[28] While these proposals are relatively expensive in budgetary terms – about $2 billion annually – the EITC is simply the most efficient and effective policy intervention available for rewarding work performed by those at the margins of the economy. While somewhat less efficient, increasing the minimum wage would also immediately improve the condition of Hispanic low-wage workers, with negligible budgetary impact.

Increasing health insurance coverage for low-wage workers should be another objective for policy-makers. Increasingly for Latino and other low-wage workers, there is a growing consensus that some form of universal health insurance coverage is the best solution, although short-term prospects for its enactment are highly uncertain. In the interim, various other policy options for increasing low-wage workers' access to health care should be explored, including expansion of eligibility for Medicaid and the Children's Health Insurance Program (CHIP), expansion of tax and other incentives for employers who choose to offer health benefits, and additional support for community-based health care providers. One approach which would seem to hold great promise for Latinos would be the extension of CHIP coverage to the parents of eligible children – those in families between 100% and 200% of the federal poverty level.[29] In addition, other types of proposals, including voucher-type mechanisms that would subsidize low-income families' access to private health insurance, also appear to be worthy of further exploration.

A related issue involves unions. As is noted in several chapters in this volume, the low wages and absence of benefits that characterize many of the jobs held by Hispanic workers could be addressed through collective bargaining agreements if Latinos were better represented in unions. Thus, unions should make a concerted effort to increase the proportion of Hispanic workers in the ranks of organized labor. Moreover, public policy can make a difference here as well. For one thing, there is growing evidence that the enforcement of immigration laws prohibiting the hiring of undocumented persons is undercutting the ability of unions to organize in many low-wage industries, and thus removes economic incentives for employers to improve wages and working conditions. These policies should be reformed, not so much to benefit unauthorized workers but precisely because all workers – including U.S. citizens and legal residents – in these low-wage sectors would benefit from collective bargaining. Furthermore, Hispanic organizations in general have not been active participants in policy debates involving other policy-related barriers to union organizing; this research suggests that they should be.

In addition, more needs to be done to encourage and support low-wage workers to engage in skills development and "lifelong learning" efforts. Many immigrant workers already participate in English language classes, but such courses are heavily over-subscribed and many are held in locations and at times which make them inaccessible to low-wage workers. Substantial increases in public support for English language and literacy training make sense, particularly for community-based programs that are accessible and responsive to the target population. Since the state-of-the-art in English language and literacy development is quite well-advanced, substantial improvements in the employability of Latino and other foreign-born workers are eminently achievable, given sufficient resources.

Given the premium that the rapidly-changing nature of the economy places on skills development, additional measures may be called for. While a number of policies have been enacted recently to support workers' acquisition of education and training, there is evidence that most low-wage workers are not aware of them. One useful step might involve the provision of basic information about lifelong learning opportunities to low-wage workers. For example, under current law, most employers are required to post notices in the workplace advising employees of their rights under the Fair Labor Standards Act and other laws. It may make sense to require the posting of similar notices informing low-wage workers about the availability of public support for education and training opportunities. In addition, expanded tax-based and other incentives for workplace-based education and training should be explored, perhaps on a pilot basis. This is another highly promising area for collaborations between employers and community groups. Expansion of worksite-based opportunities for education and skills development should be one form of "fringe benefit" that enlightened employers seeking to retain good workers might wish to pursue; conversely, many community groups are well-positioned to provide such courses.

A fourth area that this volume underscores is **the need to advance effective elements of the nation's equal employment opportunity framework.** Traditional civil rights enforcement mechanisms and affirmative action in employment have played important roles in the economic progress made in recent years by African Americans and women. On the one hand, Latinos share a fundamental interest in that agenda with these groups. Indeed, some knowledgeable observers have argued that broader coalitions involving traditional civil rights groups and new immigrants are essential to further advancements in laws and policies promoting equal opportunity.[30] On the other hand, it appears that Hispanics overall have not benefited proportionately from the implementation of the traditional civil rights agenda to-date. The emerging evidence of improvement in the status of young Latina workers, however, suggests that the nation's progress toward gender equity may be reaching the current generation of Hispanic women entering the workforce. Based on this evidence, perhaps interested policy-makers, as well as Hispanic organizations and advocates, should consider placing greater emphasis on gender-focused employment policies in the future. Moreover, while the future of affirmative action in employment is somewhat unclear, the continuing and chronic underrepresentation of Latinos in public employment should be amenable to affirmative-action-based remedies, particularly at the federal level.

Regarding other effective responses to employment discrimination, NCLR has published a long list of policy recommendations on this subject[31]; having said that, the research in the civil rights field suggests that new strategies probably are needed to make substantial progress in reducing labor market discrimination. One promising, albeit highly controversial, strategy would be to integrate paired testing techniques described above with immediate enforcement, such that bias uncovered through paired tests of employers could be used as evidence in a discrimination complaint or lawsuit. This practice has been successful in addressing housing discrimination, but its use in the employment context is constrained by both legal and policy considerations.

High levels of both economic and social "return" are achievable if the nation embraces and implements the "investment in workers" approach, suggested in this chapter. Particularly in the context of a strong economy, record federal budget surpluses, a growing understanding that worker productivity will be key to national prosperity in the new millennium, and the growing awareness of the importance of Latino workers to the economy, these investments are well within the nation's capacity.

# NOTES

1.  National Council of La Raza, *Index of Hispanic Economic Indicators*, Washington, DC: July 1997. See also Rodriguez, Gregory, *The Emerging Latino Middle Class*, Pepperdine University Institute for Public Policy and AT&T, October 1996; Humphreys, Jeff, *Hispanic Buying Power by Place of Residence: 1990-1997*, University of Georgia, Selig Center for Economic Growth, 1997; and Myers, Bill, "It's a small business world," *USA Today*, July 30, 1999, Page 1B.

2.  Myers, Dowell, *Immigration: Fundamental Force in the American City*, Fannie Mae Foundation, Housing Facts and Findings, Winter 1999; Rodriguez, Gregory, From *Newcomers to New Americans: The Successful Integration of Immigrants into American Society*, Washington, DC: National Immigration Forum, July 1999; Moore, Stephen, *A Fiscal Portrait of the Newest Americans*, Washington, DC: National Immigration Forum and the Cato Institute, July 1998; Muller, Thomas, *Immigrants and the American City*. A Twentieth Century Fund Book, New York: New York University Press, 1993.

3.  Pérez, Sonia M. with Eric Rodríguez, *U.S. Hispanic Demographic Profile: Developments, Implications, and Challenges*, Washington, DC: National Council of La Raza, April 1998.

4.  Chapa, Jorge, and Dawn A. Jahn, et al., "Latino Poverty: Not Just An Immigrant Issue," Association of Public Policy Analysis and Management Conference, Washington, DC, October 1993; and Chapa, Jorge, "The Myth of Hispanic Progress: Trends in the Educational and Economic Attainment of Mexican Americans," *Journal of Hispanic Policy*, Vol. 4, 1989-1990, pp.3-18.

5.  del Pinal, Jorge and Audrey Singer, "Generations of Diversity: Latinos in the United States," *Population Bulletin*, vol. 52, no. 3, Washington, DC: Population Reference Bureau, Inc., October 1997.

6.  *Latinos and Economic Development in California,* op.cit.

7.  Ibid.

8.  Morris, Milton and Gary Rubin, *Immigrants and African Americans: Research Findings and Policy Responses*, New York: New York Association of New Americans, forthcoming, 2000.

9.  Miranda, Leticia, *Latino Child Poverty in the U.S.*, Washington, DC: Children's Defense Fund, 1991.

10. U.S. Bureau of the Census, Current Housing Reports, *Moving to America – Moving to Homeownership*, Washington, DC, September 1997.

11. Hayes-Bautista, David, "The Latino Social Paradox," Presentation to the NCLR Board of Directors Strategic Planning Retreat, Cuernavaca, Mexico, April 1998.

12. These studies are summarized in Gonzales, Claire, *The Empty Promise, The EEOC and Hispanics*, Washington, DC: National Council of La Raza, December 1993.

13. Cross, Harry, Genevieve Kenny, Jane Mell and Wendy Zimmerman. 1990. *Employer Hiring Practices: Differential Treatment of Hispanic and Anglo Job Seekers*. Washington, DC: Urban Institute Press.

14. Bendick, Jr., Marc, Charles W. Jackson and Victor A. Reinoso, *Measuring Employment Discrimination through Controlled Experiments*. Washington, DC: Fair Employment Council of Greater Washington, Inc., January 1993.

15. Fix, Michael and Raymond J. Struyck (eds.), *Clear and Convincing Evidence*, Washington, DC: Urban Institute, 1993.

16. Pérez, Sonia M. and Deirdre Martínez, *State of Hispanic America 1993: Toward a Latino Anti-Poverty Agenda,* Washington, DC: National Council of La Raza, July 1993.

17. Cattan, Peter, "The Diversity of Hispanics in the U.S. Work Force," *Monthly Labor Review*, August 1993.

18. *1999 Retirement Confidence Survey, Summary of Findings*, Washington, DC: Employee Benefits Research Institute, June 15, 1999.

19. Black, Sandra E. and Lisa M. Lynch, "Human Capital Investments and Productivity," *American Economic Association Papers and Proceedings*, Vol. 86, No. 2, May 1996.

20. Sorenson, Stephen, Dominic J. Brewer, Stephen J. Carroll, and Eugene Bryton, "Increasing Hispanic Participation in Higher Education: A Desirable Public Investment," Santa Monica, CA: The RAND Corporation, 1995.

21. López, Elías, Ramírez, Enrique, and Refugio I. Rochín, *Latinos and Economic Development in California*, Sacramento, CA: California Research Bureau, June 1999.

22. Ibid.

23. Myers, David, and Schirm, Allen, *The Impacts of Upward Bound: Final Report for Phase I of the National Evaluation*, Washington, DC: Mathematica Policy Research, Inc., April 1999.

24. National Council of La Raza, "Hispanic Participation in Federal TRIO Programs," Washington, DC, April 1998.

25. National Council of La Raza, "Hispanic Participation in Selected Anti-Poverty Programs," Washington, DC, July 1997.

26. McKay, Emily Gantz, *The Forgotten Two-Thirds: An Hispanic Perspective on Apprenticeship, European Style*, Washington, DC: National Council of La Raza, 1993.

27. Calculation made by the National Council of La Raza based on Current Population Survey data. The EITC also pushed more than 600,000 Hispanic children above the poverty level that year. For more information, see National Council of La Raza, "Hispanic Working Poor and the Earned Income Tax Credit," Census Information Center, Washington, DC, January 1999.

28. National Council of La Raza, Issue Brief, *Hispanic Families and the Earned Income Tax Credit*, Washington, DC, February 2000.

29. This idea was proposed most recently in President Clinton's 2000 State of the Union Address. Some caution is probably in order regarding this strategy. Although Latinos are disproportionately eligible for the CHIP program, their actual enrollment levels have been disappointing due to a variety of regulatory and implementation issues.

30. See, for example, Morris and Rubin, op. cit.

31. See Gonzalez, op.cit.

# REFERENCES

## Chapter 1, Siles and Pérez

Carliner, Geoffrey, "The Wages and Language Skills of U.S. Immigrants," Cambridge, MA: National Bureau of Economic Research, Working Paper No. 5763, September 1996.

Hamilton, Gayle, Thomas Brock, Mary Farrell, Daniel Friedlander, and Kristen Harknett, *Evaluating Two Welfare-to-Work Program Approaches: Two-Year Findings on the Labor Force Attachment and Human Capital Development Programs in Three Sites,* Washington, DC: U.S. Department of Health and Human Services, Administration for Children and Families, Office for the Assistant Secretary for Planning and Evaluation, December 1997.

Hecker, Daniel, "Earnings of College Graduates, 1993," *Monthly Labor Review*, December 1995.

Holzer, Harry, *What Employers Want – Job Prospects for Less-Educated Workers*, New York: Russell Sage Foundation, 1996.

Knouse, Stephen B., Paul Rosenfeld, and Amy L. Culbertson, *Hispanics in the Workplace*, Newbury Park, CA: Sage Publications, 1992.

Levine, Robert, "Social Time and the Pace of Life in Four Continents," *Social Science Newsletter*, 70, 2, Summer, pp. 71-76, 1985.

McManus, Walter, William Gould, and Finis Welch, "Earnings of Hispanic Men: The Role of English Language Proficiency," *Journal of Labor Economics*, pp.101-130, April 1983.

Morales, Rebecca and Frank Bonilla, *Latinos in a Changing U.S. Economy,* Sage Series on Race and Ethnic Relations, Vol. 7, Newbury Park, CA: Sage Publications, 1993.

Pagán, José A. and Gilberto Cárdenas, "The Role of Occupational Attainment, Labor Market Structure, and Earnings Inequality on the Relative Earnings of Mexican Americans: 1986-1992," *Hispanic Journal of Behavioral Sciences*, Vol. 19, No. 3, August 1997.

Pérez, Sonia M. and Denise De la Rosa Salazar, "Economic, Labor Force, and Social Implications of Latino Educational and Population Trends," *Hispanic Journal of Behavioral Sciences*, Vol. 15, No. 2, May 1993.

Reimers, Cordelia W., "Labor Market Discrimination against Hispanic and Black Men," *The Review of Economics and Statistics*, Vol. 65, Issue 4, November 1983.

Rivera-Batiz, Francisco L., "The Effects of Literacy on the Earnings of Hispanics in the United States," *Hispanics in the Labor Force, Issues and Policies*, Edwin Meléndez, Clara Rodríguez, and Janis Barry Figueroa, eds., New York: Plenum Press, 1991.

Rumbaut, Ruben G., "Immigrants from Latin America and the Caribbean: A Socioeconomic Profile," CIFRAS No. 6, the Julián Samora Research Institute, Michigan State University, East Lansing, Michigan, April 1995.

Trejo, Stephen J., "Why Do Mexican Americans Earn Low Wages?" *Journal of Political Economy*, Vol. 105, No. 6, 1997.

U.S. Department of Commerce, Bureau of the Census, *1990 Census of Population – Social and Economic Characteristics, United States*, November 1993.

U.S. Department of Commerce, Bureau of the Census, *1980 Census of Population – General Social and Economic Characteristics, United States Summary,* December 1983.

U.S. Department of Labor, Bureau of Labor Statistics, "Charting the Course to 2006 – Labor Force Industry Occupation," *Monthly Labor Review*, Vol. 120, No. 11, November 1977.

U.S. Department of Labor, Bureau of Labor Statistics, *Employment and Earnings*, Vol. 44, Number 1, January 1997.

Zavodny, Madeline, "The Effects of Official English Laws on Limited-English-Proficient Workers," Federal Reserve Bank of Atlanta, Working Paper 98-4, April 1998.

## Chapter 2, Morales

Ali, Eve, "Economic Change in the Chicago Metropolitan Area," a report of the University of Illinois at Chicago Center for Urban Economic Development, December 1996.

Bendick, M. Jr., C.W. Jackson, V.A. Reinoso, and L.E. Hodges, "Discrimination Against Latino Job Applicants: A Controlled Experiment," *Human Resource Management,* 30, 1991, pp. 469-484.

Blank, Rebecca M., *It Takes a Nation: A New Agenda for Fighting Poverty*, New York: Russell Sage Foundation, 1997.

Boisjoly, Johanne and Greg J. Duncan, "Job Losses Among Hispanics in the Recent Recession," *Monthly Labor Review*, June 1994, pp. 16-23.

Carnoy, Martin, Hugh M. Daley, and Raúl Hinojosa Ojeda, "The Changing Economic Position of Latinos in the U.S. Labor Market Since 1939," in Rebecca Morales and Frank Bonilla (eds.), *Latinos in a Changing U.S. Economy: Comparative Perspectives on Growing Inequality*, Newbury Park, CA: Sage Publications, 1993.

Carnoy, Martin, *Faded Dreams: The Politics and Economics of Race in America,* Cambridge: Cambridge University Press, 1994.

Center on Budget and Policy Priorities, *Shortchanged: Recent Developments in Hispanic Poverty, Income and Employment*, Washington, DC: CBPP, November 1988.

Cross, Harry, Genevieve Kenney, Jane Mell, and Wendy Zimmermann, *Employer Hiring Practices: Differential Treatment of Hispanic and Anglo Job Seekers*, Washington, DC: The Urban Institute Press, 1990.

del Pinal, Jorge and Audrey Singer, "Generations of Diversity: Latinos in the United States," *Population Bulletin,* Vol. 52, No. 3, Washington, DC: Population Reference Bureau, Inc., October 1997.

Enchautegui, María, "Policy Implications of Latino Poverty," Washington, DC: The Urban Institute, 1995.

Fix, Michael and Raymond J. Struyk (eds.), *Clear and Convincing Evidence: Measurement of Discrimination in America*, Washington, DC: Urban Institute Press, 1992.

Goldberg, Carey, "Hispanic Households Struggle as Poorest of the Poor in U.S.," *The New York Times*, January 30, 1997.

Grier, E.S. and G. Grier, *Minorities in Suburbia: A Mid-1980s Update*, Washington, DC: Report of the Urban Institute Project on Housing Mobility, March 1988.

Heckman, James J. and Peter Siegelman, "The Urban Institute Audit Studies: Their Methods and Findings," in Michael Fix and Raymond J. Struyk (eds.), *Clear and Convincing Evidence: Measurement of Discrimination in America,* Washington, DC: Urban Institute Press, 1992.

Hispanic Association of Corporate Responsibility, *1993 HACR Corporate Study: Hispanics in Corporate America*, Washington, DC: HACR, 1993.

James, Franklin J., and Steve W. Del Castillo, "Measuring Job Discrimination by Private Employers Against Young Black and Hispanic Males Seeking Entry Level Work in the Denver Metropolitan Area," unpublished report, University of Colorado, 1991.

Kasarda, John D., "Urban Industrial Transition and the Underclass," *The Annals of the American Academy of Political and Social Science*, Vol. 501, pp. 26-47, January. 1989.

Knouse, S.B., "The Mentoring Process for Hispanics," in S.B. Knouse, P. Rosenfeld and A.L. Culbertson (eds.), *Hispanics in the Workplace*, Newbury Park, CA: Sage, 1992.

Kristof, Kathy M.V., "Why Attend College? Start With Earnings," *The Los Angeles Times*, August 8, 1992.

Meléndez, Edwin, Francoise Carre, and Evangelina Holvino, "Latinos Need Not Apply: The Effects of Industrial Change and Workplace Discrimination on Latino Employment," *New England Journal of Public Policy*, Special Issue, Latinos in a Changing Society, Part 1, Spring/Summer 1995.

Mincy, Ronald B., "The Urban Institute Audit Studies: Their Research and Policy Context," in Michael Fix and Raymond J. Struyk (eds.), *Clear and Convincing Evidence: Measurement of Discrimination in America,* Washington, DC: Urban Institute Press, 1992.

Morales, Rebecca and Frank Bonilla (eds.), *Latinos in a Changing U.S. Economy: Comparative Perspectives on Growing Inequality*, Newbury Park, CA: Sage Publications, 1993.

National Commission for Employment Policy, "Training Hispanics: Implications for the JTPA System," Report Number 27, Washington, DC, January 1990.

National Council of La Raza, "Hispanic Participation in Federal Anti-Poverty Programs," Issue Brief, Washington, DC, July 1997.

National Council of La Raza, *Index of Hispanic Economic Indicators*, Washington, DC, July, 1997.

National Council of La Raza, "Working Poor Hispanics and the Earned Income Tax Credit (EITC)." Poverty Project Fact Sheet, Washington, DC, June 1995.

Orfield, Myron, "Mapping the Future," Chicago, IL: Julie E. Hamos and Associates, 1996.

Reich, Robert B., *The Work of Nations: Preparing Ourselves for 21st Century Capitalism*, New York: Alfred A. Knopf, 1991.

Reyes, M.L. and J.J. Halcon, "Racism in Academia: The Old Wolf Revisited," *Harvard Educational Review*, 58, 1988, pp. 299-314.

Schindler, Graham, Philip Israilevich, and Geoffrey Hewings, "Chicago's Economic Transformation: Past and Future," *Economic Perspectives*, Vol. 19, Issue 5, Chicago: Federal Reserve Bank, September/October 1995.

Torres, Andrés and Frank Bonilla, "Decline Within Decline: The New York Perspective," in R. Morales and F. Bonilla, *Latinos in a Changing U.S. Economy: Comparative Perspectives on Growing Inequality*, Newbury Park, CA: Sage Publications, 1993.

Torres, Andrés, "Latinos and Labor: Challenges and Opportunities," *New England Journal of Public Policy*, Vol. 11, No.1, Spring/Summer 1995.

U.S. Bureau of the Census, *Current Population Reports*, pp. 60-188, 1996.

U.S. Department of Commerce, International Trade Administration, *U.S. Industrial Outlook 1994*, Washington, DC, January, 1994.

U.S. Department of Labor, *Report on the American Workforce,* Washington, DC, 1995.

U.S. General Accounting Office, *Immigration Reform*, Washington, DC, 1990.

U.S. Merit Systems Protection Board, *Fair & Equitable Treatment: A Progress Report on Minority Employment in the Federal Government*, Washington, DC, 1996.

Weinberg, Daniel H., "A Brief Look at Postwar U.S. Income Inequality," *Current Population Reports: Household Economic Studies*, P60-191, Washington, DC: U.S. Bureau of the Census, June 1996, pp. 3-4.

## Chapter 3, Chapa and Wacker

Acevedo, Dolores and Thomas J. Espenshade, "Implications of a North American Free Trade Agreement for Mexican Migration into the United States," *Population and Development Review.* December 1992, Vol. 18, No. 4, p. 729.

*Austin American Statesman*, "Peso's drop hurts South Texas business," April 15, 1995, p. D1.

Boisjoly, Johanne and Greg J. Duncan, "Job losses among Hispanics in the recent recession," *Monthly Labor Review*, June 1994, Vol. 117, No. 6, p. 6.

Borjas, George, "Hispanic Immigrants in the U.S. Labor Market: An Empirical Analysis," in Tienda, Marta, *Hispanic Origin Workers in the U.S. Labor Market: Comparative Analyses of Employment and Earnings*, Madison, Wisconsin: University of Wisconsin and the U.S. Department of Labor, 1981.

Bowie, Chester E., Lawrence S. Cahoon, and Elizabeth A. Martin, "Evaluating changes in the estimates, (Overhauling the Current Population Survey)," *Monthly Labor Review.* September 1993, Vol. 116, No. 9, p. 29.

Brauer, David A. and Susan Hickok, "Explaining the growing inequality across skill levels," *Federal Reserve Bank of New York Economic Policy Review*, January 1995, Vol. 1, No. 1, p. 65.

Bregger, John E. and Cathryn S. Dipp, "Why is it necessary to change? (Overhauling the Current Population Survey)," *Monthly Labor Review*, September 1993, Vol. 116, No. 9, p. 3.

Cárdenas, Gilberto, Jorge Chapa, and Susan Burek, "San Antonio in the World Economy," in Frank Bonilla and Rebecca Morales (eds.), *Latinos in a Changing Economy*, Sage Publications: Beverly Hills, CA, 1993.

Carnoy, Martin, "Education and Racial Inequality: The Human Capital Explanation Revisited," *Economics of Education Review,* Vol. 15, No. 3, 1996.

Carnoy, Martin, and Wei Min Gong, "Women and Minority Gains in a Rapidly Changing Local Labor Market: The San Francisco Bay Area in the 1980's," *Economics of Education Review,* Vol. 15, No. 3, 1996.

Castro, Felipe G., "Families at Risk: Unemployment Stress in Latino and Anglo Men, Women, and Children," in *New Directions for Latino Public Policy Research*,

Austin, TX: IUP/SSRC Committee for Public Policy Research on Contemporary Hispanic Issues, the Center for Mexican American Studies, The University of Texas at Austin, 1990.

Cattan, Peter. "The diversity of Hispanics in the U.S. work force," *Monthly Labor Review* (August 1993).

Chapa, Jorge, "The question of Mexican-American assimilation: socio-economic parity or underclass formation?" *Public Affairs Comment*, 1989.

_____. "The myth of Hispanic progress," *Harvard Journal of Hispanic Policy*, Vol. IV, pp. 3-18, 1990.

_____. "The increasing significance of class: longitudinal trends and class differences in the socio-structural assimilation of third and third-plus generation Mexican Americans," *The Peopling of the Americas* International Union for the Scientific Study of Population: Liege, Belgium, Vol. 2, pp. 489-521, 1992.

Chiswick, Barry R., "Hispanic Men: divergent paths in the US labor market," *Monthly Labor Review* (November 1988).

Cornelius, Wayne A. and Phillip L. Martin, "The Uncertain Connection: Free Trade and Rural Mexican Migration to the United States," *International Migration Review*, Vol. 28, No. 3, p. 484.

Day, Jennifer Cheeseman, *Population Projections of the United States by Age, Sex, and Hispanic Origin*. U.S. Bureau of the Census. Current Population Reports, Series P25-1130. U.S. Government Printing Office: Washington, DC.

De Anda, Roberto M., "Unemployment and Underemployment among Mexican-origin workers," *Hispanic Journal of Behavioral Sciences*, Vol. 16, No. 2 (May).

DeFreitas, Gregory, *Inequality at Work: Hispanics in the U.S. Labor Force*. Oxford University Press: New York.

Dunne, Nancy, "Mexican shock waves," *The Financial Times*, January 31, 1995, p. S7.

Fix, Michael and Raymond J. Struyck (eds.), *Clear and Convincing Evidence: Measurement of Discrimination in America*. The Urban Institute Press: Washington, DC, 1993.

Grebler, Leo, Joan Moore and Ralph Guzman, *The Mexican American People*. New York: The Free Press, 1970.

Grubb, Norton W. and Robert Wilson, "Trends in wages and salary inequality, 1967-1988," *Monthly Labor Review*, September 1993, Vol. 115, No. 6, p. 23.

Harrison, Roderick J. and Claudette E. Bennett, "Racial and Ethnic Diversity," in Reynolds Farley, ed. *State of the Union, America in the 1990's. Volume Two: Social Trends.* Russell Sage Foundation: New York, 1995.

Hayes-Bautista, David, Werner Schink, and Jorge Chapa, *The Burden of Support.* Stanford Univ. Press: Stanford, CA, 1988.

Hershey, Robert D., "Weakness in Jobs Signals Slowing of the Economy," *New York Times*, February 4, 1995, p. A1.

_____. "Bias hits Hispanic workers," *New York Times*, April 27, 1995, p. C1.

Hirsch, Barry T., and Edward J. Schumacher, "Labor Earning, Discrimination and the Racial Composition of Jobs," *Journal of Human Resources*, Vol. 27, No. 4 (Fall 1992).

Holmes, Steven A., "A Surge in Immigration Surprises Experts and Intensifies a Debate," *New York Times*, August 30, 1995, p. A1.

Howell, David R. and Susan S. Weiler, "Trends in Computerization, Skill Composition and Low Earnings: Implications for Education and Training Policy," Paper presented at the October 1994 Association for Public Policy Analysis and Management Meetings in Chicago, IL, 1994.

Johnston, W.B. and A.H. Packer, *Workforce 2000: Work and Workers for the Twenty-first Century.* Hudson Institute: Indianapolis, IN, 1987.

Kasarda, John D., *Urban Underclass Database: An Overview and Machine Readable File Documentation.* Social Science Research Council: New York. Update, 1993.

Kenney, Genevieve M. and Douglas A. Wissoker, "An Analysis of the Correlates of Discrimination Facing Young Hispanic Job-Seekers," *The American Economic Review*, Vol. 84, No. 3, June 1994, pp. 674-683.

Kraul, Chris, "Peso's Silver Lining: Mexico Nets Huge Surplus With U.S., But There's a Price to Good News: 700,000 (Mexican) Jobs Lost," *Los Angeles Times*, April 20, 1995, p. D1.

Lawrence, Robert Z, "U.S. wage trends in the 1980's: the role of international factors," *Federal Reserve Bank of New York Economic Policy Review*, January 1995, p. 18.

Lemieux, Josh, "Border Patrol Records Increase in Number of Arrests in Valley," *Austin American Statesman*, March 21, 1995, p. B5.

Levy, Frank, "Income and Income Inequality," in Reynolds Farley, ed. *State of the Union, America in the 1990's. Volume One: Economic Trends.* Russell Sage Foundation: New York, 1995.

Lippert, John, "Peso's Fall Sends Jobs, Not Goods, to Mexico," *Austin American Statesman*, March 18, 1995, p. D3.

Lowell, B. Lindsay, Jay Teachman, and Zhongren Jing, "Unintended Consequences of Immigration Reform: Discrimination and Hispanic Employment," *Demography*, Vol. 32, No. 4, November 1995, pp. 617-628.

Lucas, Tamara, Rosemary Henze, and Ruben Donato, "Promoting the Success of Latino Language-Minority Students: An Exploratory Study of Six Schools," *Harvard Education Review,* Vol. 60, No. 3, August 1990.

Martin, Phillip L. "Trade and Migration: The Case of NAFTA," *Asian and Pacific Migration Journal,* Vol. 2, No. 3, p. 329.

Marshall, Ray, "Education for Minorities and the National Interest," from *Education that Works: An Action Plan for the Education of Minorities.* Quality Education for Minorities Project, Washington, DC, 1990.

Maxwell, Nan L., "Occupational Differences in the Determination of U.S. Workers' Earnings," *American Journal of Economics and Sociology,* October 1987.

McKee, Nancy P., "Learning and Earning: Education and Well-Being in a Texas Border Barrio," *Urban Education,* Vol. 24, No. 3, October 1989.

McMurrer, Daniel P., and Isabel V. Sawhill, *The Effects of Economic Growth and Inequality on Opportunity.* Washington, DC: The Urban Institute, 1997.

Moore, Joan, "Is There a Hispanic Underclass?" *Social Science Quarterly*, Vol. 70, p. 265, 1989.

National Center on Education and the Economy, *America's Choice: High Skills or Low Wages.* National Center on Education and the Economy: Rochester, NY, 1990.

National Council of La Raza, "Hispanic Unemployment Issue Brief," Washington, DC: October 1997.

*New York Times* "Mexican's Boxcar Journeys Alarm U.S. Border Officials," June 11, 1995, p. A18.

Nusser, Nancy, "NAFTA's Effect So Far: Jobs, Trade Headed South," *Austin American Statesman*, July 20, 1995, p. C1.

Office of Management and Budget, *America's Children: Key Indicator of Well-Being*. Federal Interagency Forum on Child and Family Statistics, Washington, DC, 1997

O'Regan, Katherine M., "The Effect of Social Networks and Concentrated Poverty on Black and Hispanic Youth Unemployment," *Annals of Regional Science,* Vol. 27, No. 4, December 1993.

Orum, Lori S., *Making Education Work for Hispanic Americans*. Los Angeles, California: National Council of La Raza, 1988.

Osterman, Paul, and Brenda Lautsch, *Project Quest: A Report to the Ford Foundation*. Boston: MIT Sloan School of Management, 1996.

Quality Education for Minorities Project, *Education That Works: An Action Plan for the Education of Minorities*. Cambridge, Massachusetts: MIT, 1990.

Rasell, Edith, Barry Bluestone, and Lawrence Mishel 1997, *The Prosperity Gap: A Chartbook of American Living Standards. 1997.*

Reich, Michael, "The Economics of Racism," in *Problems in Political Economy: An Urban Perspective*, ed. Gordon, David M., Lexington, Mass: Heath, 1977.

Rendon, Laura I., and Richard O. Hope, *Educating a New Majority: Transforming America's Educational System for Diversity.* San Francisco, CA: Jossey-Bass, 1996.

Rendon, Laura I., and Nora Amaury, "Hispanic Students: Stopping the Leaks in the Pipeline," *Educational Record* (Fall 1987-Winter 1988).

Roe, Frederick, "Plunge of the Peso and Hard Times to Follow May Spur Surge of Mexican Immigration to U.S.," *Wall Street Journal*, January 6, 1995, p. A2.

Romero, Gloria J., Felipe G. Castro and Richard C. Cervantes, "Latinas Without Work: Family, Occupational, and Economic Stress Following Unemployment," *Psychology of Women Quarterly*, Vol. 12, No. 3 (September 1988).

Rumberger, R. W., "Dropping Out of High School: The Influence of Race, Sex, and Family Background," *American Education Research Journal*, Vol. 20, 1983.

*San Antonio Light*, "A Thousand Lives." Special Report, November 11, 1990 through November 18, 1990.

Tienda, Marta, "Hispanic Immigrants in the U.S. Labor Market: An Empirical Analysis," in *Hispanic Origin Workers in the U.S. Labor Market: Comparative Analyses of Employment and Earnings,* ed. Tienda, Marta. Madison, Wisconsin: University of Wisconsin and the U.S. Department of Labor, 1981.

Tienda, Marta, *Hispanic Origin Workers in the U.S. Labor Market: Comparative Analyses of Employment and Earnings.* Madison, Wisconsin: University of Wisconsin Press, 1981.

Tienda, Marta, Carl Bowman, and Mathew C. Snipp, *Socioeconomic Attainment and Ethnicity: Toward an Understanding of the Labor Market Experiences of Chicanos in the U.S.* Madison, Wisconsin: Department of Rural Sociology, University of Wisconsin, 1981.

Tienda, Marta, and Sheri Hsueh, "Earnings Consequences of Employment Instability Among Minority Men," *Population Research Center Discussion Paper Series*, No. 94-11, June 1994, University of Chicago, National Opinion Research Center [NORC], Population Research Center: Chicago, Illinois.

Tienda, M., and L. Ding-Tzann, "Minority Concentration and Earnings Inequality," *American Journal of Sociology*, Vol. 93, No. 1, 1987.

U.S. Bureau of the Census, *Population Profile of the United States, 1995.* Current Population Reports, Series p. 23-189. U.S. Government Printing Office: Washington, DC.

U.S. Department of Education, "Are Hispanic Dropout Rates Related to Migration?" Washington, DC, 1993.

Velez-Ibañez, Carlos, "U.S. Mexicans in the Borderlands: Being Poor Without the Underclass," in Joanne Moore and Raquel Pinderhughes, eds., *In the Barrios: Latinos and the Underclass Debate.* Russell Sage Foundation: New York, 1993.

Wilson, Kenneth L., and Alejandro Portes, "Immigrant Enclaves: An Analysis of the Labor Market Experiences of Cubans in Miami," *American Journal of Sociology*, Vol. 86 (September 1980).

Wilson, William, *The Increasing Significance of Class.* The University of Chicago Press: Chicago, 1980.

_____. *The Truly Disadvantaged.* The University of Chicago Press: Chicago, 1987.

_____. *When Work Disappears.* New York: Alfred A. Knopf, 1996.

## Chapter 4, Grenier and Cattan

Bean, Frank D. and Marta Tienda, *The Hispanic Population of the United States.* New York: Russell Sage Foundation, 1987.

Borjas, George J., "Do Blacks Gain or Lose from Immigration?" in *Help or Hindrance? The Economic Implications of Immigration for African Americans,* eds. Daniel Hamermesh and Frank D. Bean, pp. 51-74. New York: Russell Sage Foundation, 1998.

_____. *The Economic Progress of Immigrants.* National Bureau of Economic Research Working Paper 6505. Cambridge, MA, 1998.

_____. "The Economics of Immigration," *Journal of Economic Literature.* 32 (December 1994): pp. 1667-1717.

_____. "National Origin and Skills of Immigrants in the Postwar Period," in *Immigration and the Workforce,* eds. George Borjas and Richard Freeman, pp. 17-47, Chicago: University of Chicago Press, 1992.

_____. "Assimilation, Changes in Cohort Quality, and the Earnings of Immigrants," *Journal of Labor Economics.* 3 (October 1985): pp. 463-489.

Borjas, George J. and Richard B. Freeman, "Findings We Never Found," *New York Times,* December 10, 1997.

Borjas, George J., Richard B. Freeman, and Lawrence Katz, "How Much Do Immigration and Trade Affect Labor Market Outcomes?" *Brookings Papers on Economic Activity.* 1: pp. 1-67, 1997.

Butcher, Kristin F. and Anne Morrison Piehl, "Immigration and the Wages and Employment of U.S.-Born Workers in New Jersey," in *Keys to Successful Immigration: Implications of the New Jersey Experience,* edited by Thomas J. Espenshade, pp. 119-138. Washington, DC: Urban Institute Press, 1997.

Camarota, Steven A., "The Effect of Immigrants on the Earnings of Low-Skilled Native Workers: Evidence from the June 1991 Current Population Survey," *Social Science Quarterly.* 78 (June 1997): pp. 417-431.

_____. "The Labor Market Impact of Immigration: A Review of Recent Studies," Center for Immigration Studies Backgrounder No. 1-98, Washington, DC, 1998.

Center for Immigration Studies, "The Wages of Immigration," Center Paper 12, 1998.

Chapa, Jorge, and Dawn A. Jahn et al., "Latino Poverty: Not Just an Immigrant Issue," presented at APPAM Conference, October, 1993.

Chiswick, Barry, "The Effect of Americanization on the Earnings of Foreign-Born Men," *Journal of Political Economy.* 86 (October 1978): pp. 897-921.

Cohen, Yinon, Tzippi Zach, and Barry Chiswick, "The Educational Attainment of Immigrants: Changes Over Time," *The Quarterly Review of Economics and Finance.* pp. 37: 229-243, 1997.

DeFreitas, Gregory, *Inequality at Work: Hispanics in the U.S. Labor Force.* New York: Oxford University Press, 1991.

_____. "Hispanic Immigration and Labor Market Segmentation," *Industrial Relations.* 27: pp. 195-214, 1988.

DiNardo, John, "Comments and Discussion," *Brookings Papers on Economic Activity* I: pp. 68-76, 1997.

Duleep, Harriet Orcutt and Mark C. Regets, "The Elusive Concept of Immigrant Quality: Evidence from 1970-1990," The Urban Institute, Program for Research on Immigration Policy, Washington, DC, 1996.

_____. "Measuring Immigrant Wage Growth Using Matched CPS Files," *Demography* 34 (May 1997): pp. 239-249.

_____. "The Decline in Immigrant Entry Earnings: Less Transferable Skills or Lower Ability?" *The Quarterly Review of Economics and Finance.* 37: pp. 189-208, 1997.

Duleep, Harriet Orcutt and Phanindra V. Wunnava, eds., *Immigrants and Immigration Policy: Individual Skills, Family Ties and Group Identities.* Greenwich, Conn.: JAI Press, Inc., 1996.

Enchautegui, Maria, "Immigration and County Employment Growth," *Population Research and Policy Review.* 16: pp. 493-511, 1997.

_____. "Effects of Immigrants on the 1980-1990 U.S. Wage Experience," *Contemporary Economic Policy.* 13 (July 1995): pp. 20-38.

Espenshade, Thomas J., ed., *Keys to Successful Immigration: Implications of the New Jersey Experience.* Washington, DC: The Urban Institute Press, 1997.

Hinojosa-Ojeda, Raul, Martin Carnoy, and Hugh Daley, "An Even Greater 'U-Turn': Latinos and the New Inequality," in *Hispanics in the Labor Force.* pp. 25-52, New York: Plenum Press, 1991.

Hsueh, Sheri and Marta Tienda, "Gender, Ethnicity and Labor Force Instability," *Social Science Research.* 25: pp. 73-94, 1996.

_____. "Earnings Consequences of Employment Instability Among Minority Men," *Research in Social Stratification and Mobility.* 14: pp. 39-69, 1995.

Jaeger, David A., "Skill Differences and the Effect of Immigrants on the Wages of Natives," BLS Working Paper 273 (December 1995).

Jensen, Leif, "Secondary Earner Strategies and Family Poverty: Immigrant-native Differentials, 1960-1981," *International Migration Review.* 25: pp. 113-139, 1991.

Kposowa, Augustine, "The Impact of Immigration on Unemployment and Earnings among Racial Minorities in the U.S.," *Racial and Ethnic Studies.* 18, 1995.

LaLonde, Robert and Robert Topel, "Immigrants in the American Labor Market: Quality, Assimilation, and Distributional Effects," *American Economic Association Papers and Proceedings*, pp. 297-302, 1991.

McDonald, James Ted and Christopher Worswick, "Job Tenure, Cohort, and Macroeconomic Conditions," *Industrial and Labor Relations Review* 51: pp. 465-504, 1998.

Melendez, Edwin, Clara Rodriguez, and Janis Barry Figueroa, eds., *Hispanics in the Labor Force: Issues and Policies.* New York: Plenum Press, 1991.

Myers, Dowell and Cynthia J. Cranford, "Temporal Differentiation in the Occupational Mobility of Immigrant and Native-Born Latina Workers," *American Sociological Review.* 63 (February 1998): pp. 68-93.

National Council of La Raza, "Hispanic Poverty: How Much Does Immigration Explain?" Proceedings from the National Council of La Raza's Poverty Project Roundtable, November 27, 1989, Washington, DC.

National Council of La Raza, *Unlocking the Golden Door: Hispanics and the Citizenship Process.* Policy Analysis Center, Washington, DC, 1991.

National Research Council, *The New Americans: Economic, Demographic, and Fiscal Effects of Immigration.* Washington, DC: National Academy Press, 1997.

Perez, Lisandro, "Immigrant Economic Adjustment and Family Organization: The Cuban Success Story Reexamined," *International Migration Review.* 20: p. 20, 1986.

Piore, Michael, *Birds of Passage.* Cambridge: Cambridge University Press, 1979.

Portes, Alejandro, ed., *The Economic Sociology of Immigration: Essays on Networks, Ethnicity, and Entrepreneurship.* New York: Russell Sage Foundation, 1995.

Portes, Alejandro and Alex Stepick, *City on the Edge: The Transformation of Miami.* Berkeley, CA: University of California Press, 1993.

Reimers, Cordelia, "Unskilled Immigration and Changes in the Wage Distributions of Black, Mexican, American, and Non-Hispanic White Male Dropouts," in *Help or Hindrance?* Daniel S. Hamermesh and Frank D. Bean, eds., pp. 107-148. New York: Russell Sage, 1998.

_____. "The Progress of Mexican and White Non-Hispanic Immigrants in California and Texas, 1980-1990," *The Quarterly Review of Economics and Finance.* 37: pp. 315-343, 1997.

Reitz, Jeffrey G., *Warmth of the Welcome: The Social Causes of Economic Success for Immigrants in Different Nations and Cities.* Boulder: Westview, 1998.

Rivera-Batiz, Francisco, "English Language Proficiency, Quantitative Skills and the Economic Progress of Immigrants," pp. 57-78, in *Immigrants and Immigration Policy: Individual Skills, Family Ties, and Group Identities*, edited by Harriet Duleep and Phanindra V. Wunnava. Greenwich, CT: JAI Press, 1996.

Ruggles, Steven and Matthew Sobek, *Integrated Public Use Microdata Series: Version 2.0*, Minneapolis: Historical Census Projects, University of Minnesota, 1997, http://www.ipums.umn.edu.

Rumbaut, Ruben G., "Origins and Destinies: Immigration to the United States Since World War II," pp. 15-45, in Darrell Y. Hamamoto and Rodolfo D. Torres (eds.), *New American Destinies.* New York: Routledge, 1997.

Schoeni, Robert F., *The Effect of Immigrants on the Employment and Wages of Native Workers: Evidence from the 1970s and 1980s.* RAND, 1997.

Schultz, T. Paul, "Immigrant Quality and Assimilation: A Review of the U.S. Literature," *Journal of Population Economics.* 11: pp. 239-252, 1998.

Silvestri, George T., "Occupational Employment Projections to 2006," *Monthly Labor Review.* 120: pp. 58-83, 1997.

Simon, Julian L., "The Case for Greatly Increased Immigration," *Public Interest.* 102: pp. 89-103, 1991.

_____. *The Economic Consequences of Immigration.* Oxford: Basil Blackwell, 1989.

Smith, James P. and Barry Edmoston, eds., *The New Americans: Economic, Demographic, and Fiscal Effects of Immigration.* Washington, DC: National Academy Press, 1997.

Sorensen, Elaine and Maria Enchautegui, "Immigrant Male Earnings in the 1980s: Divergent Paths by Race and Ethnicity," in Barry Edmonston and Jeffrey Passel, eds., *Immigration and Ethnicity: The Integration of America's Newest Arrivals.* Washington, DC: Urban Institute Press: 1994, pp. 139-161.

Tienda, Marta, "Immigration and Native Minority Workers: Is There Bad News After All?" pp. 345-352 in Daniel S. Hamermesh and Frank D. Bean, eds., *Help or Hindrance?* New York: Russell Sage, 1998.

Tienda, Marta and Zai Liang, "Poverty and Public Policy: What Do We Know? What Should We Do?" IRP Conference Paper, University of Wisconsin-Madison, 1992.

U.S. Bureau of the Census, *The Foreign-Born Population in the United States*, CP-3-1. Washington, DC: Department of Commerce, 1993.

_____. *Persons of Hispanic Origin in the United States.* CP-3-3. Washington, DC: Department of Commerce, 1993.

U.S. Commission on Immigration Reform, "Becoming an American: Immigration and Immigrant Policy, A Report to Congress (Executive Summary). Washington, DC, 1997.

Valenzuela, Jr., Abel, "Hispanic Poverty, Is It an Immigrant Problem?" *Hispanic Journal of Social Policy.* 5: pp. 59-82, 1991.

Waldinger, Roger, *Still the Promised City?* Cambridge, Mass.: Harvard University Press, 1996.

Waldinger, Roger and Greta Gilbertson, "Immigrants' Progress: Ethnic and Gender Differences Among U.S. Immigrants in the 1980s," *Sociological Perspectives* 37. 3: pp. 431-444, 1994.

## Chapter 5, Reimers – no references

## Chapter 6, Santos and Seitz

Anderson, Ronald, Sandra Zelman Lewis, Aida L. Giachello, Lu Ann Aday, and Grace Chiu, "Access to Medical Care Among the Hispanic Population of the Southwestern United States," *Journal of Health and Social Behavior*, Vol. 22, March 1981, pp. 78-89.

Budd, John W., and Brian P. McCall, "The Effect Of Unions On The Receipt Of Unemployment Insurance Benefits," *Industrial and Labor Relations Review*, Vol. 50, No. 3, 1997, pp. 478-492.

Employee Benefit Research Institute, "Boom Times A Bust For Retirement Assurances: Results of the 1998 Retirement Confidence Survey," *News Release*, Washington, DC, June 2, 1998.

Ford, Jason, "State-Mandated Employee Benefits: Conflict With Federal Law?" *Employee Benefits Survey: A BLS Reader*, Washington, DC: U.S. Government Printing Office, 1995.

Fronstein, Paul, Lawrence G. Goldberg, and Philip K. Robins, "Differences In Private Health Insurance Coverage For Working Male Hispanics," *Inquiry*, Vol. 34, Summer 1997, pp. 171-180.

Fullerton, Howard N., Jr., "Labor force 2006: Slowing down and changing composition," *Monthly Labor Review*, Vol. 120, No. 11, 1997, pp. 23-38.

Goldstein, Bruce, "An Overview Of Migrant And Seasonal Farmworkers In The 1990s," Washington, DC: Farmworker Justice Fund, Fall 1995.

Hirsch, Barry T., David A. MacPherson, and J. Michael Dumond, "Workers' Compensation Recipiency In Union And Nonunion Workplaces," *Industrial and Labor Relations Review*, Vol. 50, No. 2, 1997, pp. 213-236.

Levine, Chester, "Employee Benefits: Growing In Diversity And Cost," *Occupational Outlook Quarterly*, Vol. 37, 1994, pp. 38-42.

Morales, Rebecca, and Frank Bonilla, editors, *Latinos in a Changing U.S. Economy: Comparative Perspectives on Growing Inequality*. Newbury Park, CA: Sage Publications, 1993.

Nichols, Marion E., Isaac Shapiro, and Robert Greenstein, *Unemployment Insurance in States with Large Hispanic Populations*. Washington, DC: Center on Budget and Policy Priorities, 1991.

Sloane, Arthur A., and Fred Witney, *Labor Relations*. Saddle River. NJ: Prentice Hall, 1997.

Smith, James P., *Unequal Wealth and Incentives to Save*. Santa Monica, CA: Rand Corporation, 1995.

Snyder, Donald C., "The Economic Well-Being Of Retired Workers By Race And Hispanic Origin," pp. 67-78, in R.V. Burkhauser and D.L. Salisbury, eds., *Pensions in a Changing Economy*. Employee Benefit Research Institute, 1993.

Social Security Administration, "Income sources by age, sex, race, and Hispanic origin: Percent of persons aged 55 or older with money income from specified sources, 1994," Table I.9 (PDF file), 1995.

Social Security Administration, "Relative importance of income sources by sex, marital status, race, and Hispanic origin: Percentage distribution of aged units 65 or older receiving particular sources of income, 1994," Table VI.B.4 (PDF file), 1995.

U.S. Department of Labor, Bureau of Labor Statistics, "Employer Costs For Employee Compensation - March 1996," *News Release* #96-424, October 10, 1996.

U.S. Department of Labor, Bureau of Labor Statistics, *Employment and Earnings*. January 1998.

U.S. Department of Labor, Bureau of Labor Statistics, "Lost-Worktime Injuries: Characteristics And Resulting Time Away From Work," *News Release* #97-188, June 12, 1997.

Valdez, R. Burciaga, Hal Morganstern, E. Richard Brown, Roberta Wyn, Chao Wang, and William Cumberland, "Insuring Latinos Against the Cost of Illness," *Journal of the American Medical Association*, Vol. 269, No.7, February 17, 1993, pp. 889-894.

## Chapter 7, Meléndez and Falcón

Cave, G., H. Bos, F. Doolittle, and C. Toussaint, *JOBSTART: Final Report On A Program For School Dropouts*. New York: Manpower Demonstration Research Corporation, 1993.

Falcón, L. and E. Meléndez, *Social Network-Found Jobs And The Labor Market Outcome Of Latinos, Blacks, and Whites.* Boston: Mauricio Gastón Institute for Latino Community Development and Public Policy, University of Massachusetts, Boston, 1996.

Grubb, W.N., *Learning to Work: The Case for Reintegrating Job Training and Education.* New York: Russell Sage Foundation, 1996.

Harrison, B. and M. Wiess, *Workforce Development Network: Community-Based Organizations and Regional Alliances.* Thousand Oak: Publications, Inc., 1998.

Hollister, R.G., *The Minority Female Single Parent Demonstration: New Evidence About Effective Training Strategies.* New York: Rockefeller Foundation, 1990.

Joyner, C.C., *Employment And Training: Successful Projects Share Common Strategy* (testimony before the Subcommittee on Human Resources and Intergovernmental Relations, Committee on Government Reform and Oversight, House of Representatives). Washington, DC: U.S. General Accounting Office, 1996.

Kerachsky, S., *The Minority Female Single Parent Demonstration: Making A Difference –Does An Integrated Program Model Promote More Jobs And Higher Pay?* Washington, DC: Mathematica Policy Research, 1994.

Kirschenman, J., P. Moss, and C. Tilly, "Employer Screening Methods and Racial Exclusion: Evidence from New In-depth Interviews with Employers," paper presented at the Russell Sage Foundation Conference on "Searching for Work/Searching for Workers," September 28 and 29, 1995, New York City.

Meléndez, E., *Working on Jobs: The Center for Employment Training.* Boston: Mauricio Gastón Institute, University of Massachusetts, Boston, 1996.

Meléndez, E., and B. Harrison, "Matching the Disadvantaged to Job Opportunities: Structural Explanations for the Past Successes of the Center for Employment Training," *Economic Development Quarterly*, Vol. 12, No. 1, pp. 3-11, Sage Publications, 1998.

Moss, P. and C. Tilly, "Informal Hiring Practices, Racial Exclusion, and Public Policy," paper presented at the *Politics and Society* policy conference, November 16, 1996, New York City.

Morales, R., *Project QUEST: An Embedded Network Employment and Training Organization.* Boston: Economic Development Associates Consortium, 1996.

Osterman, P. and B.A. Lautsch, *Project QUEST: A Report to the Ford Foundation.* Cambridge: Massachusetts Institute of Technology, Sloan School of Management, 1996.

Seigel, B. and P. Kwass, *Jobs and the Urban Poor: Publicly Initiated Sectoral Strategies.* Somerville: Mt. Auburn Associates, Inc., 1995.

Stokes, R., *Model Welfare-to-Work Initiatives in the United States: Effective Strategies From Moving TANF Recipients From Public Assistance To Self-Sufficiency.* Report prepared for the Connecticut Business and Industry Association by RSS Associates, 1996.

U.S. Department of Labor, *What's Working (And What's Not): A Summary Of Research In The Economic Impacts Of Employment Training Programs.* Washington, DC: U.S. Government Printing Office, 1995.

Zabrowski, A. and A. Gordon, *Evaluation Of Minority Female Single Parent Demonstration: Fifth Year Impacts At CET.* New York: Mathematica Policy Research, for the Rockefeller Foundation, 1993.

## Chapter 8, Pérez and Kamasaki – no references

# INDEX

## A

## B

# D

# E

# F

# G

# H

# S

Suburbs, 52
    Suburban growth, 49
"Successful segment" of Latino society, 213
Sun belt, 47
Supply, 36

# T

Talent Search, 226
Taste model, 76
Tax relief, 160
Teaching, 158
Technical occupations, 48
    Technical sales and administrative support, 20, 24-25, 42-43
Temporary employment agencies, 202
Tennessee, 54
Tertiary sector of economy, 15-17
Texas, 89-90, 95, 99, 101, 104-05, 143, 179-180, 221, 224, 227
    Texas border region, 73
Textile, apparel, furnishing industries, 19
Title I Compensatory Education Program, 226
Tracking, 56
Training opportunities (as a benefit), 164, 171, 177, 229
Transfer payments, 160
Transportation, 17, 38-39
Transportation and public utilities, 25
Transportation, lack of, as a barrier, 203
Truck drivers, 118
Two-parent, working families, 212

# U

U.S. Bureau of Labor Statistics, 44, 55, 71, 77, 164, 183
U.S. Bureau of the Census (See "Census")
U.S. Department of Commerce, 92
U.S. Department of Justice, 60
U.S. Department of Defense, 32
U.S. Department of Labor, 26, 44, 81, 204, 218
U.S. labor force growth, 12-13
U.S.-born Hispanics, 45

# National Council of La Raza
# Hispanic Employment Policy Project
# Academic Advisory Committee Members

**Dr. Jorge Chapa**
Indiana University
Bloomington, IN

**Dr. José E. Cruz**
State University of New York at Albany
Albany, NY

**Dr. Sheldon Danziger**
School of Public Policy
The University of Michigan
Ann Arbor, MI

**Dr. Guillermo Grenier**
Florida Center for Labor Research and
Studies
Florida International University
Miami, FL

**Dr. Edwin Meléndez**
Milano Graduate School of Management
and Urban Policy, and Community
Development Research Center
New School for Social Research
New York, NY

**Dr. Cordelia Reimers**
Department of Economics
Hunter College
New York, NY

**Dr. Refugio Rochín**
Center for Latino Initiatives
Smithsonian Institution
Washington, DC

**Dr. Clara Rodríguez**
Division of Social Sciences
Fordham University at Lincoln Center
New York, NY

## "Ex-Officio" Members

**Raul Yzaguirre**
President
National Council of La Raza
Washington, DC

**Charles Kamasaki**
Senior Vice President
National Council of La Raza
Washington, DC

**Dr. Ronald Mincy**
Senior Program Officer
Human Development and
Reproductive Health
The Ford Foundation
New York, NY

# About the Editor and Contributors

**Peter Cattan** was a labor force analyst at the U.S. Bureau of Labor Statistics prior to joining Florida International University's Center for Labor Research and Studies.

**Jorge Chapa** is Professor and founding Chair of the Latino Studies Department at Indiana University. He has scores of publications reflecting his research focus on the low rates of Hispanic educational, occupational, and economic mobility, and on the development of policies to improve these trends.

**Luis M. Falcón** is Associate Professor of Sociology and Director of Graduate Studies in the Department of Sociology at Northeastern University in Boston, MA. Dr. Falcón has research interests in the areas of labor markets, migration, urban poverty, and Latino gerontology.

**Guillermo J. Grenier** is Director of the Center for Labor Research and Studies and Associate Professor of Sociology at Florida International University. He has published widely on immigration and labor issues.

**Charles K. Kamasaki** is Senior Vice President for the Office of Research, Advocacy, and Legislation at the National Council of La Raza and is responsible for overseeing policy and advocacy activities on a wide range of issues, including civil rights, education, poverty, immigration, and housing. He has written and lectured widely on these issues.

**Edwin Meléndez** is Professor of Management and Urban Policy and Director of the Community Development Research Center at the Robert J. Milano Graduate School of Management and Urban Policy at the New School for Social Research. He has conducted considerable research in the areas of economic development, labor markets, and poverty, and has published numerous scientific papers and other works.

**Rebecca Morales** is an Associate in Morales and Associates, a consultancy in economic development, and a visiting Professor at San Diego State University, Department of Economics. She previously served as Director of the Center for Urban Economic Development at the University of Illinois, Chicago. Dr. Morales' areas of expertise include economic development, community development, industrial development, and urban development, both domestically and internationally.

**Sonia M. Pérez,** Deputy Vice President of Research at the National Council of La Raza, has studied and written about the social and economic status of Latinos in the U.S. for the past ten years. She is especially interested in policy-oriented research and community-based efforts to help reduce poverty and improve the economic prospects of Latinos in the U.S. and in Puerto Rico.

**Cordelia Reimers**, a labor economist with a long-standing research interest in earnings differences among ethnic, racial, and nativity groups, is Professor of Economics at Hunter College and the Graduate School of the City University of New York.

**Richard Santos** is an Associate Professor of Economics at the University of New Mexico; he also has faculty affiliations with the Southwest Hispanic Research Institute and the College of Pharmacy. His research interests include Hispanic employment and health care issues.

**Patricia Seitz** is the Coordinator of the sociology program at Albuquerque Technical-Vocational Institute and Community College; her research interests focus on the effects of race, ethnicity, and gender on employment and earnings.

**Marcelo E. Siles** is the Director of the Social Capital Initiative, Institute for Public Policy and Social Research; Assistant Professor, Center of Integrative Social Studies; and a Senior Research Associate with the Julian Samora Research Institute at Michigan State University. His research focuses on the role of social capital in economic transactions, and on social and economic analyses of Latinos in the United States.

**Craig Wacker** is currently employed as a research analyst with the Texas Center for Educational Research (TCER). Before coming to TCER, he worked first as a research associate with the Carnegie Foundation for the Advancement of Teaching, and later as a budget and policy analyst for the public education team of the Texas Legislative Budget Board.

# NCLR Board of Directors

Chair

**Ramón Murguía**
Attorney at Law
Murguia Law Offices
Kansas City, MO

First Vice-Chair

**José Villarreal**
Partner
Akin, Gump, Strauss,
Hauer, & Feld, L.L.P.
San Antonio, TX

Second Vice-Chair

**Lillian Cruz**
Executive Director
Humanidad, Inc.
Rocky Hill, CT

Secretary/Treasurer

**Roger Cázares**
President/CEO
MAAC Project
National City, CA

Executive Committee

**Cordelia Candelaria**
Professor, Department
of English and Chicano
and Chicana Studies
Arizona State
University
Tempe, Arizona

**Amancio J. Chapa, Jr.**
Executive Director
Amigos Del Valle, Inc.
Mission, TX

**Rita Di Martino**
Vice President
Congressional Relations
Federal Government
Affairs
AT&T
Washington, DC

NCLR President
and CEO

**Hon. Raúl Yzaguirre**
President and CEO
National Council
of La Raza
Washington, DC

General Membership

**Mari Carmen
Aponte, Esq.***
Washington, DC

**Zulma X. Barrios**
Vice President, Latin
America Leadership
The Gallup
Organization
Lincoln, NE

**Fernando Flores**
Chairman & CEO
Business Design
Associate
Alameda, CA

**Irma Flores-Gonzales***
Consultant
Embudo, NM

**Humberto Fuentes**
Executive Director
Idaho Migrant Council
Caldwell, ID

**Hon. Robert W. Gary**
Retired President
Allstate Insurance
Lake Forest, IL

**Linda Lehrer**
Consultant
East Hampton, NY

**Hon. Guillermo
Linares***
Councilman
New York, NY

**Mónica C. Lozano**
Associate Publisher and
Executive Editor
*La Opinión*
Los Angeles, CA

**Raymond Lozano**
Manager of
Community Affairs
Michigan Consolidated
Gas Company
Detroit, MI

**Dr. Herminio Martínez**
Professor and
Executive Director
Bronx Institute
Lehman College/CUNY
Bronx, NY

**Yvonne Martínez Vega**
Executive Director
Ayuda, Inc.
Washington, DC

**Pedro Narezo**
Chairman
Tallahassee Hispanic
Embracement
Organization, Inc.
(THEO)
Tallahassee, FL

*Term expires July 2000

**Hon. René Oliveira**
Representative
Texas State House of
Representatives
Brownsville, TX

**Daniel Ortega, Jr., Esq.***
Partner
Ortega & Associates, P.C.
Phoenix, AZ

**Cecilia Sánchez
de Ortiz**
Denver, CO

**Hon. Angel Luis Ortiz***
City Councilman
Philadelphia, PA

**Hon. Deborah Ortiz**
Senator
California State Senate
Sacramento, CA

**Verma Pastor**
Program Director
WestEd Southwest
Comprehensive Center
Phoenix, AZ

**Edward Reilly**
President and CEO
Big Flower Holdings,
Inc.
New York , NY

**Deborah Szekely**
Founder/Chairman of
the Board
Eureka Communities
Washington, DC

**María Elena
Torralva-Alonso***
Consultant & Interim
Director
Guadalupe Cultural
Arts Center
San Antonio, TX

**Arturo G. Torres***
Chair of the Board
& CEO
Play By Play Toys
& Novelties
San Antonio, TX

**Hon. Esteban Torres**
Former Congressman
West Covina, CA

**Kenneth I. Trujillo**
City Solicitor
City of Philadelphia
Philadelphia, PA

**Hon. Ricardo Urbina**
United States
District Judge
U.S. District Court for
the District of Columbia
Washington, DC

**Charles E. Vela, M. Sc.***
Senior Science Advisor
IIT Research Institute &
Executive Director,
Center for the
Advancement of
Hispanics in Science &
Engineering Education
Potomac, MD

**Carmen Velásquez**
Executive Director
Alivio Medical Center
Chicago, IL

**Ann Marie Wheelock**
Senior Vice President
Fannie Mae
Pasadena, CA

**Emeritus Directors**

**Herman E. Gallegos**
Trustee Emeritus
National Council of
La Raza
Brisbane, CA

**R.P. (Bob) Sánchez, Esq.**
Attorney at Law
McAllen, TX

**Gilbert R. Vásquez,
C.P.A.**
Vasquez and Company
Los Angeles, CA

**Legal Counsel**

**Christopher R.
Lipsett, Esq.**
Partner
Wilmer, Cutler and
Pickering
Washington, DC

**Frank Medina**
Partner
Wilmer, Cutler and
Pickering
Washington, DC

*Term expires July 2000*